FOOTBALL IN BALTIMORE

Football in Baltimore

HISTORY AND MEMORABILIA

Ted Patterson

With photography by Edwin H. Remsberg
and a Foreword by Raymond Berry

The Johns Hopkins University Press   Baltimore and London

The Johns Hopkins University Press
2715 North Charles Street
Baltimore, Maryland 21218-4363
www.press.jhu.edu

A catalog record for this book is available from the British Library.

Library of Congress Cataloging-in-Publication Data

Patterson, Ted.
    Football in Baltimore : history and memorabilia / Ted Patterson ; including photography by Edwin H. Remsberg.
      p.   cm.
    Includes index.
    ISBN 0-8018-6424-0 (alk. paper)
      1. Football—Maryland—Baltimore—History. 2. Baltimore Colts (Football team)—History. 3. Football—Collectibles—Maryland—Baltimore. I. Title.
GV959.53.B2 P27 2000
796.332′64′097526—dc21   00-020068

To my friend and colleague J O H N S T E A D M A N,
who has carried the torch for football in Baltimore,
on all levels, as its chronicler and its conscience,
for over half a century

CONTENTS

Color inserts appear following pages 72 and 200.

FOREWORD

It was July 1955 when I reported to the Baltimore Colts training camp for my first year in professional football. There was no way I could know what the coming years were going to bring. None of us—players, coaches, owner Carroll Rosenbloom, the people of Baltimore and Maryland—none of us realized we were all going to experience a rare and unforgettable era, and we were going to experience it together. I don't think any of us could then have foreseen the bond that would form between this team and its fans—a bond that would cross all lines whether economic, racial, cultural—and would be a powerful unifying force for an entire state.

The perspective of years has made it clearer to me how fortunate I was to arrive in Baltimore when I did. Mr. Rosenbloom was a people person. Don Kellett, the general manager, was the perfect man to head the effort to reach out to the people of Baltimore. The Colts organization did a masterful job of public relations. Mr. Rosenbloom's decision to hire Weeb Ewbank put the football operations in the hands of a man who not only would get the players he needed but give them a winning system of football—a combination that is very difficult to find. Weeb's masterstroke was recognizing the potential of John Unitas and signing him as a free agent. I have told myself over the years, "You were in the right place at the right time with the right people." Now I realize all of us who were a part of this special time can make that statement.

Very few people ever get a chance to be part of something like all of us did during those days. It is something to really be grateful for.

Raymond Berry

PREFACE

In my 27 years in Baltimore I don't know how many times I've heard the phrase, "Baltimore is really a football town"—this despite the Orioles' unparalleled success at the gate. Unfortunately, the very same month I arrived in Baltimore to become sports director of WBAL Radio, January 1973, Johnny Unitas was sent packing for San Diego. So, except for the three year play-off span of 1975, 1976, and 1977, I didn't get a chance to see firsthand Baltimore's love affair with football and the Colts. What I unfortunately experienced was the erosion of Colt football under the ownership of Bob Irsay, which of course culminated with the team's midnight Mayflower ride to Indianapolis in March 1984.

Needless to say, I didn't have to be here in person to know about the Colts' popularity not only in Baltimore but across the country. They had an appealing group of players who were impossible not to like. Johnny Unitas, Lenny Moore, Raymond Berry, Gino Marchetti, Big Daddy Lipscomb, and Art Donovan were part of a great collection of talented athletes who stayed together over a long period of time, preceding the Dallas Cowboys as "America's Team."

We saw the kind of idolatry that surrounded the love affair with the Colts in the 1982 movie *Diner,* directed by Baltimore native Barry Levinson. Colts fan Eddie Simmons made his bride-to-be, Elise, pass a test on Colt trivia before he'd marry her. The "diner guys" talked Colt football as they ate their french fries and gravy. And when Simmons got married, the organ played a slower version of the Colt fight song while the decor, from the dresses of the bridesmaids to the flower arrangements, was dominated by the blue and white colors of their beloved pro football team.

As first the voice of Morgan State football in 1978 and then the U.S. Naval Academy in 1983, beginning a 14-year stint, I saw the great tradition of college football perpetuated in the Baltimore area. In telecasting the Loyola–Calvert Hall game on Thanksgiving, I saw the fervor of high school football and the thrill the players got in playing on the hallowed turf of Memorial Stadium. It was the high schools that helped start it all in the waning years of the last century, joined by Johns Hopkins, Navy, Western Maryland, and the University of Baltimore. Navy–Notre Dame became a basic staple every other year in Baltimore. So did regular visits from the University of Maryland.

Baltimore has experienced it all when it comes to football. No other town can boast of championships in three leagues: the National Football League, the United States Football League, and the Canadian Football League. Now the Ravens hope to carry on the tradition in their new Camden Yards stadium. The Army-Navy game, college football's ultimate rivalry, has been played in Baltimore twice and a third meeting will ensue in 2000.

Football in Baltimore has had a proud history; in the pages that follow, this history will come alive thanks in part to both posed and action photographs as well as the myriad pieces of memorabilia that have survived the ages. Sit back and enjoy. It's time for the kickoff.

ACKNOWLEDGMENTS

A book of this magnitude could not have been possible without the efforts of many dedicated people, from fans to front office officials, coaches, the media, and the players themselves. First and foremost, I'd like to thank Baltimore's premier football historian, John Steadman, for his cooperation, his knowledge, and his generous support of this project. John helped on several fronts, from the college game to the pros. Vince Bagli also helped out with his recollections of Loyola–Calvert Hall, his affection for college football and the Naval Academy, and his well-known love of the Baltimore Colts.

Bob Lumsden, "Mr. Poly," who spanned the ages as a player and coach at his alma mater, was a key contributor to the City-Poly section, as well as to the history of other high school teams. Bob's vast collection of material on Poly and its rivalry with City was of great help in writing that chapter. The remarkable Howard "Dutch" Eyth, now in his 90s and a walking tribute to the joys of a clean life in athletics, reminisced about his 43 years at McDonogh. Local author and historian Paul Baker recalled his memories of playing for Mount St. Joseph in the late 1940s, the matchups with Patterson, and games at Baltimore Stadium.

Thanks go to former Navy sports information director Tom Bates and associate athletic director Eric Ruden; Maryland sports information director Chuck Walsh and his assistant Kevin Messenger; longtime Morgan State sports information director and friend Joe McIver; Johns Hopkins athletic director Tom Calder and sports information director Ernie LaRossa; Ravens public relations director

Kevin Byrne; former Baltimore Stallions publicist Mike Gathigan; sportscaster-historian Phil Wood; Ed Hargadan Jr., who recalled his high school years playing for his father at Loyola; and archivists Frayda Salkin of McDonogh and Liz Dausch of Gilman, who were extremely helpful in unearthing material on the 80-plus-year rivalry of Gilman and McDonogh. Thanks also to Ernie Accorsi, former Colts public relations director and assistant general manager, for his support, interest, and friendship.

Several collectors, all good friends, helped supplement the memorabilia sections with some spectacular pieces of Baltimore's football past. Dr. Richard Cohen, Blair Jett, Wayne Johnson, Ron Menchine, and Charles Winner all gave us peeks at their fabulous collections. Photographer Edwin Remsberg took the many memorabilia pictures and Naval Academy photographer Phil Hoffman provided photos of the Midshipmen. Michael Patterson deserves kudos for his proofreading and computer talents.

Over the past 20 years I have had an opportunity to interview many of the great figures from Baltimore's football history. The following individuals have generously shared their remembrances: Earl Banks, Johnny Unitas, Lenny Moore, Gino Marchetti, John Mackey, Arthur Donovan, Raymond Berry, Alex Sandusky, Johnny Sample, Tom Matte, Bert Jones, Stan White, Bruce Laird, Earl Morrall, Weeb Ewbank, Don Shula, Ordell Braase, Jim Parker, Alan Ameche, Glenn Davis, Joe Namath, Don Joyce, L. G. Dupre, Milt Davis, Ted Hendricks, Jim O'Brien, Art DeCarlo, Ted Marchibroda, Robert Irsay, Dick Modzelewski, Buddy Young, John Steadman, Vince Bagli, Paul Baker, and Dutch Eyth. Unless otherwise noted, all quotations from these individuals are from my interviews with them.

Last but not least, I'd like to thank Bob Brugger of the Johns Hopkins University Press for his encouragement, his support, and his unwavering belief in this project.

FOOTBALL IN BALTIMORE

ONE

The Early Years

Baltimore is of course known for its contributions in professional football with the fabled Colts of the 1950s, '60s and '70s. But almost 40 years before the National Football League was formed in an auto showroom in Canton, Ohio, on a hot summer's night in 1920, and over 65 years before the Colts made their debut in the All-America Football Conference in 1947, the city was playing and enjoying the game of football. Of course, the game that was played then bore no resemblance to the game of today. It is Great Britain that began the modern versions of football as an offshoot of rugby, and in the 1890s the game wasn't much more than a pushing-and-shoving match. Colleges like Princeton, Rutgers, Columbia, Harvard, and Yale fielded the first teams. The legendary Walter Camp helped refine the game at Yale and for over 30 years, from 1878 until his death in 1925, was a dominant force as a coach and rule-maker. It was Camp who devised a system of downs: If a team could gain five yards on three tries, it could keep the ball. This idea, along with the introduction of the scrimmage, earned Camp the title of "father of American football."

The game took hold for several reasons. First and foremost was its ruggedness and the thrill of bodily contact. It was also a game of surprises and deception which brought both delight and despair in quick order. The fact that it was played in the colorful and brisk fall season was another lure.

The roots of football in Baltimore are to be found at Johns Hopkins University, Mount Washington, the Baltimore Medical College,

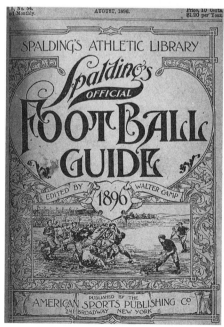

at the Naval Academy and nearby St. John's College in Annapolis, and at a few prestigious high schools, headed by Baltimore Polytechnic Institute and Baltimore City College (which had its thirteen-member team pictured in the 1906 edition of the *Spalding Official Football Guide*, a first for a local high school). City College, however, was fielding a competitive team long before that, playing the Naval Academy as early as 1894. The City boys lost 30-6, but that was no disgrace, considering Penn State mustered only six points in playing the Mids to a 6-6 tie the week before.

Johns Hopkins organized its first football team in 1881, playing in Druid Hill Park and later Clifton Park and using rules more akin to rugby than the game that we know today. After a year of learning the game, Hopkins met the Baltimore Athletic Club on October 7, 1882. The BAC won 4-0. Undaunted, Hopkins hosted Navy on Thanksgiving with snow on the ground. Navy, wearing canvas jackets, broke a scoreless tie with two second-half touchdowns to defeat the boys from Hopkins. A year later, on Thanksgiving Day 1883, Hopkins knocked off the Midshipmen for their first-ever football win. By 1888, playing at Oriole Park on Greenmount Avenue and Sixth Street, Johns Hopkins was beating the likes of Princeton, Navy, and the University of Virginia.

In 1896, former 1888 Johns Hopkins captain and halfback Paul J. Dashiell received a full-page picture in the Spalding *Official Football Guide* as a member of the National Football Rules Committee. The guide was edited by Walter Camp, who spent a large portion of the contents trying to justify the physical nature of the sport, which was under attack by many as being too violent. In fact, President Teddy Roosevelt, in a February 1907 speech at Harvard (reprinted in the 1908 Spalding *Guide*), defended the new game.

> There is no justification for stopping a thoroughly manly sport because it is sometimes abused. We cannot afford to turn out college men who shrink from physical effort or from a little physical pain. Courage is a prime necessity for the average citizen if he is to be a good citizen. Athletics are good, especially in their rougher forms, because they tend to develop such courage. They are good also because they encourage a true democratic spirit: for on the athletic

opposite page

An early Johns Hopkins eleven, the team of 1891, perched comfortably on wrestling mats.

Paul Dashiell, who helped bring football to both Johns Hopkins and the Naval Academy, is pictured in the 1896 Spalding *Football Guide*.

Cover of 1896 Spalding *Guide*.

field the man must be judged, not with reference to outside and accidental attributes, but to that combination of bodily vigor and moral quality which go to make up prowess.

Johns Hopkins finally cracked the team photo portion of the Spalding *Guide* in 1902.

In 1888 Dashiell moved on to the Naval Academy, where he became chairman of the Rules Committee and became known as the father of Navy football. He would remain on the committee for nearly three decades. In 1904, Dashiell began a three-year run as Navy head coach, posting a glittering 25-5-4 record, including 10-1-1 in 1905. (Also in 1904, Hopkins blanked its bigger neighbor to the south, the University of Maryland, 23-0.) Dashiell cut quite a swath across the early fabric of college football in the state of Maryland. For one thing, he played ten years of college football at St. John's College in Annapolis, Johns Hopkins, and Lehigh. Besides playing and coaching, Dashiell was a member of the Rules Committee for 27 years and helped outlaw the dangerous flying wedge in 1894. In 1904, he helped make the forward pass legal.

For a long period of time, the Hopkins Blue Jays more than held their own against Maryland in football. Football fell on hard times at Hopkins during World War I, however, with most able-bodied men in military uniforms, not football gear. In 1918, further hampered by a flu epidemic, the Blue Jays played only three games, beating St. John's of Annapolis, losing to Western Maryland, and playing Maryland to a scoreless tie. A highly respected coach, Dr. Ray Van Orman, was hired away from Cornell after the 1919 season to rebuild Hopkins football. Van Orman, who would coach from 1920 through 1933, brought Hopkins back to the big time, playing schools like Syracuse, Georgetown, and Virginia.

In 1921, Hopkins won the mythical state championship, defeating in-state opponents Mount St. Mary's and Western Maryland. One of the reasons was versatile Bill Wood, who transferred to West Point after the 1921 season and became one of Army's all-time greats, on and off the field. Reaching the rank of general, Wood later returned to coach the Cadets.

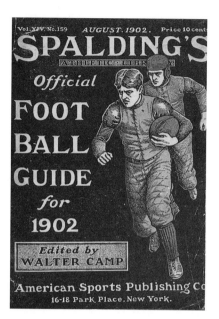

Cover of 1902 Spalding *Guide*.

In 1922, the Blue Jays played Maryland on Thanksgiving Day at Baltimore Stadium. In 1923, the game ended in a tie as did the next two Turkey Day games with Maryland. In 1924, Hopkins, led by Doug Turnbull, Tom Magill, and Walker Taylor, played Maryland to a 0-0 tie. They tied again at 7-7 in 1925, as underdog Hopkins held down the favored Terrapins. Then came a 17-14 win for Maryland in 1926, followed in 1927 by a 14-13 victory for Hopkins. It was a closely fought series that brought the Hopkins campus to a fever pitch every season. "All Maryland" great Gardner Mallonee anchored the line in that golden era of Hopkins football, playing both ways. Another standout was quarterback Bobby Lyons, who kept Maryland off balance with his passing and his place-kicking. Hopkins' fortunes began falling in the late 1920s, however, with Western Maryland, Maryland, and Navy coming to the forefront. Hopkins was becoming more noted for its dominance in lacrosse although Mallonee, assisted by Jack McNally, rekindled interest in Hopkins football in the late 1930s. In his book *Recreation and Athletics at Johns Hopkins*, published in 1977, G. Wilson Shaffer wrote about a letter sent to *Sunpapers* sports editor Jesse Linthicum from a fan in 1937. Wrote Jesse:

He came down from New York Saturday to see Navy and Notre Dame play in one of the standout games of the day. Figuring he would be able to obtain a ticket at the box office, this fan had made no reservation. Much to his surprise the Stadium was sold out. He drove out to Homewood to watch Johns Hopkins and here's the impression he took back to New York: "Arriving in Baltimore yesterday and not being able to secure even a fair seat for the Navy–Notre Dame show, I decided to drive out to Johns Hopkins and take a gander at their famous simon-pure athletic setup. I saw a peppy, scrappy, clean-looking bunch of youngsters play a good game of ball. But I also saw something else. I saw a boy named (Charley) Rudo, Jesse. That game should have been called 'Swarthmore versus Rudo.' He must have averaged four yards a try on the offensive and he was in on nine out of every ten tackles on the defense. Pound for pound he's as good as any back I've seen this year. Send one of your boys out there next week and see if I'm not right. Aside from Rudo, the thing that impressed me most was the sight of people walking right into the stadium without any semblance of a ticket—and not looking guilty about it. If Johns Hopkins University is a good sample of the simon-pure in athletics, then I'm all for it."

Rudo, who went on to manage a successful sporting goods operation, had starred for City College before enrolling at Hopkins. Thanks largely to the efforts of Rudo, Bill Vickers, Bill Day, John Milligan, and other mainstays, Hopkins put together five straight winning seasons leading into World War II, from 1937 through 1941. Longtime Baltimore sports columnist and football historian John Steadman says that some of his earliest recollections were of going to Johns Hopkins games, because it didn't cost anything to get into Homewood Field. "If you wrote a postcard to Hopkins early in the year, they'd send you a complimentary ticket that was gratis for all events played at Hopkins," recalls the dean of Baltimore sportswriters. "I remember watching Hopkins play a great Drexel team, coached by Walter Halas, the brother of Chicago Bears owner and coach George Halas. Drexel hammered Hopkins pretty good. Anchoring the Drexel line was Cameron Snyder, who grew up about three blocks from the Homewood campus and who would later cover the Baltimore Colts for the *Sunpapers* for over 30 years."

By 1906, City College was playing an 11-game schedule against college teams such as the Maryland Agricultural College in College Park, as well as local high school rivals such as Poly, Mount St. Joseph's, and Sparrows Point. Poly, then known as the Baltimore Manual Training School, began fielding teams against the wishes of faculty and administration and was not even allowed to use the school name, for fear it would discredit them. Although Poly's renowned rivalry with City dates back to 1889, poor record-keeping makes it hard to trace the exact scores. In fact, game programs throughout the years state that before 1903, when scores began to be officially recorded, City won all the games. That's because City was playing several college teams and considered Poly nothing but a practice game.

The first recorded score between City and Poly was from the 1901 game, won by City 5-0 at Union Park. Poly's first win over City wasn't until an 11-0 shutout in 1908. The game was witnessed by 2,000 fans at Oriole Park on November 20, 1908, and the win gave Poly the Interscholastic Championship of the East. Except for those early years and a tough stretch in the late '30s and early '40s, Poly has more than held its own. The Poly-City rivalry precedes such famous rivalries as Army-Navy (1890), Ohio State–Michigan (1897), and Penn-Cornell (1892). Only Boston English and Boston Latin have maintained a high school series for the same length of time. Only Princeton-Rutgers and Harvard-Yale have gone on longer in the college ranks. All that's known of the first game in 1889 is that the City JV team played Poly at Clifton Park and won the first of six unreported games. By 1895, City was playing a 16-game schedule against mostly college teams and once again had their scrubs play Poly to a scoreless tie.

One of the most famous Poly-City games was on November 20, 1926, at the Baltimore Stadium on 33rd Street. With over 20,000 fans in the stands, the game was scoreless heading into the fourth quarter. Poly's Harry Lawrence, who had already missed two dropkicks, tried a third from the 30 yard line and split the uprights for a 3-0 win. Lawrence later, after a stellar career at Bucknell, became a legendary coach at City College. One of Lawrence's protégés at Bucknell, George Young, coached City in the '60s and later coached as an assistant for the Colts and headed the front office of the New York Giants. When City lost its city-wide status and became a zoned school in the '70s, the Black Knights' fortunes fell. They dropped 17 straight to Poly from 1970 to 1986 and were outscored 464-71 before George Petrides brought City back to prominence. Game programs and tickets for City-Poly, as well as Loyola–Calvert Hall, were comparable to the college programs of the era. In many years they were oversized magazines packed with photos of the players, coaches, bands, and administrators. Mayors such as Theodore McKeldin and Thomas D'Alesandro Jr. sent greetings and welcomed fans to the annual clashes of Baltimore's football might.

Advertisers ranged from Koontz Creamery to Glenn L. Martin Aircraft to Brandau's Clothing on Greenmount Avenue. Tickets were

Team photos from City-Poly program, 1926.

THIRTY-EIGHTH ANNUAL FOOTBALL GAME
CITY-vs-POLY

BALTIMORE STADIUM
Saturday, November 20th, 1926

SOUVENIR PROGRAM   PRICE 10 CENTS

City-Poly program, 1926.

printed on heavy stock and were more impressive than those of most of the colleges and practically all of the pro teams.

Former player and coach Bob Lumsden has been on the field, the sidelines, or in the stands for over 60 City-Poly games since 1932, when he watched from the stands as his older brother Milt played for Poly. Lumsden began playing at Poly in 1938 as a sophomore tailback and coached several sports, including football and baseball, before retiring as athletic director in 1980. He served as head football coach from 1949 through 1966. "In my years as coach we used to draw over 30,000 fans at Memorial Stadium for City-Poly," he remembers. "There were only eight public high schools and most kids went to either Poly, City, Forest Park, or Southern. There were 3,000 boys at Poly and 3,000 boys at City and the fervor for the schools was community wide, not just East Baltimore or in the county." The game became a tradition on Thanksgiving Day, a tradition that Lumsden says began by accident. "We had to move the game from a Saturday because the Naval Academy wanted to play the Army-Navy game in 1944 on the same date. Loyola and Calvert Hall, the other great rivalry, who played on Thanksgiving, were kind enough to let us follow them on Thanksgiving afternoon and it stayed that way for the next 50 years." That 1944 game ended in a 7-7 tie with crowd estimate anywhere from 27,000 to 35,000.

Lumsden, now 79 and living in retirement in Baltimore County, lost his first game to City as head coach, 26-12 in 1949, but starting in 1950 won five straight and nine of ten. His overall record against City was 11-7. He wishes, like all coaches, that he could have done better. "Coaches create their own pressure but when you're attached to a school as much as I've been attached to Poly, it was like life and death when we played City." Dubbed "Mr. Poly" because of his longevity and devotion to Poly, Lumsden has some particularly vivid City-Poly memories. "The 1950 win, 12-0, which broke a four-game losing streak, was great and so was the 1959 win, also 12-0, because that team was one of the greatest in Poly history, when you look at speed, size, and ability," recalls Lumsden. "The 1962 team, which later that year played a team from Miami in the Orange Bowl, was also a favorite."

BALTIMORE CITY COLLEGE FOOTBALL SQUAD, 1926

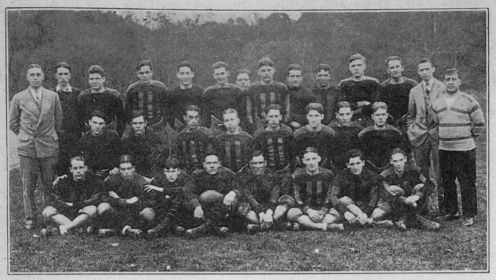

FRONT ROW (Sitting)			MIDDLE ROW			BACK ROW (Standing)				
No.	Name	Pos.	No.	Name	Pos.	No.	Name	Pos.		
33	Wilbourne, H. M.	R. E.	..	Baker, Wm.	R. G.	..	Armstrong, H. E. Asst. C.		12 Dummer, R.	L. E.
14	Mallard, G. B.	R. E.	31	Gibson, A. R.	R. G.	..	Streett, C.	Asst. Mgr.	.. Carter	
28	Parker, Wm.	R. H.	17	Hipp, Wm.	F. B.	8	Benson, H. H.	L. T.	.. Stevenson, A. F.	F. B.
15	Morris, J. D. Capt.	L. G.	3	Proffitt.	L. H.	19	Warlow, F. W.	R. T.	23 Robertson, J.	L. G.
34	Noonan, M. F.	L. H.	13	Green, L.	Q.	..	Klein, B.	L. G.	.. Leidig, F.	L. T.
5	Lloyd, F.	Q.	2	Helm, O.	R. T.	4	Thomas, S.	C.	.. Laudeman, W.	Mgr.
35	Feldman, M. B.	L. E.	..	Bower,	L. G.	32	Gordy, L.		.. Goddard, H.	Coach
9	Kircher, F.	L. E.	20	Borchers, H.	C.					

BALTIMORE POLYTECHNIC INSTITUTE FOOTBALL SQUAD, 1926

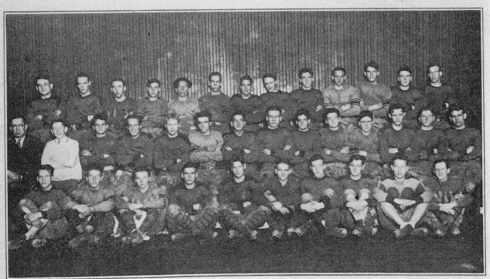

TOP ROW (Left to Right)			2ND ROW (Left to Right)			3RD ROW (Left to Right)			OTHER PLAYERS		
No.	Name	Pos.	No.	Name	Pos.	No.	Name	Pos.	No.	Name	Pos.
4	Fisher	T.	..	Geo. Hoban	Coach	8	Hoffert	T.	..	McClaskey	Lin
10	Keyes	T.	..	Boone	Asst. Coach	..	Sullivan		..	Magill	
20	Uhrig	G.	27	Miller	C.	..	Heffner		..	Taliaferro	
28	Limpert	H. B.	12	Doernerberg	G.	1	Lawrence	H. B. & Q. B.	..	Bialoskorski	
7	Kamphaus	E.	3	Boyd	T. & G.	35	Bishop	H. B.	..	Kantman	Lin
2	Pearce	E.	6	Di Massia	T. & G.	16	MacCubbin	C.	17	Johnson	
4	Pugh	H. B.	6	Rosenberg	F.	13	Kirby	T. & G.	5	Porter	
14	Parks	C.	7	Bledsoe	H. B. & C.	8	Linck	E.	..	Young	H.
10	Carvel	T.	11	Turnbull	Q. B.	32	Mitchell	Q. B.	7	Kamphaus	
12	Grondell	G.	1	Stayer	H. B.				22	Hoffstetter	
6	Besore	H. B.	5	Henderson	H. B.				4	Weitzel	
			310	Usinger, Capt.	T.						
			33	Pollard	F. B.						
			2	Powell	C.						

POLY CITY

IN THE STADIUM AT
BALTIMORE
SATURDAY - NOVEMBER - 19 - 1927
PRICE 15 CENTS

High school football was at its zenith in Baltimore in the years after World War II and into the 1950s. "We'd play night games at Memorial Stadium against Calvert Hall, Loyola, and others and draw 15,000 or more," says Lumsden. "It was a town thing, a family thing, and a community thing because the schools were all closely associated. The kids knew the kids on the other teams, the families knew the families, and they were just big, fun events."

Lumsden had an effect on many of the young men he coached. For every great player there were eight or ten who had limited ability but were made better players and human beings because of their association with "Mr. Poly." Some of the great ones that come to mind: "The play of Roland Savage, the play of Ernie Torain, the play of competitors like Ed Stuckrath, the Spangler brothers Bill and John, Jack Scarbath, and Harry Olszewski, was something I'll never forget," says a wistful Lumsden. In the mid-1940s, a 125-pound kid from the Hamilton section of Baltimore came out for football. He played center. The next year he weighed 145 pounds as a sophomore and still played center. One day in practice, Lumsden, then an assistant coach, saw the kid pick up a ball and throw it. "I told Bill McLean, the head coach, 'I don't think that kid's going to be a center.'" Lumsden was right. The kid from Hamilton was Jack Scarbath, who became a star quarterback at Poly and went on to become an All-American first-team quarterback at Maryland under Jim Tatum.

"To this day," says Lumsden, who retired in 1980, "many kids going back to 1945 and 1946 stop by to visit, call me, send me letters, take me places." Former Lumsden stars include Tubby Smith, the first black ball player at Lumsden's alma mater, High Point College. When Smith left Georgia to take over as head basketball coach at the University of Kentucky, his successor, Ron Jersa, was the son of Lumsden's all-scholastic pitcher at Poly in 1949. "So what goes around, comes around." Lumsden picked Augie Waibel to follow him. Waibel coached at Poly for thirty-one years, compiling 280 wins and a 22-4 advantage over City.

Another great rivalry in Baltimore is Loyola–Calvert Hall, played on Thanksgiving at either Municipal Stadium, Homewood Field, Ori-

opposite page

Poly-City program, 1927.

ole Park, Memorial Stadium, or, in 1998, the Ravens' new stadium at Camden Yards. It began in 1920 with Calvert Hall winning 9-3, and after Loyola's 40-6 conquest at the Ravens Stadium in 1999, which was their 11th straight win and 14th out of 15 in the series, the Dons lead the overall series 42-30, with eight ties. In that first game on November 12, 1920, Calvert Hall fullback Louis Walker, who formerly played for Loyola, scored all his team's points on a first quarter field goal and fourth quarter touchdown. The game was tied 3-3 with five minutes left when Loyola fumbled on the Calvert Hall 5 yard line. Calvert Hall marched upfield when, from his own 40, Walker caught a pass from Ray Brooks and raced 35 yards for the winning score.

In 1925, Loyola had one of its greatest seasons, blanking unbeaten City College 25-0, and, after scoreless ties with the Hall in both 1923 and 1924, Loyola shut out Calvert Hall in 1925, 7-0.

In 1940, Loyola and Calvert Hall played another memorable game. The teams were scoreless at halftime. At the beginning of the second half, the Cardinals blocked one of Len Kelly's kicks deep in Loyola territory. Three plays later Dick Waldt, whose son Jobie also quarterbacked Calvert Hall, heaved a 28-yard pass to Bob Filippeli in the end zone for the score. The try for the point after was blocked, making the score Calvert Hall 6, Loyola 0. From this point on, the Cardinals never threatened while the Blue and Gold (Dons didn't become the Loyola nickname until 1944) had the ball in Calvert Hall territory several times but couldn't dent the goal line, tossing two interceptions. They did muster a safety but lost to the Hall 6-2. Fans leaving this Thanksgiving morning game got on the streetcar and made their way home; within an hour they would have an early edition of the *News-Post* or the *Evening Sun* with the first quarter score of the Poly-City game. Those were magic times.

Loyola dominated the series from the state championship season of 1943 through 1963, winning 18 of 21 games. Ed Hargaden began a 15-year association with Loyola in 1942, coaching the legendary Bob Williams, who quarterbacked the Notre Dame Fighting Irish and became an All-American in 1950. Another great Hargaden product was his son Ed Jr., who had been in the locker room as a young boy, a player in 1953 through 1955, and then an alumnus. He re-

opposite page

Running back John Spangler helped lead Poly to a 14-6 win over City in 1962.

Legendary Poly coach Bob Lumsden on sideline, 1964.

Poly's 1959 team shut out City 12-0.

Official Program 25c

CALVERT HALL
vs.
LOYOLA

Thursday
November 24, 1949

STADIUM
Baltimore, Md.

LON KELLER

membered his father giving the same speech every year before the big game with Calvert Hall. "He would gather the players together and after some quick comments about the game plan, would get deadly serious and address the seniors playing their last game for him. 'Boys,' he would say, 'there is only one thing I wish for today. I wish that when this game is over, that you can walk off this field with pleasant memories.' The coach then explained what pleasant memories meant," continued Ed Jr. "It meant that you played your last game with reckless abandon, holding nothing back, playing like your last breath of air depended on it, trying to perform things that you never dreamed could happen. The coach then promised that if you could do that, you would be assured of pleasant memories and that they would last a lifetime." Against Calvert Hall Ed Jr. played on three Loyola winners, and after the last one in 1955, a 32-7 trouncing that enabled the Dons to win the MSA championship, the emotion of it hit him in the locker room. "All I could do is quietly slip into the men's room and lock myself into a stall where I wept quietly. I knew I would have pleasant memories, but I also knew that it was OVER. I would never be able to wear a Loyola football uniform again—only in my memories."

Loyola played the highly touted Boys Town team of Nebraska and Father Flanagan fame in 1945, hosting the 8-0 team from Omaha at Baltimore Stadium before 20,000 fans. Led by flashy African American halfback Ken Morris, who dashed 88 and 99 yards for touchdowns, Boys Town won 26-0.

Tracy Mehr took over from Hargaden in 1957, and during his six-year tenure, his teams never fell to Calvert Hall. Loyola's Henry Blaha was the league's star runner in the early 1960s. In 1961 he scored 118 points—32 on Thanksgiving morning in a 38-12 win. Joe Brune, who played tackle at Loyola in the early 1950s, took over as coach at Loyola in 1967 and is still at the helm, 33 years later. He coached the Dons in the Golden Anniversary game and in the Diamond Anniversary showdown in 1994.

Calvert Hall has also had its share of coaching legends. "Dutch" Lentz coached during the 1920s and also coached the basketball team to 59 straight wins. Nick Burtscher coached undefeated teams in

opposite page

Noted illustrator Lon Keller drew the cover of the 1949 Loyola–Calvert Hall program.

1932 and 1934. Joe Mellendick played for Loyola in the 1930s and then coached George Young, Tom Scott, Joe Carroll, and Frank O'Brien to win the 1948 game 13-0 over the Dons. Former Colt Bob Nowaskey coached in the early 1950s, and George Young from 1954 to 1958. Augie Miceli won 101 games from 1974 through 1987 and beat the Dons seven straight times. Bill Mackley and Lou Eckerl have carried on the tradition in recent years. Perhaps the strangest game in the series was in 1989 when Loyola won 15-12 without benefit of a first down. They had two long runs for touchdowns.

In 1949, as a high school freshman at Mount St. Joe, Paul Baker watched his alma mater rout favored Patterson 24-0 before over 20,000 fans at Baltimore Stadium. In 1944 as a nine-year-old, Baker, who would go on to play for the Mount and later coach several area high school and college basketball teams, watched in awe with his dad as Army beat Navy. "It was freezing cold and we collected several splinters on the stadium bleachers," remembers Baker, "but it didn't matter as we sipped our hot chocolate and dined on corned beef sandwiches from Nate's and Leon's on North Avenue. The whole scene, from the cadets and midshipmen marching on, to watching Glenn Davis and Doc Blanchard lead Army to victory, was spellbinding."

Baker talks about the 1949 Patterson–Mount St. Joe's clash as if it were yesterday. "Patterson was a juggernaut in those years under Irv Biasi," remembers Paul. "They had a 29-game win streak heading into their game with Mount St. Joe's, who had their best team ever. Like Patterson, they were kids from East Baltimore, so it was literally a neighborhood game. It was scheduled for a Friday night but a huge Nor'easter storm forced postponement until Monday afternoon. There would have been 30,000 there on Friday night." Baker remembers St. Joe blocking a kick on the opening series and running it in for a touchdown. Over a dozen players in the game went on to play major college football. "St. Joe's had it all that year," says Baker. "They had two backs who ran the 100-yard dash in 10 flat. In fact one ran it in 9.8 and neither of them were the leading ball carriers on the team. The coach was Vic Wojcihovski, who had played for

Patterson–Mount St. Joseph program cover, 1949.

Notre Dame in the mid-1930s as a running back. He was a mean, tough guy. Not a great coach, but he had the persona of a leader of men. All his players respected him greatly." Baker went on to play for Mount St. Joe's as a 140-pounder and played a half dozen games at Baltimore Stadium. The next year, 1950, Patterson again played Mount St. Joe's in the stadium and the game finished in a 7-7 tie. Patterson's Dick Bielski, who went on to a great career at Maryland and played with the NFL Colts, Cowboys, and Eagles, ran 50 yards for a touchdown with Bobby Benzing, the Mount's best all-around player, on his back unsuccessfully trying to wrestle him down over the last 20 yards.

Gilman and McDonogh have waged war on the gridiron since 1914. In 84 meetings the Greyhounds of Gilman hold the advantage, 50 wins to 29 losses with five ties. No games were played in 1916 or in 1918 during World War I. McDonogh, founded in 1873 in rural Pikesville as a military school for boys from poor backgrounds, began playing football in 1887. With colors of orange and black, they played their first game on December 7, 1889, hosting Carey School. Mc-Donogh was leading 19-4 when the game was "called" because Carey had to catch a train home.

Gilman opened its doors in the fall of 1897 in Roland Park and in 1914 hosted McDonogh in the first game of the series, winning 35-0. The average weight of the Gilman players was 148 pounds, to 133 for the "Pikesvillians," as McDonogh was then known. Gilman dominated the first 16 games of the series, winning 14, 13 by shutouts. There was also a 0-0 tie in 1919, with the lone McDonogh win, 6-0, coming in 1927. John Joh recovered a fumble for the only touchdown of the game and McDonogh's first win in the series. It also capped an unbeaten season for the 225-boy school that included a 20-0 win over City and its 3,500 boys.

One of the reasons Gilman dominated in the early years was that every boy was required to play football. Led by runner-kickers Tripp Haxall and Ray Scarlett, Gilman beat Poly at Homewood Field to go unbeaten and win the 1917 city championship. The 1921 Gilman squad, quarterbacked by all-time great Jake Slagle, rolled to a perfect 8-0 season that featured a 45-0 trouncing of McDonogh. In 1931, Gilman blanked the Cadets 27-0 on their way to the state championship. In 1940 at Homewood Field, Gilman blanked McDonogh 25-0 on a muddy field as the one-two punch of captain George Franke and Joe Moore accounted for three touchdowns. The Gilman defense didn't allow McDonogh inside the 30 yard line all day.

In 1962, Gilman, coached by Reddy Finney, knocked off unbeaten McDonogh 21-6 to go unbeaten for the first time in 41 years.

Gilman captain John Claster gained 128 yards on 31 carries and scored 14 points to give him 116 for the season.

The 1967 Greyhounds, Finney's last team before he became headmaster, rolled over all nine opponents by an average score of 41-9. Assistant coach Nick Schloeder then took over as head coach.

McDonogh fielded seven teams in weight classes of 65, 75, 85, 95, 105, 118, and 130 pounds, as well as the varsity. McDonogh's fortunes began to pick up in 1932 when Herb Armstrong and Howard C. "Dutch" Eyth took over as varsity coaches. Armstrong had played professional baseball and became a top college football official. Eyth had played football at Carnegie Tech, and in 1927 helped Tech upset Knute Rockne's Notre Dame Fighting Irish, 27-7. In 1930, Rockne's last season before perishing in a plane crash, Notre Dame went a perfect 10-0, including a 21-6 win over Carngie Tech in the new Notre Dame stadium. Tech's only touchdown was scored on a 75-yard run by "Dutch" Eyth.

The Depression was gripping the country in 1931, and nearing graduation Dutch had sent out over 100 resumes, without much luck. He got a tip that McDonogh in Baltimore was looking for a teacher, preferably with experience in athletics. "I jumped at it," recalls Eyth, now an amazingly spry 92. "I ended up staying for 43 years, 29 as athletic director and living right on the grounds."

McDonogh followed its 1932 win over Gilman with a 33-0 win in 1933, going unbeaten for the second year in a row and topping the 1932 season by going unscored upon. In 1938, 6,000 fans watched as the Cadets blanked Gilman 13-0 in the newly dedicated John McDonogh Stadium. Dutch remembers taking all the different teams—the 65-, 75-, 85-, 95-, 105-, 118-, and 130-pound teams—along with the JV and varsity over to Episcopal School in Alexandria, Virginia at nine o'clock in the morning; they'd play all day, ending with the varsity game at 3 P.M.

"We had a nice rivalry with Gilman," remembers Dutch, who also refereed college games for 33 years. "It's always been a good rivalry. At first the two schools genuinely disliked each other but once I became athletic director, with help from Reddy Finney, I tried to help civilize the relationship." Dutch's final team in 1953 beat Gilman

19-7 to go unbeaten and win the MSA championship for the first time since 1936. They outscored the opposition 217 points to 7.

Navy and Maryland have enjoyed rich football associations with the city of Baltimore. Navy's first-ever game, on December 11, 1879, was a 0-0 tie with the Baltimore Athletic Club on the Academy superintendent's cow pasture. The game resembled soccer more than football and was organized by William John Maxwell of the class of 1881. From his experience with sails Maxwell knew that canvas was extremely slippery when wet, and so he designed a sleeveless canvas jacket for the players that would make them difficult to grasp when they began to sweat. His ingenuity was hailed by Walter Camp, who dubbed Maxwell the designer of the first football uniform. On this first football game in Annapolis, the *Baltimore American and Chronicle* newspaper reported in its December 12 edition:

> The game, played under Rugby rules, was a battle from beginning to end—a regular knock down and drag out fight. Both sides became immediately excited and the audience was aroused to the highest pitch of enthusiasm by the spirited contest. The ball oscillated backward and forward over the ground without any material result.
>
> The scrimmages were something awful to witness—living, kicking, scrambling masses of humanity surging to and fro, each individual after the leather oval. If a Baltimorean got the ball and started for a run he was unfailingly caught by one of the brawny Cadets and dashed to earth with five or six men falling on him. The Middies were never allowed to get hold of the ball at all.

When Maxwell graduated in 1880, there was nobody at the Academy to keep the football flame burning until 1882 when Navy's first coach, Vaulx Carter, put a team together and challenged the Clifton Football Club of Baltimore to a game on a snowy Thanksgiving Day, November 28. The Middies won the game 8-0 and the "Cliftons" really were the boys from Johns Hopkins, who played under a club name because of the coldness of the Hopkins authorities toward foot-

opposite page

Pepper Constable, captain of the 1931 Gilman team, has the ball at left while the McDonogh defender does a pirouette in midair. Constable was named All-State in 1930 and 1931.

The McDonogh varsity lines up with their future replacements and younger classmates, circa mid-1930s.

THE W.B. & A. ELECTRIC LINE IS THE ONLY ROAD WHOSE CARS RUN THROUGH THE STREETS OF ANNAPOLIS TO THE GRAND STAND AT NEW NAVY FOOT BALL FIELD. CARS LEAVE FROM GRAND STAND AT CLOSE OF GAME. BE SURE AND GET ROUND TRIP TICKETS FROM BALTIMORE AND WASHINGTON.

Postcard shows game action in Annapolis with an inset of the Baltimore and Annapolis Railway, 1911.

ball. A midshipman named George Washington Street from Wisconsin had the distinction of making the first Navy score in football history. The November 29, 1882, *Baltimore American* talked about the second half, saying the rest period had apparently "stiffened the Cliftons, for the Academy, making a vigorous spurt, got the ball through them and Street scored a touchdown." In the first half the ball reportedly sailed over the seawall at one point and had to be retrieved by boat before the game could continue. The November 29 *Baltimore Sun* reported that Hopkins wore worsted jerseys with black and light blue stripes, white knee pants, and long blue stockings. Navy wore maroon stockings, white canvas pants, and jackets with maroon lacings. Headgear had not been developed, but both teams wore a strip of leather nailed on their soles to prevent slipping.

On Thanksgiving Day 1883, Navy once again played Johns Hopkins, who by now had the blessing of their faculty, and the Blue Jays won 2-0 on a pair of one-point safeties. As in 1882, as well as in the following year, it was Navy's only game of the season. The November 23, 1883, *Baltimore American* reported that "the game began in heat and discussion and ended in quarrel and wrangle. At one point matters grew so hot that the Hopkins team was about to stop playing. The Hopkins team had the skill and light weight; the Academy team the endurance and muscle." Navy turned the tables in 1884 with a 9-0 win, but lost again to Hopkins 12-8 in 1885. Hopkins and Navy played twice in 1886, the Mids winning by 6-0 and 15-14 scores. Hopkins dominated Navy in 1888, winning 25-12. The "Hoppies" uncovered something new in the game—a cheering section which gave the team yell in unison.

Navy's gridiron fortunes began to change for the better in 1889 when the Mids won four of six games and tied another, blanking Johns Hopkins 36-0 and dominating Virginia 26-6. The Mids stopped playing Hopkins after that year and except for a pair of games against the surprising Baltimore Medical College in 1900 and 1903, didn't play a Baltimore team again until 1911 when they opened with Johns Hopkins after a hiatus of 22 years. Navy beat the Medical College 6-0 in 1900, as the future doctors turned what was supposed to be a breather into a battle royal. Nobody took the Baltimore Medics seriously in 1903 either, but the Mids were fortunate to escape with a 0-0 tie. Future Admiral "Bull" Halsey was the big gun on the Navy team in '03.

College football reached a crisis in 1909 forcing the liberalization of passing rules to open up the game. A first down would be achieved in ten yards and not five, and the downs allowed to make it went from three to four. Several players were killed in 1909, including Navy quarterback Earl Wilson, who broke his neck in the Villanova game and died six months later. Wilson had also starred in baseball, basketball, gymnastics, boxing, pole vaulting, and tennis. Cadet Eugene Byrne of Army was killed in the Harvard game and Archer Christian of Virginia was fatally injured in the Georgetown game. The Army-Navy game was cancelled, as the game came under siege for its roughness.

Johns Hopkins found Navy to be a much more formidable opponent when they resumed play in 1911, with the Mids winning 27-5, the first points allowed by Navy in two years. Seven more Navy shutouts followed, including a 3-0 win over Army. The next year, 1912, was much different, as the Mids barely escaped with a 7-3 win over Hopkins. In 1919, Navy played Johns Hopkins for the last time, rolling over the Blue Jays 66-0.

Navy's days of playing teams from Baltimore were almost over, but their days of playing games in Baltimore were just beginning. The

A newspaper rotogravure of the 1919 Naval Academy football team.

reason was a brand new stadium constructed on 33rd Street in North-east Baltimore on the same spot where Memorial Stadium now sits. At the urging of Mayor William Broening in the fall of 1921, the sta-dium was built in only seven months after a site was selected. Sites considered included Clifton Park, Druid Hill Park, Wyman Park, the abandoned Mount Royal Reservoir at North and Mount Royal Av-enues, and historic locales near Federal Hill and Fort McHenry. In the end, Venable Park, surrounded by newly constructed residential neighborhoods, was selected. In order to save on steel costs, the stadium was dug out of the ground in the form of a giant horseshoe with the open end pointed toward 33rd Street, where an administration building was constructed. Wooden planks were erected for seating over the earthen sides. Only a limited number of chair seats were installed over concrete, with most of them nearer the playing field. The wooden bleachers were at the mercy of the weather and often needed replacing. The cost to build the stadium: a thrifty $458,000.

Municipal Stadium opened on December 2, 1922, when 50,000 fans turned out to see the Army's 3rd Corps Area play the Quantico Marines. Before the game, a procession of 12,000 soldiers and Marines marched to the stadium from the Mount Royal Railroad Station. There was much ballyhoo surrounding the game, with several cabinet officials on hand from Washington. A special phone hookup was installed so that President Warren Harding and first lady Florence could get a play-by-play account of the game. Although Army's Gene Vidal scored the first points on a field goal, the Quantico team, which included several former Army Cadets and Navy Midshipmen, won the game 13-12. (The Army had suffered a similar fate the year before at Homewood Field, when they were coached by future Allied commander and president of the United States, Dwight D. Eisenhower.)

Sun correspondent Raymond Tompkins wrote about the Baltimore Stadium inaugural game in a December 3 front-page story: "United States Marines, fighting by land and air, beat the United States Army, 13-12, at football yesterday in Venable Stadium, Baltimore's mighty outdoor arena. It was a new stadium, dedicated just before the game. The crowd of over 50,000 people, who sat and stood in and around it, was seeing it in use for the first time. It is not a new stadium now. It has lived and suffered, if a giant of concrete and earth can do that. It knows the blackest depths of despair and the most golden heights of triumph, ending with a struggle that should have rocked a mountain." The crowd included over 43,000 in permanent seats, 10,000 standing along the sidelines, and 7,000 on the outside, eager to get a glimpse of the goings-on inside.

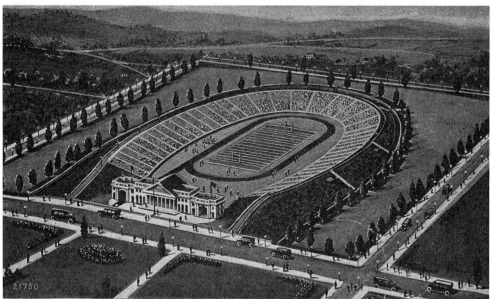

Within two years the seating capacity was almost doubled, enabling the city to host the annual Army-Navy game. The new stadium was awesome in size, encompassing some 20 acres with the playing field alone covering 7 acres. Erecting the stadium was the first big step needed to get Baltimore into baseball's and football's big leagues.

Navy wasted no time in scheduling a game in the new stadium, playing Princeton to a 3-3 tie on October 27, 1923. It was one of three ties played by the Mids in 1923, including a 14-14 standoff against Washington in the 1924 Rose Bowl and the only tie in the Army-Navy series, 0-0. Over 45,000 fans turned out at the Venable Municipal Stadium to see the underdog Mids play favored Princeton. Said the *Baltimore Sun* the next morning: "The noise cannot be described . . . like 10 tempests with a boiler factory and a couple dozen airship motors thrown in." Navy's points came from Herb Ballinger's 25-yard field goal that tied the game in the final two minutes. With the brigade of Midshipmen looking on, Princeton stopped the Mids three times inside the 5-yard line.

Navy struggled in 1924, winning just two games with a dozen new faces from the Bowl team the year before. The Mids were 30-point underdogs against Army in the annual game which was played at the new stadium in Baltimore on November 29. With President and Mrs. Calvin Coolidge looking on, Army could muster only 12 points on four field goals by captain Ed Garbisch, who missed three field goals in the first six minutes. The game ended up as a moral victory for the outmanned Midshipmen, even though they lost 12-0. Famed *New York Tribune* sportswriter Grantland Rice eloquently described the All-American Garbisch's one-man blitz of the Midshipmen in the next day's editions:

> Ed Garbisch, the big Army Captain, used his big right toe as a flaming howitzer today in the Baltimore Stadium and beat the Navy singlehanded as 80,000 people looked down upon the field of war. Probably the greatest gathering that ever saw a football battle in the East surrounded the Maryland plain as the brilliant Army center drop-kicked four field goals and came within one shot of tying the five-goal record which Brickley and Eckersall had established in

opposite page

The 1921 Navy team, captained by "Swede" Larson, came within a touchdown of winning the national championship.

An early postcard shows an artist's rendering of the new Baltimore Stadium, ca. 1924.

OFFICIAL PROGRAM
1924

27TH ANNUAL
ARMY NAVY
GAME
BALTIMORE
MARYLAND

other years. For it was Garbisch 12 and Navy 0, as the game ended under a gray, shadowy sky with a shrill wind singing its song of winter from the north. He had, after the early misses, been adjusting his famous toe to the proper range with care and coolness. He was getting nearer and nearer to his mark and when the alert Fraser blocked a Navy kick around midfield the proud citizens of Washington, Pa., where Garbisch lives, were about ready to light the old home bonfire in honor of the gallant deeds of a native son. When the Navy braced and repelled the next attack, Garbisch, from the 32-yard line, sent a dropkick spinning on its way to Army glory.

By this time the Army mule was beginning to look with envy upon a right foot of such power and precision, and the demonstration which broke out among the 1,200 Cadets came near shaking the big stadium loose from its mooring and caving down the concrete walls.

The official program for the 27th Army-Navy game featured a full-page photograph of the nation's commander-in-chief, President Calvin Coolidge, with advertisers from all over the country. On page 12, there was an advertisement for Stewart & Co., Baltimore's premier department store at Howard and Lexington Streets, "the store where you can get what you like and like what you get." Beneath the Stewart's ad was one for the Emerson Hotel, where a person could get a room with a bath for $3 and up. O'Neill's at Charles at Lexington, "where quality rules the whims of fashion," was a proud advertiser, as was Isaac Hamburger and Sons on Baltimore at Hanover Streets, "where you can score with style." The Southern Hotel proudly called itself "Army and Navy Headquarters" in its one-page ad which proudly recounted a tradition going back to George Washington and the Old Fountain Inn of colonial days on the same spot. Alex Brown & Sons of Baltimore, the oldest banking house in the United States; Baker, Watts & Co.; Hochschild Kohn; Hutzler Brothers; and Koester's honey bread were also advertisers, in amidst photos of the players, coaches, and scenes of West Point and Annapolis. Inside the front cover was a color ad for Camel cigarettes and on the back cover a Norman Rockwell–type advertisement for Black Jack

opposite page

Army-Navy game program, 1924.

chewing gum. At a cost of 50 cents, the game program was a classy keepsake.

After the 1924 Army-Navy game, the Naval Academy brass decided to play one game a season in the cavernous horseshoe in Baltimore, representing a huge payday when compared to tiny Thompson Stadium on the Academy grounds. In 1925 a heavily favored Princeton eleven, en route to the Ivy League title, came down to play Navy in Baltimore. The Tigers were badly mauled and were lucky to escape with a 10-10 tie, as the Mids played their best game of the year. Fifty-five thousand fans cheered as Navy came back in the last period to tie on Tom Hamilton's 35-yard pass to Alan Shapley.

Navy posted one of its greatest seasons ever in 1926, winning nine straight games before being tied by Army 21-21 in a classic. Sparked by quadruple threat Tom Hamilton, the Mids were recognized as the top football team in the land. Hamilton, who excelled at running, passing, punting, and dropkicking, led the Mids to five straight wins before an October 30 game against powerful Michigan, a team that had dealt the Mids their worst defeat ever the year before, 54-0, in Baltimore. Despite Michigan's being laden with All-Americans such as Benny Friedman and Benny Oosterbaan and sporting a 17-game win streak, Navy rose up and blanked the Wolverines 10-0. Howard Caldwell scored the first touchdown against Michigan in 13 games. W. Wilson Wingate wrote the next day in the *Baltimore Sun*: "Only a brilliant football team could have beaten Michigan yesterday and this is the type of team Navy sent on the field with the 1925 score of 54 to 0 still silhouetted against the skyline of memory."

Later in the season, the Mids played little Loyola College of Baltimore, which stunned the Mids by taking a 13-0 lead early in the game. Navy quickly regrouped, however, and coasted to a 35-13 victory. The Army-Navy game of 1926 was played before 110,000 fans at the dedication of Chicago's Soldier Field. Army, led by "Light Horse" Harry Wilson and Chris Cagle, hung on to a 21-14 lead late in the game when Navy mounted a final drive. Facing a fourth and five on the 8-yard line, Alan Shapley scored on a naked reverse in the final minute. Tom Hamilton, who would win the Bronze Star and the Legion of Merit for his achievements in World War II and who would

opposite page

Parker Brothers thought so much of Navy Captain Tom Hamilton they created a board game in his honor.

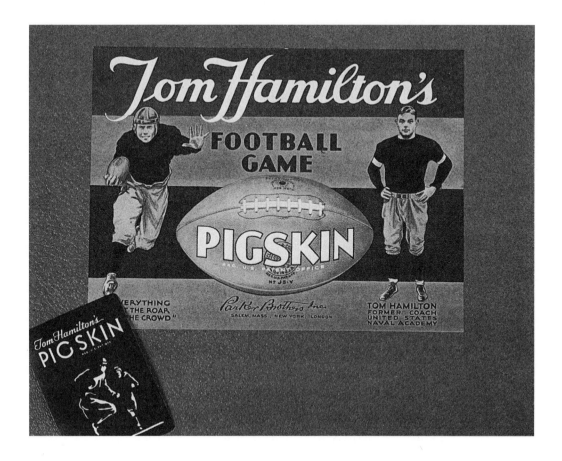

later coach the Navy football team, dropkicked the ball through the uprights for the tying point in the 21-21 standoff. There were some anxious moments at the end as Army drove to the Navy 16 but sure-footed Harry Wilson missed the field goal attempt from the 25 yard line with seconds to go, thus ending one of the greatest games in college football history. The game etched such a deep impression in the nation's sports consciousness that Parker Brothers released a board game commemorating the classic. The game was called "Tom Hamilton's Pigskin."

In 1927, Navy and Notre Dame began a tradition of yearly play that continues to the present day. The brothers Ingram, Navy athletic director Jonas and head football coach Bill, had enjoyed a great friendship with Notre Dame coach and athletic director Knute Rockne. The Irish had played Army every year since 1913; now they would play Navy as well. The fact that one of Rockne's great players, Edgar "Rip" Miller, one of the fabled "Seven Mules" on the line that featured the "Four Horsemen" backfield, was now the Navy offensive line coach, was also a plus in cementing the relationship. Rockne was interested in making Notre Dame into a national attraction, having also worked out a home-and-home series with the University of Southern California.

The longest intersectional rivalry in college football history kicked off in Baltimore on the afternoon of October 15, 1927, before over 53,000 fans, including trainloads of rooters from Chicago and South Bend. Navy grabbed an early 6-0 lead against the favorite Irish that lasted until the third quarter, but Notre Dame rallied behind Christy Flanagan's two touchdowns in the second half to win 19-6. Since that first game in 1927 the Irish have dominated the series with Navy, winning 63 games, losing nine, and tying one. Unlike the 1924 Army-Navy game program, the first Navy–Notre Dame game program had no advertising at all containing photos of school officials, coaches, and players; team pictures; lineups; records; and songs and yells.

The following year, after losing to Notre Dame 7-0 in Chicago before the largest crowd ever to witness a football game in the United States (117,000 at Soldier Field), the Mids played powerful Michigan in Baltimore and tied the Wolverines 6-6. Johnny Gannon's 75-yard touchdown run had given the Mids the lead but Michigan pulled even in the final quarter. Navy didn't rest on its laurels, crushing Loyola of Baltimore 57-0 the following week.

Notre Dame, en route to a national championship and an unbeaten season in 1929, came to Baltimore and barely got by Navy 14-7 before 80,000 fans. In 1930, the Mids played Ohio State and Southern Methodist in Baltimore, and with Rip Miller as head coach notched their first win over Notre Dame on November 4, 1933, by a score of 7-0; legendary Navy back Fred "Buzz" Borries scored the only touchdown of the game. On a defense that blanked the Irish was a big tackle named Slade Cutter, who was destined the following year to sink Army with a field goal in a 3-0 game.

With Navy playing Notre Dame every other year in Baltimore and other college powers coming to town at least once and oftentimes

opposite page

The first Navy–Notre Dame game, October 15, 1927. Program cover and ticket.

NAVY
vs
NOTRE DAME

FOOTBALL GAME
To Be Played by Teams Representing

Univ. of Notre Dame
AND
U. S. Naval Academy

BALTIMORE STADIUM
BALTIMORE, MARYLAND

Saturday, October 15, 1927
2.30 p. m.

PRICE $3.00
Tax Exempt

THIS TICKET WILL NOT ADMIT TO STADIUM
UNLESS ADMISSION STUB IS ATTACHED

SCHNEIDEREITH & SONS, BALTIMORE

WEST SIDE
NAVY
GATE
6
SECTION
XB
ROW
8
SEAT
38
(OVER)

BALTIMORE STADIUM
OCT. 15 · 1927

twice a season, the city was starting to grow in prominence as a major league town. Up until Navy began playing Army, Notre Dame, Michigan, and other national opponents, Baltimore's only moment in the national limelight had been the Preakness Stakes in May. Navy was an excellent drawing card and the relationship between the Academy and the Baltimore Park Board was a warm one for several decades. Navy scheduled its glamour opponents for play in Baltimore because of the bigger gates. Ohio State, Michigan, Notre Dame, North Car-

olina, Maryland, Cornell, Penn State, Southern Cal, Duke, Yale, Georgia Tech, Northwestern, and many others came to Baltimore.

Yale and Navy played in a classic at Municipal Stadium on October 17, 1936. Navy lost 12-7 before 53,000 fans in a game that featured a controversial play by that year's Heisman Trophy winner, Larry Kelley. Navy led 7-6 in the third quarter, and after a Navy punt and fumble a mad scramble for the football ensued. Just as Navy's Sneed Schmidt was about to fall on the ball, Kelley kicked it toward the Navy goal line and then fell on the ball at the Navy 2. Despite Navy's protestations, Kelley's kick was ruled inadvertent and Clint Frank, who would win the Heisman in 1937, scored the winning touchdown.

Many local businesses got into the spirit of having big-time college football in its own backyard, running different promotions for ticket discounts or just wanting to be part of the pomp and color. Miller Brothers, called "The Place to Eat" and a longtime restaurant fixture on West Fayette Street in Baltimore, would change its menu covers to commemorate a big Navy game. On November 7, 1936, it was Navy–Notre Dame, and the menu cover featured a football action scene with a diagonal blue and gold stripe. Inside was the regular menu featuring full meals for less than a dollar. Navy blanked the Irish 3-0 in 1936 as Bill Ingram, son of Jonas, dropkicked a 25-yard field goal in the third quarter to account for the only points of the game. At halftime, coach Tom Hamilton, in his third season as Navy coach (he would leave after 1936, but return in 1946 and 1947), fired up his team at halftime by telling his team, "Remember, there are 12 of you out there—John Paul Jones is out there with you, the entire Navy is out there with you. They're watching you. Don't let them down."

In 1937, Navy and Harvard played to a 0-0 tie and again Miller Brothers printed a colorful souvenir menu, replete with an action game photo and blue and crimson pennants in tribute to each school.

Emory "Swede" Larson, who had played on four teams that never lost to Army, took over as Navy coach in 1939 and one of the great eras in Navy history was launched, a six-year period in which the Mids sported numerous All-Americans and vied for national champi-

Navy-Yale program, 1936.

opposite page

The 1935 Navy–Notre Dame game, won by the Irish 14-0, seen in overhead view of jam-packed Baltimore Stadium. Thirteen members of the Navy team were later killed in action during World War II.

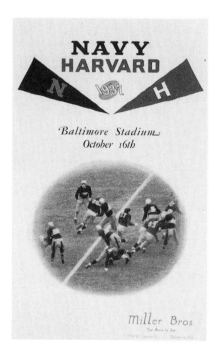

Miller Brothers restaurant issued colorful souvenir menus of important Navy games in Baltimore.

onships. They blanked Army in both 1939 and 1940 and, after beating them 14-6 in 1941, just a week before Pearl Harbor, shut them out again in both 1942 and 1943. In 1943, only a loss to Notre Dame kept the Mids from an unbeaten season.

The 1941 Navy–Notre Dame game in Baltimore was another classic in the series. Many of the Navy players were just months away from entering military service and would become war heroes. But in 1941 they were concerned with football and coach Larson called the game with Notre Dame in Baltimore "the best played and most thrilling" of all the games he had coached. Actor Pat O'Brien was in attendance at the game, having just portrayed legendary Notre Dame coach Knute Rockne on the silver screen. Navy was hard-pressed to stop the all-around brilliance of Heisman winner Angelo Bertelli, but a drive for the tying touchdown ended at the Army 6 yard line with time running out. Because of the urgency in getting the seniors into the war effort as soon as possible, Navy turned down an invitation to play in the Cotton Bowl.

In 1944, Navy played five games in Baltimore, blanking Duke on October 14, beating Notre Dame for one of the few times, 32-13 (knocking the Irish from the unbeaten ranks in the process), and shutting out both Cornell and Purdue before hosting rival Army. In 1942, because of war restrictions, President Franklin Roosevelt ordered the Army-Navy game played in Annapolis with attendance limited to no more than 10,000 to 12,000 fans who lived within ten miles of the Maryland State House. The Office of Price Administration checked all vehicles at the game and anybody not from the Annapolis vicinity was barred from entry. Wartime gas rationing limited car travel, and travel by train was discouraged because space was needed for military personnel. Because the Corps of Cadets was unable to travel to the game, half of the Brigade of Midshipmen were ordered to cheer for Army, which added to the bizarre circumstances surrounding the game. In 1943 the game was played in similar circumstances before 15,000 at Michie Stadium at West Point with Hal Hamberg and the Mids blanking the Cadets 13-0. Army had wanted to move the game to Yankee Stadium, where earlier that season the Cadets played Notre Dame before 70,000 fans. But their pleas went unanswered and Navy, anchored by All-America linemen Don Whitmire and George Brown, upset the favored Cadets on their home turf.

In 1944, Navy lost its opener to North Carolina Pre-Flight 21-14, led by future pro great Otto Graham, before thrashing Penn State the following week 55-14. They outscored Penn, Cornell, and Purdue by a combined 106-0. Led by Hal Hamberg, Ben Martin, Clyde "Smackover" Scott, Don Whitmire, Bobby Jenkins, and Jack Martin, Navy buried Notre Dame 32-13 in Baltimore. The following week Army clobbered Notre Dame and it was evident that the top-ranked Cadets and second-ranked Mids would decide the national championship.

The collision of the nation's two best teams had one hitch. It was slated to be played in Annapolis at Thompson Stadium, which could hold only 19,000 fans, as part of President Roosevelt's decision to alternate the game during the war between the two military schools. A campaign from press, fans, and politicians urged that the game be moved to a larger stadium. Naval officials settled upon Baltimore because the Brigade could go to the game by boat or bus and the Cadets could come down the Hudson and the East Coast by boat.

The Brigade arrived for the December 2, 1944, game by boats sailing up the Chesapeake Bay and Army came by troopships that were escorted by four Navy destroyers. After arriving in the harbor, "The Long Gray Line" marched up Charles Street to the stadium on 33rd Street. One of the stipulations for buying tickets to the game was that fans had to live within ten miles of Baltimore and each had to purchase a war bond to promote the war effort. All of the 71,000 tickets were sold in one day. Fifteen private boxes, each with just six seats, were sold to major businesses for a million dollars each. The total war bond figure was over $58 million. For John Steadman, the game represented one of his greatest disappointments. "I went down to the stadium the morning of the game, not having the money to buy a ticket," he remembers, painfully. "I walked around casing the joint and there was so much security there was just no way to get in. Usually we'd go over a fence, or under one, or climb a poplar tree outside. It was a bitter cold day, so I went home and listened to the game on radio. My brother had more tenacity than I did and he got in and saw the game."

As it turned out, the game was probably the most important sports event held during the war. Navy lost two of its greatest stars, Don Whitmire and Bobby Jenkins, to early injuries while Army was led by its famed backfield of the "Touchdown Twins," Mr. Inside (Doc Blanchard) and Mr. Outside (Glenn Davis) and completed its first undefeated season since 1914 with a 23-7 win. Davis, who ran for a 50-yard touchdown, called it his greatest career moment. "We had lost five straight to Navy and scored only one touchdown in the five games. Navy was the only team standing in the way of an unbeaten season and a national championship. Before the game Coach [Red] Blaik read a wire from an Army general in the South Pacific, which said 'Win for all the soldiers . . . fighting for us.' A chill went up and down our spines, and we charged out fighting mad." Later that night in Baltimore, while the Cadets celebrated their victory, Coach Blaik received another wire, this one from General Douglas MacArthur in the Pacific Headquarters. It read: "The greatest of all Army teams. We have stopped the war to celebrate your magnificent success. Signed, MacArthur." Blaik later called the win and the telegram from MacArthur the high points of his coaching career. After the season, a booklet was given to each player on the Army team and in it was inscribed the following message: "Seldom in a lifetime's experience is one permitted the complete satisfaction of being part of a perfect performance. To all the coaches, the 23-7 is enough."

That 1944 Army-Navy game wasn't the last great Navy appearance in Baltimore. The Mids continued to play several games every season in the cavernous 33rd Street stadium. In 1945 alone they beat Georgia Tech 20-6 in a night game, Michigan, and Wisconsin in Baltimore. Admiral William "Bull" Halsey, hero of the Pacific and of Navy's 1902 and 1903 football teams, attended the Michigan game, won by the Mids 33-7.

Navy fell on hard times after the war as several star players left for other less demanding schools. They managed only five wins against 28 losses and three ties from 1946 through 1949. Still, the Mids were a fixture in Baltimore. The procession of the Brigade of Midshipmen marching from Clifton Park up the Alameda to 33rd Street and through the main gates of the stadium became an impor-

Maryland and Navy played several times in Baltimore before their rivalry ended.

tant fall ritual. In '49, the stadium, renamed Babe Ruth Stadium for one year, was beginning a transformation into what eventually became Memorial Stadium. The rotting wooden seats were gradually being replaced by concrete and steel in a process that took several years to complete.

In 1950, Navy hired Eddie Erdelatz as coach and things began to improve. The Mids beat Southern Cal in Baltimore in 1950. By 1954 Navy was playing in the Sugar Bowl and beating Ole Miss. One of their last great Baltimore wins was achieved in 1956 when they crushed Notre Dame 33-7. Erdelatz coached Navy to a 40-14 win over Maryland at Memorial Stadium in 1958 and Wayne Hardin did the same against the Terps in his first season at the helm in 1959 with Joe Bellino running roughshod. Navy's last game at Memorial Stadium for over 25 years was a 35-3 win over Air Force in 1960. There was a brief return to Baltimore in 1986 and 1988 when popular mayor (and later Maryland governor) William Donald Schaefer teamed with local promoter Lou Grasmick to bring the Navy–Notre Dame game back to town. Navy, quarterbacked by the late Alton Grizzard, lost to the Irish 33-14 in '86 and 22-7 in '88. Beginning in October 1923, Navy has played 67 times in Baltimore and has compiled a 28-30-9 record. On June 4, 1999, Navy and Army held a joint press conference at the new PSINet Stadium to announce that the 101st Army-Navy game would be played in Baltimore in 2000. Fifty of the past 54 games had been played in Philadelphia; for the first time in 56 years the classic would be returning to Baltimore.

The third official game the University of Maryland football team ever played took place at Clifton Park in Baltimore on November 5, 1892. Johns Hopkins proved a rude host, winning 62-0. Then known as the Maryland Agricultural College, the Aggies were no match for the seasoned Hopkins team. By the next season, however, the Farmers, as they were also called, were posting a 6-0 record including an 18-0 win over Baltimore City College, which would be the only high school team in the Maryland Intercollegiate Football Association (formed in 1894). In the ensuing early years of Maryland football, the Aggies played Johns Hopkins, the Baltimore Medical College, and

Navy's Joe Bellino won the
1960 Heisman Trophy.

the University of Maryland at Baltimore on a fairly regular basis. In
1899, the Hoppies of Johns Hopkins routed the Aggies in Baltimore
40-0. Hopkins blanked the Aggies again in 1901 and 1902 at Oriole
Park. In 1905, Maryland opened with a 20-0 win over Baltimore Polytechnic Institute but in 1906 the Mount Washington Athletic Club, a
sandlot team comprised of former stars, surprised the Farmers 29-0
on a muddy field in Baltimore.

Johns Hopkins again posted shutouts over Maryland in '08 and
'09 at Clifton Park before the Aggies tied the Hoppies in 1910. A dis-
placed tooth figured in the outcome. In the waning moments of the

game Hopkins was driving on the Maryland 8 yard line. They faced a second down and two yards when suddenly a Hopkins guard named Schrieber dashed for the bench to drop off a tooth he had lost during the preceding play. The referee penalized Hopkins ten yards and they were unable to regain the yardage. A field goal attempt was blocked and the game ended 11-11. From 1892, when they first began playing, until 1934, when Maryland blanked Hopkins at Baltimore Stadium, the Terrapins and Blue Jays would play 32 games, 11 of them at the vast Baltimore Stadium, with Maryland having the edge, 16-11-5. The game between Maryland and John Hopkins became a Thanksgiving tradition. Sixteen times the two teams played on Thanksgiving, with 11 of the last 12 games in the series at Baltimore Municipal Stadium. After Thanksgiving Day ties at Baltimore Stadium in '23, '24, and '25, and a Hopkins win at Homewood Field in 1927, the Terrapins, under famed coach Harry "Curley" Byrd, won the last seven games of the series before it came to a merciful end.

One of the classic games in the series occurred on Thanksgiving Day 1915, when 13,000 fans, the biggest crowd in Homewood Field history, watched the Hoppies of Johns Hopkins post a 3-0 win. Neither team could move the ball, but the Hoppies prevailed when a halfback named Hoffman kicked a field goal from the Maryland 15 yard line after having missed his previous eight field goal attempts in succession.

Like the Naval Academy, Maryland scheduled other opponents for games in Baltimore. Byrd, who coached Maryland from 1911 through 1934 and who helped develop the forward pass when he quarterbacked Georgetown in 1909, while in pursuit of his law degree, began his long career at Maryland when the school had only 300 students. He knew that Baltimore was loaded with talent and began scheduling either City or Poly for reasons other than the game at hand. Maryland blanked City College in 1913, 27-10. The Engineers' best player was a squat Dutchman named Ridgeley Wilson Axt. Axt would later star for Byrd at Maryland, so Curley got an early glimpse of his future talent by playing Baltimore's best high schools. Poly blanked the Aggies 6-0 in 1914, but Maryland returned the favor the next year 31-0.

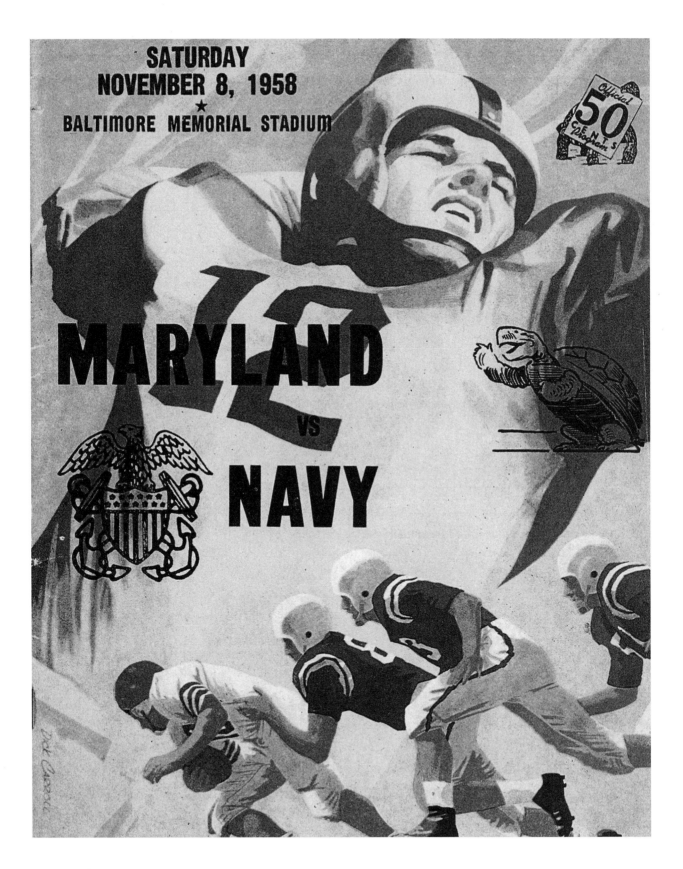

Western Maryland College, which began playing Maryland back in 1893, also began scheduling games in Baltimore, often against the Aggies. Reduced to a six-game schedule in 1918 because of World War I, Maryland shut out Western Maryland 19-0 in Baltimore. A few weeks later, on November 23, Maryland and Western Maryland both played in Baltimore, but not against each other. In a rare double-header at Homewood Field, the Aggies, now known as Maryland State, beat a stubborn St. John's of Annapolis team 19-14, while the Green Terrors cruised over Hopkins 28-0. Just five days later on Thanksgiving, Maryland and Hopkins played to a 0-0 tie at Home-wood Field. In 1919, every nook and cranny of Homewood was occupied as over 15,000 watched Maryland blank Hopkins 14-0, the eighth straight season in which Hopkins failed to score a point on Maryland.

While the new stadium was being erected a few blocks to the north, Maryland played twice in 1921 down the street at Oriole Park. The Old Liners lost 16-7 to North Carolina and then, because of Hopkins' unwillingness to play Maryland (because of a dispute over the eligibility of a Maryland player), took on North Carolina State in a driving rainstorm at Oriole Park with the game ending in a 6-6 Thanksgiving Day tie.

In 1922, Maryland opened their season at Homewood Field against the 3rd Army from Baltimore, a collection of former West Pointers who outweighed the Old Liners by 20 pounds a man. Nevertheless, Maryland prevailed 7-0. Their first stadium appearance was the final game of the 1923 season, in which they tied Hopkins 6-6 on Thanksgiving Day. The game, on November 29, came just five days after Byrd Stadium was dedicated in College Park.

Beginning in 1924, Maryland began playing at least once, and of-tentimes twice a year, in the 33rd Street stadium. They lost to North Carolina 16-0 on a rainy Halloween Day in 1925 and later tied Hopkins on Thanksgiving. In 1927, Hopkins won its first game over Maryland since 1915 before over 18,000 jubilant fans at Homewood Field. The win was achieved when Hopkins blocked a try for the point after on Maryland's second touchdown.

opposite page

Navy and Maryland used to play on an annual basis in Baltimore before the series ceased.

Maryland and Western Maryland clashed often in Baltimore.

BALTIMORE STADIUM   OCTOBER 24, 1942

Official Program
Price 25 Cents

UNIVERSITY OF
MARYLAND vs. WESTERN MARYLAND
COLLEGE

Maryland played back-to-back games at Baltimore Stadium in 1929, beating Johns Hopkins 39-8 on Thanksgiving and then losing 12-0 to Western Maryland (capping a brilliant 11-0 campaign for coach Dick Harlow and the Green Terrors). Maryland followed the same format in 1930, with similar results. They shut out Hopkins on Thanksgiving but lost to Western Maryland again on a late touchdown 7-0, as Harlow's powerhouse completed a 9-0-1 season that included wins over St. John's and Loyola at Municipal Stadium.

The 1931 Maryland team was one of Byrd's best, losing only at Vanderbilt and tying Kentucky while winning eight games as "Shorty" Chalmers and "Bozie" Berger led the Old Liners to easy wins over Johns Hopkins (35-14) and Western Maryland (41-6) at Municipal Stadium. In 1932, Maryland played three times at the Stadium, losing to the Buzz Borries–led Navy team 28-7, blanking Johns Hopkins 23-0, but losing to Western Maryland and its greatest ever player, All-American Bill Shepherd, 39-7. In 1934, Byrd's last year as coach as he began his ascendency to president of the University, Maryland shut out three opponents in Baltimore. The first to bow was Florida (21-0), followed by Virginia Military (23-0) and, in the final game of the series, Johns Hopkins (19-0).

A busy year at the Stadium was 1935, as Maryland played five games there and Western Maryland four. Maryland beat Virginia Tech 7-0, lost to North Carolina 33-0, lost to Indiana 13-7, tied Syracuse on Thanksgiving 0-0 in a sea of mud, and got some measure of revenge against Western Maryland by winning 22-7.

Western Maryland began a new era in 1935 without the legendary Bill Shepherd and with new coach Charlie Havens replacing the departed Dick Harlow. The Green Terror had gone 8-0-1 in 1934, Shepherd's and Harlow's last year, including a 40-0 shellacking of Boston College at Baltimore Municipal Stadium. In 1935, the Green Terror lost to Bucknell, but beat North Dakota and Georgetown before losing the finale to Maryland at the Stadium. In 1936, Western Maryland played twice at the Stadium, including a 12-0 whitewash of Maryland to end the season. On October 24 of that year, Western Maryland played St. Mary's of Texas at the Stadium, a game attended by young John Steadman. "St. Mary's of Texas had been the subject of a cover story in either the *Saturday Evening Post* or *Collier's*," recalls Steadman. "The coach was a fabled character by the name of Mo Sims, who dressed the team in red, white, and blue uniforms. The team was like a barnstorming team that traveled in a red, white, and blue bus. It turned out that most of the players had exhausted their eligibility in other places. Sims changed the players' names. They were playing under phony transcripts. He had convinced the order of Catholic priests and brothers that ran the college in San Antonio that he could make St. Mary's the Notre Dame of Texas. It never happened, of course. Western Maryland won the game 32-12."

The next week, St. Mary's played out in North and South Dakota as they played all road games. Tex Maule, who later covered the NFL for *Sports Illustrated* magazine, played on that team and Steadman once asked him about that season. He said on the way to the next game they'd find a flat area along the road, a farmer's field, stop the bus, have a short workout and go back on the bus without showering and keep riding into the night. St. Mary's soon drifted into college football oblivion, never to be heard from again.

Maryland played Washington and Lee on Thanksgiving Day at the stadium in 1936, 1937, and 1938, winning all three in close, hard-fought fashion. The 1938 game, won by Maryland 19-13, was waged in a driving sleet storm that held the attendance below 1,000. 1937 saw one of the great upsets of the year when the Terrapins blanked 17th-ranked Syracuse 13-0 at the Stadium, sending the Orangemen to their first loss of the season. The Terrapins rolled to an 8-2 record that year. Municipal Stadium hosted Maryland's 14-7 Thanksgiving Day win over Rutgers in 1940 and a 50-0 bombardment by number fourth-ranked Duke over the Terps early in the 1941 season. That same season the Terps tied Western Maryland 6-6 and barely beat Washington and Lee on Thanksgiving 6-0.

Clark Shaughnessy, developer of the "T" formation, was hired to coach the 1942 Terps and they rolled to a 7-2 season that included a 51-0 pasting of Western Maryland in what turned out to be the Green Terror's final appearance at Municipal Stadium. That was also their final game with Maryland. The Green Terror continued its series with Johns Hopkins and the two teams continue to play each other in the traditional last game of the season.

In 1943 at Municipal Stadium against Wake Forest, a last-second pass from 17-year-old quarterback Johnny Makar from his own end zone was hauled in by Dick Tuschak at his own 35, and behind great blocking Tuschak scooted down the sideline for the winning touchdown as the gun sounded in a 13-7 Maryland victory.

After a two-year hiatus, Maryland returned to Baltimore in 1946, and led by former Baltimore schoolboy stars Lu Gambino and Vern Siebert, outclassed Washington and Lee at Municipal Stadium, 24-7. It wasn't until 1951, during the fabulous era of Jim Tatum, that Maryland next played in Baltimore. En route to a perfect 10-0 season and a 28-13 victory over Tennessee in the Sugar Bowl, the Terps, who would finish ranked third in the nation, easily outdistanced Navy 40-21 behind the quarterbacking of Baltimore product and Heisman hopeful Jack Scarbath. The only Mid highlight was a 100-yard punt return for a touchdown by Frank Brady that set a Navy record.

With a refurbished 45,000-seat Byrd Stadium on their campus at College Park, Maryland didn't venture north that often after 1950. They lost to Navy 40-14 in 1958 in what was by then Memorial Stadium, and in 1959 lost again in Baltimore to the Middies, led by 1960 Heisman Trophy winner Joe Bellino, 22-14. Maryland didn't play again in Baltimore until 1984, when they beat 20th-ranked Clemson 41-23 en route to a 9-3 season, ACC championship and Sun Bowl victory over Tennessee under the direction of coach Bobby Ross. From 1984 through 1991, Maryland played seven nationally ranked teams at Memorial Stadium, including number eight Miami in 1985, a game the Hurricanes won 29-22 behind Vinny Testaverde. There was also a 13-13 tie with 13th-ranked nemesis Penn State in 1989. The Terrapins returned to Baltimore in 1998, playing another ranked team, Georgia Tech, at the Ravens' new downtown stadium, losing to the Yellow Jackets 30-14.

Another proud Baltimore football tradition is housed on the campus of Morgan State University, where coaching legends Eddie Hurt, Talmadge Hill, and Earl Banks put together some memorable seasons and teams. After coming to Morgan in 1929, Hurt won 14 Central Intercollegiate Athletic Association championships and several national titles among the nation's black colleges before retiring after the 1959 season. In 31 seasons, Hurt's teams won 175 games, lost 52 and tied 18. From 1932 through 1939, his teams played 54 games without a defeat, one of the longest unbroken strings on record. Hurt, who retired from the faculty in 1970, also coached basketball and

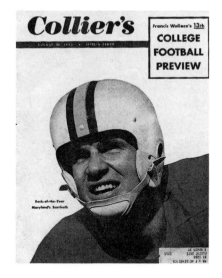

Late August 1952 and Collier's —by no means a sports magazine—got so caught up in the college game that it featured Maryland's Jack Scarbath on its cover (bright red jersey, gold-in-black helmet stripe) as "Back-of-the-Year." Next year Scarbath finished second in Heisman Trophy balloting.

track and field, where he produced eight individual NCAA champions and one Olympic champion.

A native of East Orange, New Jersey, Talmadge "Marse" Hill played football at Morgan in the mid-1920s. He never left, assisting Eddie Hurt in football and taking over the basketball reins in 1947. In 1925, playing favored Lincoln University of Pennsylvania at the old Black Sox Park in Westport, Morgan was trailing when Hill caught a pass and began streaking for the Lion goal. Julie Martin of Lincoln suddenly sprang from the Lion bench and tackled Hill. Pandemonium reigned, but Hill was given the touchdown and Morgan had won its first major victory in football. Hill went on to coach the Morgan lines for Eddie Hurt, producing the likes of New York Giant Hall of Famer Roosevelt Brown and former Baltimore Colt Charlie Robinson. Hill retired from active coaching in 1964 and from the Morgan faculty in 1972 after 42 years on the job.

When Eddie Hurt retired from coaching Morgan football after the 1959 season, Earl Banks, an assistant at Maryland State for nine seasons, took over the head coaching job. Former Colt running great Buddy Young had recommended Banks and was instrumental in his being hired. Their friendship dated back to the 1940s when they were teammates at Wendell Phillips High School in Chicago. Banks had grown up in rough circumstances in Chicago. He often went to bed hungry and said he must have lived in every apartment building in South Chicago. The family couldn't pay the rent, so they'd pack up and move on. While other kids would steal money and go to a movie, Earl went to school and eventually enrolled at Iowa, where he became an All-American player. He would later obtain a master's degree from NYU while playing for the New York Yankees of the All-America Football Conference. An injury cut Banks' career short after one year. The man they called "Papa Bear" carved out a legendary coaching career at Morgan, winning 96 games and losing 31 with a pair of ties over a 13-year span. His .839 winning percentage ranked him number one among college coaches. He posted a 31-game winning streak at one point—fourth longest in college history—had three unbeaten regular seasons, won five CIAA titles, and played in four bowl games. Twice under his tutelage the Bears led the nation in total

Renowned Morgan coach
Eddie Hurt is honored for his
25 years with the college,
receiving a silver football from
alumnus Dr. Eugene D. Byrd,
1953.

defense. In his third year as coach, Banks' team compiled an 8-1
record and the rest, as they say, is history. In 1970, Banks' Bears won
eight straight games after an opening loss to Grambling and met the
University of Delaware in the Boardwalk Bowl in Atlantic City. His
teams had post-season success in the 1965 Orange Blossom Classic,
a 36-7 win over Florida A & M, and the 1966 Tangerine Bowl, a
14-6 triumph over West Chester State.

A large photo gallery in the coach's office was a testament to the
coach's prowess. It was a "Who's Who" of pro football stars. The former All-American lineman at the University of Iowa coached Willie
Lanier, who became a Hall of Fame linebacker with the Kansas City
Chiefs, and Leroy Kelly of the Cleveland Browns, also enshrined in

Canton. Then there was Raymond Chester of the Raiders and Colts, Frenchy Fuqua of the Steelers, and George Nock of the Redskins. In a lesser category were Mark Washington, Willie Germany, Daryl Johnson, Jeff Queen, Ron Mayo, Maurice Tyler, and Ara Person.

Sitting down and talking with his players was one of Banks' strong suits. He communicated with them, instilling within each man a desire to perform at peak performance and to be great no matter what the odds. "About two days a week I talk life, not football, to my boys," said Banks, who passed away on October 27, 1993. "I tell it like it is and they know that. They know they'll hear it straight from the shoulder, with no frills or fancy talk. I tell them if they act like a man they'll be treated like one. They may come to us as boys, but they leave as men. Good men with a purpose in life." It was a tribute to Banks that he was able to recruit some of the athletes that he did, many of whom developed under his coaching. "We can't go after the real big names and recruit them like the large universities do," said Banks, while still a coach. "We can't offer them what the big schools offer. We have to tell them that they're gonna be scholars first and football players second. So they know ahead of time that they're coming to Morgan for an education. There's no doubt about it, Morgan is one of the top schools in the country, and I'm not just talking black!"

As for Banks' coaching philosophy: "I want to develop a good citizen, a man who can contribute something—give something back to society. I try to treat a boy like he's my son. I want him to tell me his troubles. At least 99% of my guys get their degrees and that's not physical education majors either. I'm talking pre-law, pre-med, business administration, etc."

Players like Lanier and Kelly didn't come to Morgan with glamour and ballyhoo. Remembered Banks, after Lanier's Hall of Fame induction,

> Willie called me two weeks before we started practice and said he wanted to come to Morgan. If others knew that he was going to become the best linebacker in football he wouldn't have come here. The big schools would have grabbed him.

opposite page

All-time Morgan State great and future Pro Football Hall of Famer Willie Lanier, number 65, standing next to coach Earl Banks, with glasses, in 1965 game. Former Colt Jesse Thomas, a Banks assistant, is at left.

Roosevelt Brown was one of Morgan's all-time greats who made the Pro Football Hall of Fame.

Morgan's "Poppa Bear," Earl Banks.

Leroy Kelly was a quarterback in high school the same year that I was looking for a good signal caller. All I could offer him was $600 in scholarship funds. He had to pay the other $600 that it cost to go here. But Kelly didn't work out too well at quarterback so I moved him to the halfback slot. He didn't like it, but he accepted the move and became my number one back as a freshman. He had a lot of natural talent that we channeled and helped to refine.

Coach Banks had a motto that he often repeated to his players: "I shall rise from that whence I came." In the long-hair era of the late 1960s, when discipline seemed to disappear and chaos reigned supreme at our nation's colleges, Banks let his players know there would be no Afro hairdos on his team. "I wanted their attention . . . and I wanted to capture their minds," said Earl. "Cutting their hair was a symbol of sacrifice, a discipline, a direction. Long hair was something these kids really wanted, and I wanted to see if they would do without it, sacrifice it to play football. They did it, so I knew they really wanted to play. It was the beginning of a direction. I guess there are times when I want more for them than they want for themselves. That drives me to read them . . . to help them achieve greatness." Banks kidded that he had the longest hair on the team in those years. He relied on two philosophies—hard work and patience. "Football players want to become superstars overnight. They must realize that hard work and patience are necessary to get to the top." Banks preached that members of minority groups, more than anyone else, have to stand up and face life head to head. "Only the biggest, the fastest, the toughest, and the smartest will be chosen for any given job. And all the skills you have must be developed to the nth degree in order to succeed." Earl Banks became a coaching legend in his adopted city of Baltimore.

A few miles north of the Baltimore city line on York Road, Towson University has a football tradition of only 30 years, but has been successful on three different levels. There have been 16 winning seasons, post-season play-offs, and a program known for producing top quarterbacks. Over the course of 20 seasons, Phil Albert coached the Tigers to a 10-0 record in 1974, 10-3 in 1976, 9-1 in 1979, and 10-1

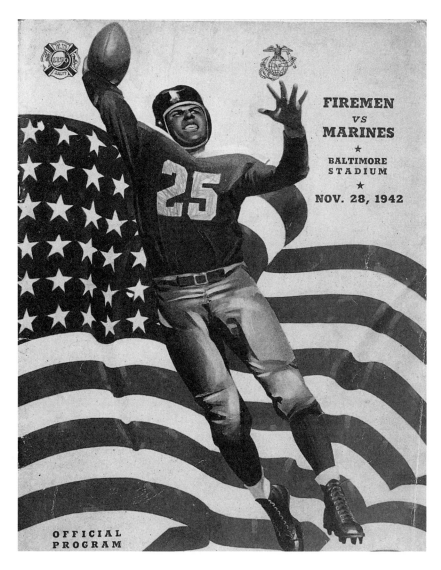

The Firemen and the Marines established a heated rivalry at Baltimore Stadium.

in 1983. Albert's record was an impressive 117-91-3. Many Tiger fans consider the 1983 team the best in school history. They blanked Morgan State 48-0, beat always tough Delaware 13-4 and held opponents to 5.8 points per game. Gordie Combs replaced Albert in 1992 and has brought the Tigers back to prominence. The Towson–Morgan State game has become a great rivalry for city-county bragging rights. Towson has produced several pro players, including punter Sean Landetta, running back Dave Meggett and fullback Tony Vinson.

For over 50 years, from Johns Hopkins and City College to Navy–Notre Dame to the annual rivalry of the Baltimore Firemen

playing the Marines of Quantico (the firemen led by the incompara-
ble "Reds" DuVall, who never went to college, and his brother
Buddy), football in Baltimore was strictly played on the amateur level.
After World War II, however, pro football, which had struggled for
years in the shadow of the more popular college game, was about to
explode onto the national scene, and nowhere would the love affair
be as intense as in Baltimore. The courtship was a rocky one in the
early years, but the marriage of the Colts and the city of Baltimore
would be one of the great human interest stories in the history of
sports.

TWO

Here Come the Colts

World War II dealt the National Football League and all of professional sports a severe blow. Pro and college football teams were decimated as players left their shoulder pads and helmets behind, donning the uniforms of the various armed services. To illustrate the slippage in attendance at NFL games, over 43,000 fans were in the stands at Wrigley Field to see the Bears win a 33-14 divisional playoff game against the Packers on the day the Japanese attacked Pearl Harbor, December 7, 1941. One week later, with the Bears and Giants playing for the NFL championship just 13,341 turned out at Wrigley Field to see Chicago take its fifth championship, 39-7.

The next year, Bears owner and coach George Halas reported in mid-season for Navy duty, as did many of his players. In 1943, the Cleveland Rams had to suspend operations because the team's owners, Dan Reeves and Fred Levy, were in the service. Pittsburgh, in similar straits, combined forces with the Eagles and became the Phil-Pitt Eagles. With rosters depleted, Bronko Nagurski came out of a six-year retirement to lead the Bears to a championship. In 1944, the Steelers changed wartime partners again, this time teaming with the Chicago Cardinals to play as Card-Pitt. The Brooklyn Dodgers ceased operations permanently. By the time hostilities ended in 1945, 638 NFL players had served their country, 355 as commissioned officers. Sixty-six were decorated and 21 lost their lives, including Giants tackle Al Blozis, who was killed by machine gun fire in France just six weeks after playing in the 1944 NFL championship game.

A program from a long-ago Baltimore league and team that played semipro football at old Oriole Park. Pictured is the fabled Red Grange.

While Baltimore was hosting top college games, such as the 1944 Army-Navy game, its involvement with professional football was sporadic. In the late 1930s Baltimore had a team in the lower-level Dixie League. The team played three seasons from 1936 through 1938 and was known as the Blue Jays. The coaches were Bull Draper and Jack McNally, with former Western Maryland coach Charlie Havens an adviser. They played at old Oriole Park on Greenmount Avenue and 29th Street and had a total payroll of $1,000 a week. The semipro Blue Jays faded away after the 1938 season. The NFL Redskins had moved from Boston to Washington by that time, and they drew the interest of Baltimore fans. Then came Pearl Harbor and World War II.

Ironically, the city's biggest enemy in acquiring a team, Redskins owner George Preston Marshall, helped bring Baltimore some notice in NFL circles. On September 30, 1945, the Redskins played the first Variety Club benefit game at Municipal Stadium, drawing 27,911 fans. On February 19, 1946, the Redskins signed a six-year contract to play an annual Variety Club game in Baltimore. On September 22, 1946, the Redskins played the Bears in Baltimore, losing 20-14, but raising over $55,000 for boys' club activities in Washington and Baltimore. In 1947, Baltimore's first season in the All-America Football Conference, the Redskins played the Packers and trailed 31-0 entering the fourth quarter. The legendary Redskins quarterback, Sammy Baugh, entered the game for the first time in the fourth quarter and rallied Washington to three touchdowns but could not prevent his team from losing 31-21.

By 1944, the NFL had been in business for 23 years. There were ten teams in the league and there was some pressure to add more, but the NFL's old guard was wary because only 4 of the franchises had ever shown a profit; more than 40 franchises had folded since the league had been formed in 1920, 12 of them in one season after a premature attempt at expansion. The answer was no, they would not expand.

In San Francisco, lumberman Tony Morabito had sought a franchise to no avail. The NFL traveled by train and California was out of the question. Many of the owners were reluctant to give permission to Dan Reeves to move his Rams from Cleveland to Los Angeles in 1946, but he, like Morabito, knew that plane travel would soon be commonplace.

In Chicago, well-known *Chicago Tribune* sports editor Arch

Ward was toying with the idea of starting up a new league to rival the NFL. Ward was a visionary, having already created the major league baseball all-star game in 1933, and the college football all-star game in 1934. Ward knew that baseball magnates Dan Topping of the Yankees and Branch Rickey of the Dodgers would be interested in making money in the fall after the baseball season. In September 1944, the *Tribune* carried a banner headline that a new league was being formed, the All-America Football Conference, to start play in 1946. At a September 2 meeting, it was announced that six teams were definite: Buffalo, Chicago, Cleveland, Los Angeles, New York, and San Francisco. In addition, Lieutenant Commander Gene Tunney, USNR, the former heavyweight champion of the world, was present as a representative from Baltimore. Tunney planned to hire former Redskins coach Red Flaherty as his coach and George Washington University athletic director Max Farrington as general manager.

Tulsa All-American back Glenn Dobbs was signed by New York, becoming the first player to be acquired by the new league. With players returning from World War II service, rosters would soon be swelled with talent. In Cleveland, millionaire taxicab tycoon Arthur "Mickey" McBride was awarded a franchise to be coached by legendary Ohio schoolboy and Ohio State Buckeye coach Paul Brown. The Cleveland Rams, who had not played in 1944, ended up winning the NFL championship in 1945, 15-14 over the Redskins, but owner Reeves convinced the other owners that he should be allowed to move to Los Angeles, saying that he lost $50,000 in Cleveland with a championship team. The move of the Rams paved the way for the Browns to move into Cleveland Stadium by themselves in 1946.

Baltimore was originally going to be one of the franchise pioneers in the AAFC. Tunney and Arch Ward had come to Baltimore, met with Mayor Theodore McKeldin and the Parks Board, and made an application to use the Stadium in 1945, but at the league's third meeting in December 1944, Ray Ryan, who owned the New York team, reluctantly withdrew from the conference because of pressing duties in the oil business. Tunney agreed to move his franchise from Baltimore to New York, but soon thereafter was ordered to duty in the Pacific, forcing him to withdraw from the league.

In April 1945, another meeting was scheduled in Chicago and it was agreed to approach NFL commissioner Elmer Layden and discuss the players' draft, salary limits, schedules, inter-league games, anti-raiding policy, etc. Mr. Layden was quoted as saying, "There is nothing to talk about until someone gets a football and plays a game." In other words, the established NFL was turning up its nose at the upstart AAFC.

In October 1945, actor Don Ameche announced that he would own the Los Angeles franchise, which would be named the "Dons." Co-owners included crooner Bing Crosby, actor Pat O'Brien, and MGM prexy Louis B. Mayer. An application from a Baltimore group headed by R. Bruce Livie and Edward Nielson was discussed. However, in a January 4, 1946, meeting in Chicago, Nielson announced that because of a delay in working out a stadium lease, Baltimore would not operate in 1946.

The following cities were awarded franchises in the AAFC for '46: Brooklyn, Buffalo, Chicago, Cleveland, Los Angeles, Miami, New York, and San Francisco. The league's first commissioner and president was "Sleepy" Jim Crowley, one of the famed Four Horsemen of Notre Dame. Another member of that legendary quartet, the aforementioned Elmer Layden, was commissioner of the National Football League. Eleanor Gehrig, the widow of the late Yankee Iron Horse, Lou Gehrig, was the first vice-president of the AAFC. The value of a club franchise was set at $10,000.

By February 1946, Commissioner Crowley revealed that the conference had 400 players under contract and challenged the NFL to a series of eight preseason games for charity. The challenge was declined. The AAFC had made a strategic decision to go head-to-head against the established NFL. The two leagues would clash particularly in Chicago, which had two NFL franchises in the Bears and Cardinals; in Los Angeles which had the Rams; and in New York, where the NFL had the Giants and the AAFC had the Yankees and Dodgers.

On August 23, 1946, the College All-Stars defeated the Los Angeles Rams, the NFL defending champions by way of Cleveland, 16-0, before more than 97,000 fans at Soldier Field. There were eight future AAFC players on the All-Stars' starting team and 40 out of 67 on the squad, compared with 16 players who had signed with the NFL. Wisconsin great Elroy Hirsch, soon to be a member of the Chicago Rockets, scored both touchdowns, one on a pass from Northwestern's Otto Graham, the future quarterback of the Cleveland Browns. On August 30, 1946, to give Baltimore a taste of the AAFC, the Buffalo Bisons beat the Miami Seahawks 23-21 before 16,664 at Baltimore's Municipal Stadium. The small crowd that came out was unknowingly seeing in the Seahawks the franchise that would become the Baltimore Colts.

On September 6, 1946, the Cleveland Browns began their four-year dominance of the AAFC by blanking Miami before 60,135 fans at Cleveland Stadium, a record for a regular season professional game in any league. On October 20, 1946, the Browns defeated the Los Angeles Dons 31-14 before another record crowd of 71,134, and on December 22, 1946, the Browns, who finished 12-2 in the Western Division, three games ahead of the runner-up 49ers, beat the Yanks 14-9 for the first AAFC championship before over 41,000 fans in Cleveland. Fans loved the wide-open football played by the AAFC. They averaged 39.5 points a game and Glenn Dobbs of Brooklyn was named MVP for his prowess as quarterback and punter.

The one big negative of the fledgling league's inaugural year was the failure of the Miami Seahawks to make a go of it in the Orange Bowl. The Seahawks won only three games, helping give Baltimore another chance to get into the league. The Miami ownership team defaulted on its obligations and the other clubs had to contribute thousands of dollars to keep the Seahawks afloat, thus adding to their own deficits or reducing their profits. Finishing with a record of 3-11, Miami's coach, Jack Meagher, resigned on October 22, 1946, and was replaced by Hamp Pool. Miami, which had to play its home games on Monday nights, was also beset by terrible weather, with rain and inclement conditions on every home playing date. Two games had to be postponed because of hurricanes. The biggest crowd to see the Seahawks play was only 9,700 fans, the smallest a paltry 2,250. On December 20, 1946, Miami was expelled from the conference for failing to meet its contractual obligations.

Officials in Baltimore were working hard, meanwhile, to come up with an ownership group and it took a flamboyant Washington businessman named Robert Ridgway Rodenberg to make it happen. The son of a former Illinois congressman and a graduate of Harvard and Babson Institute, Rodenberg had been a newspaper reporter for the long-defunct *Washington Herald* and *Capitol Daily,* working in Mexico, San Juan, and other ports of call as a correspondent; he also had had experience as a public relations executive and film producer. Rodenberg had enlisted as a private in World War II in March 1942, and came out four years later as a captain, having served with the OSS behind Japanese lines in Burma. It was during the war that Rodenberg met up with Maury Nee, a friend from Washington who was serving in naval intelligence. The two talked about the success of the Redskins and how Baltimore seemed a ripe area for pro football. Three years later, back from the war and recovered from a lengthy stay in Walter Reed Hospital for treatment of recurring malaria and black fever that he had contracted in the jungles of Burma, the 38-year-old Rodenberg made his dream a reality by becoming the principal owner of the Baltimore football club. He paid $50,000 for the franchise and the remnants of the players from the defunct Miami Seahawks. Despite the protestations of Redskins owner George Preston Marshall, who fought any accommodation with the AAFC and who was particularly incensed by the prospect of a team in his own back yard, the AAFC awarded a team to Rodenberg and his four associates, Charlie McCormick, J. C. Herbert Bryant, Maurice L. Nee, and brother William R. Rodenberg. It was estimated that the Redskins had over 7,000 season ticket holders in Maryland, the bulk of them from the Baltimore area. Also, Marshall had made money on the exhibition games in Baltimore and that was all about to end. The angry Marshall blamed longtime foe and *Washington Post* sports editor Shirley Povich and some other enemy scribes for orchestrating Rodenberg's entrance into Baltimore.

The first order of business for the new owners in Baltimore was to pick a team nickname. Rodenberg decided to let the fans pick the name and a contest was held, with the winner to receive two season tickets, a $50 bond, a lamp, and an autographed team football. Although Rodenberg favored the "Whirlaways" in tribute to the great Triple Crown champion, a panel of local media members and other dignitaries reviewed the fans' suggestions and selected the name "Colts." The winner, selected from 1,877 entries, was Charles Evans of Middle River. Two others, Jerry McDade and Maxine Cox, also submitted the name "Colts," but Evans' letter on why they should be given the name was picked by the judges.

Offices were established at 6 South Howard Street in downtown Baltimore. Rounding out the front office staff of the original Colts were seven other investors, mostly from Washington, with local investors Charles P. McCormick, R. C. "Jake" Embry, and Albert Wheltle added to the mix. The first publicity director was local raconteur and bon vivant Tommy Dukehart, who John Steadman said was an ideal man for the job because he was so likable:

> He had served in the 29th Division in Special Services during the war. He was very entertaining. A spellbinder with a deck of cards, Tommy knew every card trick in the book. The story is that John Kiernan of the *New York Times* had seen him perform in London during the war and wanted Tommy to contact him after the war because he felt he had the makings of a great nightclub act. He never took it to a professional level, however. It was just something he enjoyed. He was very clever at it. He had an excellent personality, having started at the *News-Post,* which became the *News-American.* He really hit it off with the equally fun-loving Rodenberg. If he had any weakness it was that he wasn't much on detail and when you're in that job and not interested in detail, things can get a little bit chaotic at times.

Dukehart's first Colts press guide was a primitive effort, containing mimeographed copy of player and coaching biographies; the cover depicted the team logo of a spirited, helmeted colt in colors of green and silver jumping over the goalpost. It was housed in a three-ring binder put out by the league that contained similar brochures on

The first Colt media guide was mimeographed and housed in a three-ring notebook with the other AAFC teams.

the seven other teams in the AAFC. Ticket prices for reserved seats were announced as $3.50, $2.75, and $1.50.

Steadman also feels Dukehart was the front man in the birth of the Colt fight song, written and arranged by Joe Lombardi and Benjamin Klasmer. "I have a feeling he contributed to the lyrics of the song because when he was at the *News-Post*, he would capsulize the sports events of the day in verse form. From that connection he had a pretty good idea of what a good lyric was all about." Lombardi and Klasmer worked right around the corner from the Colt offices as conductor and lead violinist at the Hippodrome Theater on Eutaw

Lefthanded quarterback Ernie Case led UCLA to a Rose Bowl berth and landed a backup QB job in Baltimore.

Billy Hillenbrand was a slashing, all-out running back for the early Colts.

They called Lamar Davis "Racehorse" for his running style after catching the football.

Street. So Dukehart had easy access to the two musicians who immortalized themselves in Baltimore football annals. "In my opinion," says Steadman, who would later work for the Colts himself, "the Colt fight song is a classic. A classic in its simplicity. I liken it to the Marine Corps Hymn because as soon as you hear the Colts song you know what you're listening to." A Colts marching band was also formed; directed by Gay Rimert and Sidney Kuff, it became an institution in Baltimore, staying together even during the absence of pro football in 1951 and 1952, and those dark years after Robert Irsay stole the team from the town in 1984. In 1947, the Colts even had a swing band under the direction of Sid Cowen.

Jack Espey of the Redskins was Rodenberg's choice as general manager, and on February 10, 1947, former Packer quarterback great Cecil Isbell signed a five-year contract to coach the Colts at $18,500 a season. Isbell was only 32 years old, having had some great seasons in Green Bay throwing passes to the legendary Don Hutson. In 1942, Isbell hit Hutson with 74 completions for 1,211 yards and 17 touchdowns. He left the NFL in 1943 to coach the backs at his alma mater Purdue and in 1944 took over the head job before being lured to Baltimore by Rodenberg and Espey. Among the assistant coaches hired by Isbell was local hero Nick Campofreda, a Loyola High School grad who played college football at Western Maryland for Dick Harlow and for the Bears, Lions, and Redskins in the NFL.

The 1947 training camp was established at Hershey, Pennsylvania. The roster, except for a few Seahawk holdovers, was almost brand-new. The quarterback was Bud Schwenk, who had backed up Otto Graham in Cleveland in 1946. Behind Schwenk was Ernie Case, who spent 42 months in the Army as a pilot, was shot down over Sardinia, and escaped from an Italian prison camp before returning home to lead UCLA to a Rose Bowl berth. Case was making $16,000, almost what Isbell was being paid, and for whatever reason, the coach didn't give Case, a little lefthander at 5′ 11″, 170 pounds, much of a chance. At one halfback was Billy Hillenbrand, a former All-American at Indiana who had played with the Chicago Rockets in 1946. Ray Terrell of Mississippi and Andy Dudish of Georgia divided the other halfback spot and Bus Mertes and Frank Sinkwich, the latter a vet-

Brooklyn's Glenn Dobbs was pictured on the first ever Colts game program, 1947.

eran from Georgia and a late season pickup, shared the fullbacking. Other fullbacks were Jim Castiglia, who caught for the baseball Philadelphia Athletics in 1942 and played fullback for the Philadelphia Eagles for four years, and former City College and University of Maryland star John "Red" Wright, who turned down an offer from the New York Giants to play with his hometown team.

At one end was Hub Bechtol, dubbed one of the greatest ends in the history of the Southwestern Conference while at Texas. At the other end was fan favorite Lamar "Racehorse" Davis, who became one of the top pass catchers in the league. Rodenberg spared no expense in paying his players and going first class. He even hired legendary CBS sportscaster Ted Husing to broadcast the play-by-play, paying him a reported $1,000 a game, an amazingly high fee for the time. Although Husing was polished and professional, his lack of preparation was noticeable and color commentator Bill Dyer filled in many of the gaps. The fact that Husing was also broadcasting Army games on Saturdays gave him little time to devote to the fledgling pro team in Baltimore.

The first game the Colts played was a preseason game in Hershey with the Buffalo Bills, with the Bills winning 29-0. They also lost to the Browns in Akron 28-0 in the week leading up to the September 7 opener against the Brooklyn Dodgers in Baltimore. Baltimore fans didn't exactly grab on to the new team in town with fervor. Municipal Stadium was only a bit over a third full with a crowd of 27,418 on a humid, rainy day to watch the silver-and-green-clad Colts entertain the Dodgers. The opening kick provided a bizarre beginning as Dodger return man Elmore Harris, a product of nearby Morgan State, fumbled at the 25 yard line when hit by Hub Bechtol. The ball popped into the air and was fielded by Dodger lineman Harry Buffington, who plodded toward midfield, then was spun around and began heading toward his own goal line. When Buffington realized his mistake he threw the ball away. It ended up in the clutches of Colt fullback Jim Castiglia, who stepped over the goal line to score the first touchdown in Baltimore Colts history. Augie Lio, another early fan favorite, kicked the point after. (Years later, while scouting a game at the Houston Astrodome, Buffington told John Steadman that the following night, while driving to a team meeting in Brooklyn, he was pulled over for driving the wrong way on a one-way street.) Despite the muddy field, the Colts triumphed by a 16-7 margin. Billy Hillenbrand provided the crowd a thrill by returning the second half kickoff 96 yards for a touchdown—two touchdowns, both on kick returns! After defeats at San Francisco and Cleveland, the Colts returned on

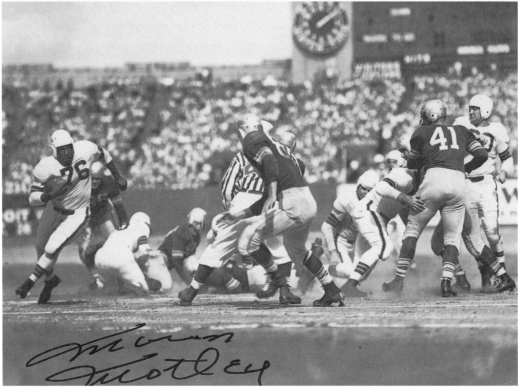

September 28 and before 51,583, a Baltimore record crowd for a professional game, lost to Buddy Young and the New York Yanks 21-7.

Outside of a 28-28 tie with San Francisco on October 5, and a 14-7 late season win over the Chicago Rockets, the 1947 inaugural season at 2-11-1 was hugely disappointing. The Colts drew 199,661 fans for their seven home games, sixth in the league ahead of Chicago and Brooklyn. Schwenk finished second in the league in passing behind Otto Graham, leading the conference in attempts and completions, while the one-two punch of Racehorse Davis and Billy Hillenbrand finished fourth and fifth in pass receiving with 46 and 39 catches, respectively. Davis caught ten for 89 yards against the 49ers alone. Hillenbrand finished third in punt returns and fourth in kick returns. Cleveland won its second straight AAFC championship in a repeat of the year before, 14-3, over the Yankees before over 60,000 at Yankee Stadium.

For a Colt souvenir hunter, there wasn't much to pick from in 1947. For a dollar, a fan could buy a game program, a pennant, and a ribboned button and still have some change left over. The game program had a green and silver look and featured a close-up of a top Colt or opposing player on the cover. Inside were player thumbnail biographies, photos, rosters, and advertisements. There was a feature on "Duke," the big white stallion that stood beneath the south goal post while his rider Jack Watts trumpeted the entry of the Colt squad before the kickoff. Later in the season the Colts issued an oversized team photo with the 34-man roster, something their Oriole baseball counterpart had been doing for several years. Fans could also write in for 8 × 10 glossy photos of the players, which were sent out free of charge.

The party-loving Rodenberg probably needed a good stiff drink when he got the tab for the 1947 season. Thanks to bonuses and salaries to lure players from the long-established NFL, Rodenberg took a huge bath. He and co-investor Herb Bryant lost $70,750 apiece, while the other six investors lost a total of $108,000. The lucrative deals for television and radio rights were still far down the road, so gate receipts had to pay the freight. And there just weren't enough of them in 1947.

opposite page

Rex Baumgartner of the Colts, number 54, tries unsuccessfully to block Horace Gillom's punt in Cleveland in the inaugural 1947 season.

Pulverizing Cleveland fullback Marion Motley carries around end as the Colts recoil and await the impact. Number 41 of Baltimore is Al Klug.

A green and silver Colt souvenir button, 1947.

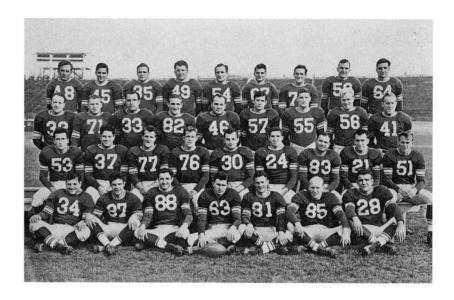

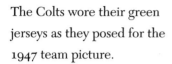

The Colts wore their green jerseys as they posed for the 1947 team picture.

Refinancing was needed, and Rodenberg, despite his protestations, was not part of it. Several of his Washington partners dropped out, leaving him holding the bag. New AAFC commissioner Jonas Ingram, the old Navy coach and former commander-in-chief of the Atlantic fleet, wanted Baltimore to stay in the league but not with Rodenberg in charge. Ingram met with Baltimore mayor Thomas D'Alesandro, telling him that the Colts, in effect, were dead but that the league wanted Baltimore. At the urging of Charles McCormick, Howard Busick (manager of the Lord Baltimore Hotel), WITH radio exec Jake Embry (a minor investor in the '47 Colts who also owned the Bullets basketball club), and others, Mayor D'Alesandro called together a group of 50 prominent Baltimore businessmen to discuss methods of keeping the franchise in Baltimore. While some of the civic leaders weren't interested, others were and a "Save the Colts" committee was formed with Busick in charge. McCormick was named chairman of the board and Embry president. William Hilgenberg and Zanvyl Krieger were named vice-presidents. The group of 17 put up $200,000 and the public matched it by pledging $200,000 in season ticket and stock purchases. Each share of stock cost $1.00, with a minimum block of 100 shares. Helping to sell the stock was the newly-formed Colts Associates group, comprised of young Baltimore businessmen who served as an auxiliary to the organization by helping players to find housing and off-season employment, running parades, and selling tickets.

Rodenberg, who died in 1994 at the age of 84, attended the April 1948 meeting that restructured the ownership and orchestrated his own financial funeral. Before he was squeezed out, however, Rodenberg made one major contribution to the cause. He gave the franchise its star quarterback of the future, Y. A. Tittle, a great pure passer out of Louisiana State who actually was a gift to Baltimore from Cleveland coach Paul Brown. Brown had Otto Graham running the show in Cleveland and didn't need Tittle, so he simply gave him to Rodenberg to help boost Baltimore's fortunes.

Baltimore needed a lot more than Tittle, and the new ownership group pleaded with the league for some talented players to improve the roster. In a "Help the Weak" program initiated by Ingram, it was decided by the league office that Baltimore would have the right to purchase guard Dick Barwegen of the New York Yanks, tackle Ernie Blandin of the Browns, and several others. A few weeks later the Colts purchased the contract of quarterback Charlie O'Rourke from the Los Angeles Dons. Isbell was retained as coach and Walter Driskill, former Maryland athletic director who had gone back to Oklahoma to assist Bud Wilkinson with the Sooner football team, was hired as the new general manager, replacing the fired Jack Espey. One of Driskill's duties was building up the number of season tickets. Sales increased from the 1947 figure of 3,700 to a total of 5,300 in 1948. A season ticket package for all seven home games in 1948 cost $21.00. Compare that to the personal seat licenses and overpriced tickets and concessions of today that run into four figures; no wonder teams were struggling financially.

The AAFC was in a dogfight with the NFL for signing top college talent. Isbell, a Texas native, was in love with University of Texas quarterback Bobby Layne and offered Layne a $10,000 bonus just to sign and a three-year contract that started at $20,000, which would have made him one of the highest paid players in the league. Isbell flew to Texas and laid out ten $1,000 bills on a bed, saying it was Layne's just for saying yes. Bobby's jaw dropped and he was going to sign with Baltimore the following day, but his coach, Dana X. Bible, pursuaded him to go with the more established Bears, who already had Sid Luckman and Johnny Lujack. Layne got far less money in Chicago and after a few years was traded to the Lions, where he carved out a Hall of Fame career.

The Colts meanwhile had young Y. A. Tittle, as well as O'Rourke and local product Dick Working at quarterback and optimism was high when training camp opened at, of all places, Sun Valley, Idaho. Certainly the most scenic training camp in pro football, Sun Valley made for some great publicity shots of Colt players with the mountains as a backdrop.

The team press guides in 1948 were reduced to a 4 × 6 size with the league guide and all the team guides contained in a leather pouch. Dukehart's 38-page effort was sponsored by American Brewery of Baltimore with beer ads inside and on the back cover. The 1948 game program, which sold for 24 cents with one cent state tax, featured a cartoon front and back cover with the green-colored Colt bucking its hind legs and stomping its horseshoes into the rear end of an opposing player. There was an ad for a Philco television set from The Hub on West Fayette Street for $424.50, and on the back cover was a Gunther's beer ad. Inside the back cover was an ad for American beer, another local brewery.

Football bubble-gum trading cards returned in 1948 for the first time since before the war, as the Bowman Gum Company of Philadelphia issued a 108-card black-and-white set. All of the cards depicted NFL players, many of them stars and some of them not, but nary a Cleveland Brown or Baltimore Colt or any other AAFC player was in the bunch.

Baltimore played three exhibition games in 1948, traveling from their Sun Valley base. The first exhibition was in Portland, Oregon, against the Los Angeles Dons, who featured former Tulsa great Glenn Dobbs and Jarrin' John Kimbrough from Texas A&M. The

Baltimore Stadium was just a year old when the Third Corps played the Scouting Fleet.

With the country at war, the 1944 Poly-City program had a patriotic theme.

Thanksgiving not only meant turkey, it meant the Loyola–Calvert Hall game in the morning.

FOOTBALL
CALVERT HALL
VS.
LOYOLA

STADIUM   NOV. 28. 1946

opposite page

Navy played many historic games in Baltimore, including this one versus Princeton in 1925. Navy's Joe Sullivan was the cover boy on the 1944 *Illustrated Football Annual.* A colorful collection of Navy ticket stubs.

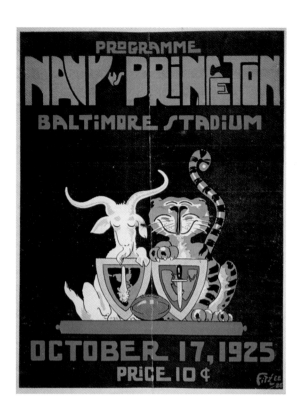

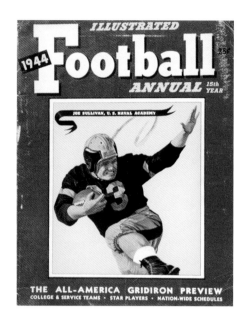

Noted illustrator
Gib Crockett painted the
Navy program covers for
over 25 years.

opposite page

The 1944 Army-Navy game, played in Baltimore, was one of the most
memorable in their long history.

The 1948 Colts programs had cartoon scenes along with an ad for WITH radio.

opposite page

The 1950 Colts were featured in their own 25¢ comic book, which included images of all the players, coaches, trainers, and front office personnel.

The sheet music to the new Colts fight song was published in the team colors of green and silver.

Popular Colt Bob Nowaskey was one of the first
Colts on a bubble-gum card. The back of Jonathan
Jenkins' card chronicled his college exploits. These
cards are from the 1950 Bowman set.

Sport magazine's full-
page tribute to the
Colts' Y. A. Tittle.
Dick Barwegan and
Tittle were part of a
national set of sports
and cowboy heroes
that were featured on
bread labels.

ART DONOVAN

The Dallas Texans 1952 press guide. The next year they were in Baltimore sporting the same blue and white colors. The cover of the 1953 Colts' press guide. Art Donovan, pictured in the 1952 Bowman trading card set, was one of several Texans who found a home in Baltimore in 1953.

The first program in 1953 had the cozy feel of a Norman Rockwell painting. The program for the Colts-Redskins that same year resembled a fall issue of the *Saturday Evening Post*.

COLTS

BEARS

Official Program 50¢

BALTIMORE
MEMORIAL STADIUM

September 27, 1953

COLTS

'SKINS

OFFICIAL PROGRAM

50¢

BALTIMORE
MEMORIAL STADIUM

Sunday, October 25, 1953

Noted New York cartoonist Willard Mullin, creator of the Brooklyn Dodger bum, did the honors on the 1953 Colts-49ers cover. The 1953 Colts-Redskins program resembled a football still life.

opposite page

Lon Keller was the most prolific and talented of the football cover illustrators.

November 6, 1954

Official Program

50¢

COLTS ★ LIONS

BALTIMORE MEMORIAL STADIUM

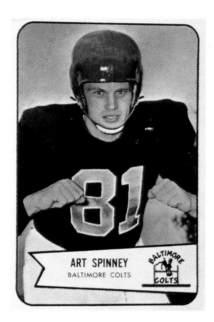

Players were still wearing blue helmets in the 1954 Bowman trading card set.

One of Lon Keller's best covers had a young boy, his mind on football, stuck at home practicing on the piano.

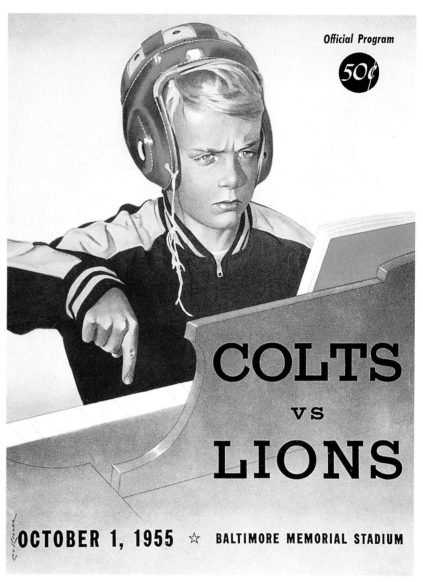

Official Program

50¢

COLTS

VS

LIONS

OCTOBER 1, 1955 ☆ BALTIMORE MEMORIAL STADIUM

opposite page

Another zany cover by the unmistakable Willard Mullin.

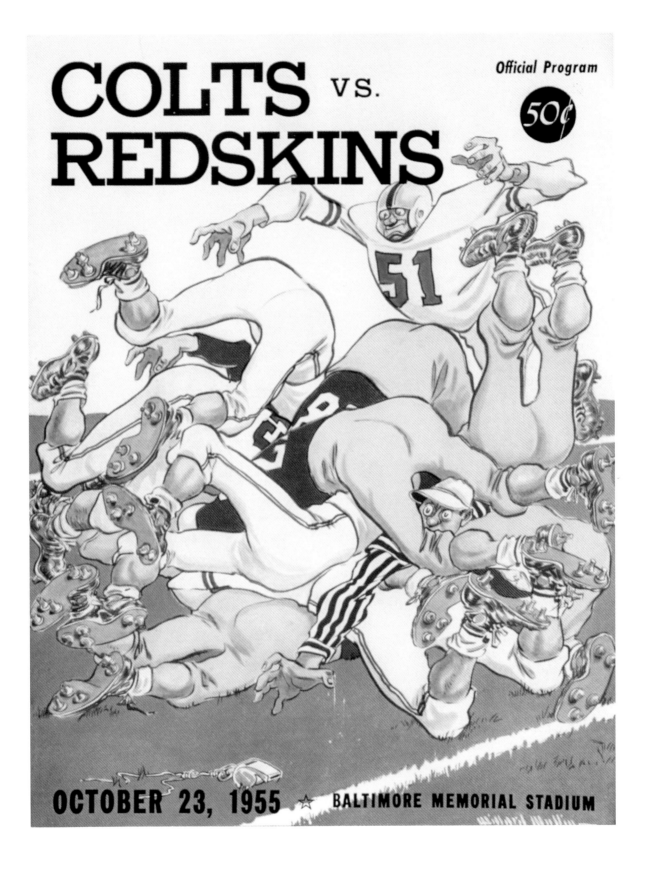

This 1957 program had a decidedly fifties look. *Right:* Lon Keller's covers were used by the pros, colleges, and high schools and were both nostalgic and timeless.

Dons led 19-7 with just a few minutes left when Isbell inserted Tittle for O'Rourke (Y. A. had joked with his roommate Windell Williams that Isbell was going to blow the game unless he put him in). Y. A. promptly tossed a touchdown pass to Racehorse Davis. The Colts got the ball back and Tittle had driven them to the 20 yard line when time ran out, with the Dons winning 19-14. After a 31-17 loss to San Francisco and a tongue-lashing from Isbell followed by several exhausting practice sessions held by the still seething coach, the tired Colts pulled off a huge win over the champion Browns in Toledo, 21-17. Thousands of victory-starved Colt fans met the team at the airport after the flight back from Toledo. The team was paraded up Charles Street, all for a game that didn't count. "You'd think we won the championship or something," said Windell Williams. "Naw," said Hub Bechtol, "Baltimore fans are always like this . . . even when we get beat. They are really something." Colt assistant coach Tarzan White referred to Baltimore as a big Green Bay.

The 1948 season was a huge success compared to the year before. The Colts opened with a thrill-packed 45-28 win over New York at Municipal Stadium. Isbell's choice at quarterback was the rookie from LSU, Yelberton Abraham Tittle. It was obvious from the outset that Tittle was something special and destined for greatness. The 21-year-old phenom completed 11 of 21 passes for 346 yards and three touchdowns while scoring one himself. He broke four conference passing records in the process.

When the regular season ended on December 5, the Colts had disposed of New York once again, as well as the Brooklyn Dodgers twice, the Rockets, Dons, and Bills, and had tied with Buffalo for the Eastern Division championship with a 7-7 record. One of the most hard-fought games was against Cleveland on October 5, a rain-soaked Tuesday in Baltimore. The wind and rain kept the fans away, but the two teams battled fiercely on the soggy field. Tittle tossed a screen pass to Hillenbrand on the Colts 22 and Billy ran 78 yards for the touchdown. The Browns matched the score, but Rex Grossman put the Colts ahead with a 40-yard field goal into the wind. The score was still 10-7 Colts with two minutes left when O'Rourke got off a poor

punt from his own 10. It traveled only 17 yards to the 27. Otto Graham threw 21 yards to Mac Speedie and then hit Dub Jones for the winning touchdown in a 14-10 win. It was a bitter defeat, but one that gave the Colts confidence that they could play with anybody.

The regular season tie with Buffalo necessitated a playoff game with the Bills in Baltimore and brought on another crisis. The Colt players were unwilling to play Buffalo unless they received a cut of the playoff swag. Embry met with player reps Ernie Blandin and Dick Barwegen and said that the game was part of their contract obligation, and besides the team was having problems staying in the black. Embry told the players that if they balked the team would just end the season at that point and forfeit the game. A player vote was taken and the "yeas" barely won out. There was dissension in the ranks between those who wanted to play and those who didn't.

The game was played on December 12 and the Colts ended up losing in controversial fashion. Late in the fourth quarter, with the Colts leading 17-14, disaster struck in the form of a disputed decision which turned the tide of the game and precipitated a near riot among the incensed Baltimore fans. Buffalo quarterback George Ratterman threw what appeared to the nearly 30,000 fans in attendance to be a completion to halfback Chet Mutryn. Mutryn pivoted away from a tackler, took about three strides, and as he did, was hit by Dick Barwegen. The ball trickled out of Mutryn's hands and was alertly scooped up by Colt tackle Johnny Mellus, who ran with it to the Buffalo 20 yard line before he pulled up, halted by the frantic sounding of horns and whistles by game officials. Head linesman Tommy Whelan ruled that Mutryn never had possession of Ratterman's pass and he called it a simple incompletion. The decision was booed lustily by the partisan, unbelieving fans, many of whom started making their angry way toward the playing field.

After order was restored, Buffalo drove to the 26 yard line. Ratterman then hit Alton Baldwin for a touchdown and a 21-17 lead with only 2:30 left to play. A desperation Tittle pass from his own 10 yard line was intercepted by Ed "Buckets" Hirsch and returned for a touchdown. Instead of controlling the ball, using up the clock, and winning, the Colts had lost a crusher because of a highly disputed call.

opposite page

Bus Mertes poses for a publicity shot at Sun Valley, 1948.

The Colts mix it up at Municipal Stadium in 1948 game action.

Y. A. Tittle was so popular he was accorded his own souvenir button.

When the gun sounded on the 28-17 Buffalo win, the Bills were in the title game despite only 11 first downs to Baltimore's 24 and 297 total yards to the Colts' 394.

The situation was tense at game's end, as some 10,000 angry fans out of the 27,327 in attendance moved from their seats along the sidelines and out onto the playing field, threatening the officials. Epithets were hurled and more than one enraged fan tried to throw punches and bottles at Tommy Whelan for the "we wuz robbed" ruling. Whelan's eye was swollen and his shirt torn. Escorted through the seething mob by players from both teams who aided the outmanned police, the officials finally made it to the dressing room.

An hour or more later, with several thousand fans still surrounding the administration building that housed the dressing rooms, the game officials were smuggled out of the stadium in the Buffalo players' bus, with the crowd yelling, "Let's Get Whelan . . . . Let's Get Whelan."

Thus ended the last exciting incident of an exciting season which saw the Colts' fortunes on the field improve by leaps and bounds. A couple of Colts players, Aubrey Fowler and Len "Tuffy" McCormick, were recognized for coming to the aid of Whelan on the field. Several Buffalo players later admitted that they felt Baltimore had gotten robbed. Cleveland annihilated the Bills in the title game in Cleveland, 49-7, before only 22,981 fans. The total dominance of the Browns was causing fan apathy in the AAFC; even in Cleveland attendance was falling.

Great strides had been made by the Colts in 1948. Dick Barwegen was picked first team All-Conference at guard and Billy Hillenbrand was selected second team halfback. Tittle was third in the league in total offense and second only to Otto Graham in passing and was named rookie of the year. He threw for 2,522 yards and 16 touchdowns, and had only nine interceptions in 289 attempts. Mertes was seventh in rushing, and Hillenbrand and Davis were third and sixth in pass receiving. Twice Tittle tossed passes good for 80 yards, one to John North against New York and the other to Racehorse Davis against Buffalo. Place-kicker Rex Grossman booted 45 straight extra points in his first season and connected on 11 of 19 field goal attempts. The longest scoring play of the season was turned in by Bob "Stormy" Pfohl, who scampered 92 yards with a punt return against the Brooklyn Dodgers.

In the souvenir department, it was another lean year with the game program, pennant, ribboned button, publicity photos by mail request, and large team photo pretty much the extent of the collectibles. A special ribboned black-and-white button picturing Baltimore's biggest star, Tittle, was sold at souvenir stands.

A new publicity director came on board for 1949: Eddie Adams took over for Dukehart, who left for a career in the new medium of broadcasting called television that had pictures along with the voices, joining WAAM-TV as sports director.

Adams' 1949 press guide contained the previous year's statistics and lengthy player profiles, including one for popular ex-Maryland star Lou Gambino, who nearly caused a big upset of the 49ers in San Francisco in 1948. "Lou came into his own," wrote Adams. "He tore off large chunks of yardage and was a constant threat to the tranquility of Frisco's head coach, Buck Shaw. Again in Los Angeles, with Tittle on the bench due to a neck injury, Gambino took handoffs from Charlie O'Rourke for good gains, and contributed greatly to a thrilling 29-14 Baltimore win." Adams wrote colorful biographies on all the key players, such as fan favorite Bob Nowaskey, and Ollie Poole of Ole Miss, who came from a great sports family. Wrote Adams: "The steady parade of various and sundry kinfolk who have preceded Ollie out of the south on the road to sports greatness includes Jim Poole of the New York Giants, Ray Poole of the Giants and Chicago Cubs, Harmon Poole of the Cubs, Barney Poole, All-America at both Mississippi and Army and Phillip, Jack and Leslie, all of whom lettered in the grid game at Ole Miss."

Based on the successful playing record in 1948 and the redoubled efforts of the Colts organization and the Colts Associates, the season ticket sale for 1949 climbed to 6,700. By this time the NFL knew the new league was more than just an idle threat; they were for real. The invincible Browns were drawing sizable crowds in Cleveland, the Dons were more than holding their own against the Rams in L.A., and the 49ers were drawing well at Kezar Stadium. The Colts of 1948 drew 224,502 fans (including the playoff game), an increase of 30 percent from the year before, but still the team finished in the red, losing a more acceptable $47,036.36.

The league-wide battle with the NFL was taking its toll and there was talk of a merger, but Baltimore, according to the rumor mill, wasn't to be a part of it. The AAFC owners met in mid-January in Chicago; before they left for the Windy City, Embry and Driskill met with Baltimore attorney John Henry Lewin, who said that the Colts couldn't be forced out of business if they had the resources and were in accordance with the league's bylaws. Embry and Driskill talked only positives at the meeting, citing higher ticket sales and more fan interest. That and the threat of legal action forced the owners to back down on dropping Baltimore. Rather, it was Brooklyn that ended up folding, thus creating an uneven number of teams.

The 1949 Colts, once again coached by Cecil Isbell, opened training camp on July 19 at Western Maryland College in Westminster, some 30 miles northwest of Baltimore. The close proximity to Baltimore made camp accessible to the fans and began a great tradition between the Colts and the quaint college town of Westminster.

Off the near divisional title the year before, expectations were high in 1949. Tittle, after all, could only get better under the tutelage of Isbell, and except for the retirement of Hillenbrand just about everybody was back. Driskill, who succeeded Embry as president, predicted the Colts would win the 1949 championship. Tittle was revered in Baltimore in the same way that John Unitas was ten years later, and when he led the Colts to an opening 28-12 preseason win over Buffalo, the fans began to think that Driskill was right about winning the title. But the bubble burst early as the Colts played their first four regular-season games on the road and lost all four by big scores. They fumbled 16 times in the four games and after the fourth loss, 35-7 in Chicago, the frenetic board of directors fired Isbell, and Driskill, already the president and general manager, was appointed coach. Driskill tried to talk the directors out of such a drastic move but once the city's newspapers began printing the news that Isbell was fired, the board went ahead and made it official, sending the sensitive Isbell into a deep depression.

Suddenly Driskill, who had engaged in heated contract discussions with several players, including Tittle, just weeks before, was now the coach. And amazingly, he benched Tittle in favor of Sam Vacanti for the first home game with Cleveland on September 25, in what was at this point called Babe Ruth Stadium. The Colts led at halftime 13-0, but a poor O'Rourke punt set up a Browns touchdown and Bill Willis' interception and return of a Vacanti pass to the 2 yard line set up another in a 14-13 Browns win. The lone victory of the season came the following week against Buffalo, 35-28, with Tittle back at the helm throwing a 79-yard touchdown pass to John North to tie the game and a 53-yard TD strike to Billy Stone with 24 seconds left. Then came six straight defeats to end the season.

Tittle felt that Driskill was making him a scapegoat for the poor season. Y. A., instead of improving on his rookie season, lost his confidence. Still, he was good enough to finish second behind Graham in passing, throwing for 2,209 yards and 14 touchdowns.

But unquestionably the Colts underachieved in 1949. They had solid personnel, including the talented former St. Mary's All-American Herman Wedemeyer, whom they picked up from the Los Angeles Dons in a bizarre transaction. The Dons were loaded with top running backs—Glenn Dobbs, George Taliaferro, Billy Grimes, and others—and the Hawaiian-born Wedemeyer, an outstanding crowd-pleasing runner, was riding the bench. The 49ers were eager to acquire Wedemeyer, who had played his college ball in the Bay area, but the Dons wouldn't trade him to their biggest rival. They approached the Colts. "How much is he making?" asked Driskill. When informed that Wedemeyer was making $12,000, Driskill declined, saying he was too expensive for the Colts. But since the Dons wanted Baltimore to have Wedemeyer, they told Driskill to pay him $8,000 and they'd make up the rest (Steadman 1958, 39). The shifty Wedemeyer led the league in kick returns and was fifth in punt returns. He led the team in rushing with a paltry 291 yards.

The 1949 game program still cost only 25 cents with two different players pictured on each cover, one from the Colts and one from

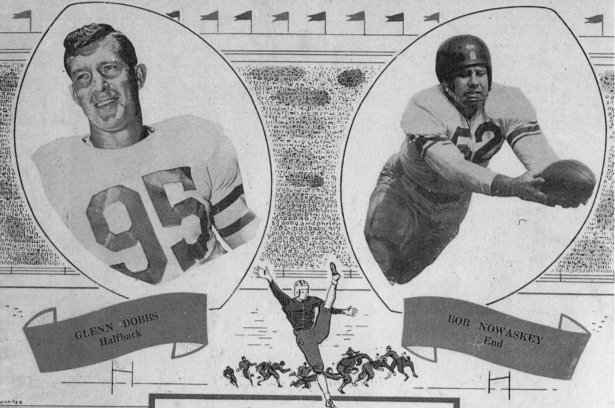

BALTIMORE COLTS

GLENN DOBBS
Halfback

BOB NOWASKEY
End

Balto. 10 VS. Los Angeles 21
LOS ANGELES DONS
Sunday, November 20th

25¢

For latest sports WITH

1230 ON YOUR DIAL

the opposition. Decked out in orange and green, an ad for WITH radio, the Colts' station, ran across the bottom of each program cover. Announcers Chuck Thompson and Bill Dyer were pictured inside the front cover in a Gunther's beer advertisement, teaming with WITH as "Two Maryland Favorites." There were player profiles and photos and a great offer from the Colts regarding the errant footballs that were kicked into the stands. To make the ownership of one of those way-ward pigskins even more desirable, all of the Colt coaching staff and players were available to "autograph any ball which is booted into the eager arms of a fan." The fan needed only to bring the ball to the Howard Street offices of the Colts. The fan would receive a receipt and within a few days that same ball, autographed by all the Colt play-ers and coaches, would be presented back to the fan on a local tele-vision show. Imagine a club doing that sort of promotion today! Other souvenirs included the team photo, 8 × 10 photos of the players which were sent out free on request, and the buttons and pennants for sale at the stadium. There were two different pennants sold by the AAFC Colts. One had the familiar frisky Colt jumping over the crossbar with helmet and football. The other, also in silver and green, featured a generic quarterback with white jersey and silver pants. Other teams used the more common running back and kicker, but only the Colts and Brooklyn Dodgers used the quarterback pennant. A fan could also write and order the All-America Football Conference Record Manual, with Otto Graham and Frankie Albert on the cover, for $1.50.

The Leaf Gum Company of Chicago, which issued a 98-card set of color trading cards in 1948, came out with a 49-card set in 1949,

opposite page

The Colts' 1949 programs featured an opposing player and a Colt on the cover.

Colt pennants were green and white with old English script lettering.

opposite page

The rare Silber's bakery trading card of Dick Barwegen.

Rex Grossman was part of the elusive Silber's bakery set of All-America Conference Colts.

Details on the contest to win an autographed football were on the back of each Silber's card.

but once again all the cards were of NFL players. There was however, a set of Colt cards issued in 1949 and they are now among the rarest of all pro football cards. In the fall of 1949 the Silber's Baking Company, with its factory on Monroe Street, one block south of North Avenue, created a set of between 17 and 20 cards, all picturing members of the Baltimore Colts. The exact number has never been substantiated. The cards were the size of playing cards, with rounded corners and the photo of the Colt player the same as the 8 × 10 glossy publicity shots made by the team. The top of each card read "Silber's Trading Card." The name of the player and his vital statistics were at the bottom. On the back of each card was the Colt home schedule and details of a contest sponsored by the bakery.

Ten-year-old Richard Cohen idolized the AAFC Colts and, along with his friends, tried to collect as many cards as he could. Richard, who lived on Lake Drive in the Druid Hill section of Baltimore, attended P.S. 61 and would often stop at Silber's to get the trading cards. "Each of their eight locations would have a pile of the cards behind the counter," remembers Richard, who is now a Baltimore neurosurgeon. "Every few days there would be a new card on the pile behind the counter and if you got to know the clerk you could usually get a card without buying anything." It was the contest that Silber's ran that drove Richard and his friends crazy. "Each card had a box on the back with a letter in it," he recalls. "The letters were S-I-L-B-E-R-S. Whoever could get a card with each letter to spell out Silber's had the choice of a Silber's cake, two tickets to Colt home games (we never figured whether it was just one game or the entire season), and an official AAFC football, signed by every member of the Colts. The trouble was," says Dr. Cohen, "they never printed any cards with the letter E, which meant there were no winners. We had tons of the other cards but no E card. By law, however, there had to have been a few printed in order to keep the promotion legal. I asked my father (Paul Cohen), who was the city building commissioner and had many contacts, if he could help me out. To make a long story short he was able to obtain one of the E cards directly from Mr. Silber." That meant that young Richard got perhaps the only official AAFC ball au-

DICK BARWEGEN
Guard—Height 6'0"—Weight 230
College—Purdue
THE BALTIMORE COLTS

REX GROSSMAN
Fullback—Height 6'1"—Weight 215
College—Indiana U.
THE BALTIMORE COLTS

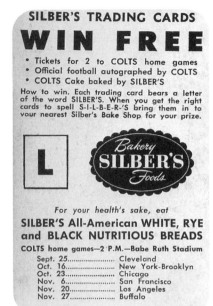

tographed by the Colts team. "I still have it," he beams proudly. "It's got Jonas Ingram's name and the entire team signed it in black pen on the brown ball."

In valuing the Silber's cards, Cohen, whose original cards were all tossed out when he left home for college, wouldn't know where to start. They are priceless, which amazes him because in 1949 there seemed to be thousands of them around Baltimore. He has managed to find 13 as he tries to reconstruct the set from his youth, but has resigned himself to not getting them all. "I know I won't get the E card because I had the only one and I handed it back in to get the ball." Richard has put numerous ads in the *Baltimore Sun* in search of the cards but hasn't gotten one reply. Just how rare are the cards? "I ran into Y. A. Tittle, one of my all-time heroes, several years ago, and showed him my Silber's card of him, which is his true rookie card," recalls Cohen. "Y. A. looked at it in amazement, saying he had no recollection whatsoever of the card. He thought, and all the price guides echo it, that his 1950 Bowman card was his rookie card. In reality it was his 1949 Silber's card." The known players in the Silber's set are

Ten Colts were picked to appear on matchbook covers in 1949. A no-no today.

Tittle, Dick Barwegen, Rex Grossman, Lou Gambino, Hub Bechtol, Stormy Pfohl, Billy Stone, Bus Mertes, Charlie O'Rourke, Windell Williams, Johnny North, Barry French, Racehorse Davis, John Mellus, Sam Vacanti, Paul Page, and Dub Garrett.

There was also a set of Colt matchbooks issued in 1949, with the players pictured on the covers. Cohen has all ten of the Colt matchbooks, which picture the players in white sport shirts rather than in uniform. "The same pictures are in the game program," adds Richard, "which means they must have asked the players to all wear white sports shirts to be photographed or else they each were given a shirt. I would go to the local pharmacy at the corner of Brookfield and Whitelock and the matchbooks would be in a bowl on the counter." The matchbooks were issued by the Maryland Match Corporation and were tinted in blue and white, not the Colt colors of green and silver. On the front was written "Buy Maryland Made Products. Ride with the Colts." The photos were on the back of each matchbook and featured players such as Tittle, Dick Barwegen, Rex Grossman, Racehorse Davis, and Herman Wedemeyer. Like the Silber's cards, the matchbook covers are extremely rare.

In 1949, the Exhibit Supply Company of Chicago, following up on their Sports Champions series of 44 the year before (which included 12 football players), began issuing a set of football cards that numbered 59 by the time they ceased in 1952. Collectors could obtain the cards for a penny in arcade machines. The $3\frac{1}{4} \times 5\frac{3}{8}$ cards featured both professional and college players in black and white and sepia tones, with Y. A. Tittle and Dick Barwegen representing the Colts. These were the first nationally produced cards featuring the Colts.

The 1-11 record of 1949 threw the franchise into another financial crisis. Despite drawing an average of 23,000 fans to their six home games the Colts lost between $80,000 and $100,000. Cleveland once again waltzed to its fourth straight AAFC championship, beating San Francisco 21-7. In four seasons, the Browns had posted 47 wins against just 4 defeats and 3 ties. Counting the postseason they were 52-4-3. Attendance was down 30 percent because of Cleveland's

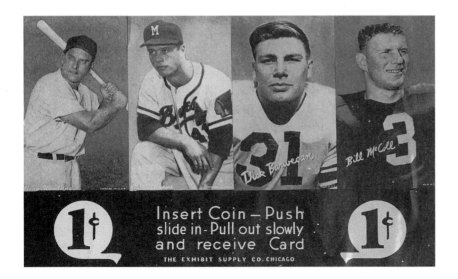

Dick Barwegen and Y. A. Tittle were featured on cards in penny arcade machines in the late 1940s.

dominance, and the biggest plunge was in Cleveland, which lost 130,000 fans from the year before.

Things were chaotic in both leagues. In Boston, before the 1949 season, Ted Collins announced that he couldn't make a go of his NFL franchise there and would move to New York. The NFL champion Eagles were sold for $250,000. AAFC commissioner Jonas Ingram resigned. The AAFC Chicago franchise got its fourth set of owners in four years. Only two AAFC teams had made money, the Browns in all but their last season and the 49ers only in their last season. The players gained big-time due to the competition between the leagues, with the average salary skyrocketing.

Merger talks were under way and it looked like a 13-team NFL circuit would result, with Cleveland, San Francisco, and Baltimore joining the 10 NFL teams. A bitter Buffalo would be left out. The Colts were angry because they'd have to pay George Preston Marshall, down the road in Washington, $150,000 in territorial damages. There was a segment of the NFL owners pitted against Baltimore, but the Colts, who had threatened legal action if they weren't included in a merger, were added as the swing team, meaning they would play the 12 other teams once.

There was a "Save the Colts" game planned in August, an exhibition with all seats at $5. The drive had barely reached the halfway mark of its goal of 50,000 tickets when the merger was signed in early March 1950. Understandably, once the Colts were in the NFL, the impetus to buy tickets wasn't as great.

A new money man entered the picture at this point. Abraham "Shorty" Watner, who along with Jake Embry was an official in the Advertising Club, took on the operation of the Colts for the 1950 season. His greatest notoriety had come in 1943 when $10,600 blew out his office window on Baltimore Street while he was talking to George Preston Marshall on the phone. Only $200 was recovered. Watner had aspirations of owning an NFL team as early as 1941 and was part of Gene Tunney's group that tried to get an AAFC team for Baltimore in 1946. As it turned out, Watner, who operated a cemetery (which he referred to as a "series of underground bungalows"), a trucking enterprise, and a railroad in successful fashion, met his match with pro football.

Despite being in the East, the Colts were placed in the National or Western division. The team sustained a key blow when Driskill resigned in May to join the McCormick Company and Clem Crowe, who had played on the fabled "Four Horsemen" Notre Dame team in the 1920s and had coached Buffalo the year before in 1949, was named the new coach. Crowe didn't have much to work with. In fact, the Colts of 1950 are ranked among the worst teams in pro football history. For one thing, Baltimore had been shortchanged when the NFL distributed talent from the defunct Yankees and Bills. Instead, the Giants and Browns took the cream of those franchises. The Giants, among others, got future Hall of Famer Arnie Weinmeister from the Yanks. Gone were stalwarts like Barwegen, who was traded right before the season to the Bears, Bechtol, Grossman, and Racehorse Davis. In their place were some aging veterans and some youngsters with promise, but very little in between. Two rookies from Boston College, Art Donovan and Art Spinney would become Colt greats down the road. But for now, this was a motley bunch. Crowe remembered walking into a huddle in an early practice session and was almost floored by the smell of alcoholic breath. "My God," protested Crowe, "not so early in the morning." "No, Coach," came the reply from a player in the huddle, "that's from last night" (Claassen 1963, 280).

Besides the regular season, the Colts had a murderous seven-game exhibition season that included three games in six days. They dropped all seven, including a 30-27 loss before only 22,000 on "Save the Colts" night and a 70-21 drubbing by the Rams in San Antonio. Things just got worse in the regular season. Tittle and company lost 11 out of 12, mostly by lopsided scores. The Rams beat them 70-27, the Cardinals won 55-13, and the Giants buried them 55-20. Cleveland blanked them 31-0. The Colts had no pass defense. Quarterback

Baltimore COLTS

BOB LIVINGSTONE
Halfback
Baltimore Colt

VS.

WASHINGTON REDSKINS
Sunday, Sept. 17th
MEMORIAL STADIUM

25¢

PRICE   24¢
MD. SALES TAX   1¢

SAMMY BAUGH
Quarterback
Washington Redskin

Jim Hardy of the Cardinals tossed six touchdown passes against the Colts in one game and Bob Shaw caught five of them. The Cardinals actually trailed 13-7 at the half before ripping off 48 second-half points to set a record. Cloyce Box of Detroit caught 12 passes for 302 yards one afternoon. Things were bad off the field too. Publicity director Eddie Adams got fed up with Watner's eccentricities and quit at midseason.

opposite page

The 1950 game programs had a red background and featured players from both teams on the covers.

The only Colt victory of the year was a 41-21 thumping of the almost-as-bad Packers on November 5 at Memorial Stadium; that snapped an 18-game losing streak going back to preseason. Down 21-10 in the fourth period, defensive backs Jim Owens, Jim Spavital, and Herb Rich picked off Tobin Rote passes for touchdowns. Spavital, also the starting fullback, scored on a 96-yard touchdown jaunt, finishing with 176 yards rushing. Herb Rich, the rookie from Vanderbilt, ended the season with an average of 22 yards on 12 punt returns, the highest seasonal average in NFL history. The Colts also finished the entire season without kicking a field goal. The only other team to achieve that mark, the Dallas Texans of 1952, would become the Colts of 1953.

Money was tight in that 1950 season in Baltimore, so when a player was injured, he wasn't replaced. The Colts were down to just 25 players at season's end, a 51-14 loss to the Yanks at Yankee Stadium before only 5,003. Fans were admitted free if they brought a toy for charity, but not even a free ticket proved to be much of a lure. Attendance in Baltimore was only 94,992 in six home games, an average of less than 16,000. The future of pro football in Baltimore again was at a crossroads. Not so in Cleveland. The Browns proved their dominance in the AAFC was no fluke, as they humiliated the defending NFL champion Eagles 35-10 in the season opener and went on to beat the Rams for the championship 30-28 on Lou Groza's last-second field goal.

The 1950 Colt game program was a solid effort in red, silver, and black. A Colt player was always on the cover along with a star from the opposition. There were excellent player profiles and photos. There was a contest in which the fan who guessed the correct number of total points scored by the Colts in 1950 would win a Philco 16-

inch television set. In this case it was wise to think small, since they scored only 213. On the back cover was an ad for Arrow beer. The first NFL Colt press guide in 1950 was compiled by Eddie Adams and featured a green, silver, and white cover that showed the Colt jumping over a crossbar with a football between his hooves. There were 1949 statistics for both the NFL and the AAFC and a nice article on the Colt band, at this point led by Bob Cissin. There were also player profiles and statistical info.

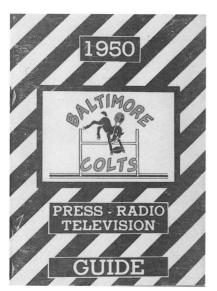

The Colts first NFL press guide was green and white with the familiar Colt logo in the middle.

Nineteen fifty marked the first year that Colt players were pictured on bubble-gum trading cards. The Bowman Gum Company of Philadelphia, after a year's hiatus in 1949, produced a 144-card color set. The cards were actual paintings of the players with all the vital statistics on the back. Colts in the set were Y. A. Tittle, Jon Jenkins, Dick Barwegen, Bob Nowaskey, Adrian Burk, Bill Leonard, Barry French, Billy Stone, and Earl Murray.

Also in 1950, a colorful comic book called "The Baltimore Colts" was produced and printed by American Visuals Corporation of New York. It sold for a quarter, and on the cover was a determined Colt ballcarrier in green and silver running to daylight. The book chronicled the formation of the Colts late in 1946, recounted the controversial playoff game with Buffalo in 1948, and gave glowing testimonials to Abe Watner. Each page highlighted a different Colt, from coach Clem Crowe to all the players (Billy Stone, Y. A. Tittle, Don Colo, Johnny North, Leon Campbell, and Bob Nowaskey among them). The artwork was first rate. There was even a section on the men who worked behind the scenes, publicity director Eddie Adams, trainer Mickey McClernon, equipment chief John Sanborne, and ticket manager Herb Wright. The inside back cover had an article on the Colt band. Not many of these comic books have survived over the years; to find one in good condition is a rarity. In 1950, a pair of Colts also graced the end wrappers of bread loaves all over the country. Bakeries found bread labels were a great vehicle for selling their products, especially among young people. There were stars from all sports as well as western cowboy heroes and Hollywood movie stars. Y. A. Tittle and Dick Barwegen were part of a 32-color set of labels that in Baltimore were found on Koester's bread. The now almost impossible to find labels also featured Sammy Baugh, Otto Graham, Sid Luckman, and Bob Waterfield.

After the dismal 1950 season, the future of the Colt franchise was up in the air. Watner was a total buffoon when it came to football, sort of an early-day but nonvindictive version of Robert Irsay. At the annual NFL meeting on January 18, 1951, in Chicago, Watner, who had been vacillating on whether to keep or disband the Colts, made his decision. After asking for player assistance from the other teams and being refused, he announced he was getting out. The league gave him $50,000 for his assets, meaning all the players on the roster. Tittle was the biggest plum, and was picked by the 49ers to replace Frankie Albert. Even the club's helmets were sold, to the Green Bay Packers. Crowe had gone to the Chicago meeting as the coach of the Colts and came home without a team. He hadn't seen a paycheck in a month and had bills to pay on his farm in Eden, New York. Crowe confronted Watner that night and among other things berated him for treating him and his assistants "like dogs" (Steadman 1997, 105–6).

Embittered fans in Baltimore took the news of the Colts' demise hard. While Watner headed for a Florida vacation, his Pikesville home was vandalized twice. Five days after the team was disbanded, the board of directors held an emergency meeting. Top Baltimore business leaders such as Jake Embry, Victor Frenkil, William Hilgenberg, Zanvyl Krieger, and Charles McCormick were in attendance. Each man pledged $500 to form a legal fund to get the team back. They felt they had a strong case, that Watner lacked legal authority to dissolve the franchise and that the league had been an accomplice in the deed. NFL commissioner Bert Bell admitted that the league had acted too harshly and ruled that Baltimore could get the Colts back if they cleared all debts, put up $200,000, and appointed one man to run the franchise. The league would also agree to return all the original Colt players and let them pick first in each round of the draft. But nothing happened. Finally, on November 1, 1951, ten months after the Colts had folded, attorney William Macmillan, representing the board of directors and the city of Baltimore, filed suit against Watner and the NFL. Baltimore didn't want money, it wanted a football team. The Boston–turned–New York Yanks had been available, but owner Ted Collins sold the franchise to Dallas interests instead and they became the Texans for the 1952 season. NFL owners were excited to be heading for a football-rich state in Texas. All except one: Pittsburgh's venerable Art Rooney had doubts. He was in Baltimore's corner, and as events would soon prove, he was right.

THREE

Back to Stay

Once again Baltimore was a pro football castoff, faced with re-grouping and winning back the confidence of the National Football League. Watner had sold out both the board of directors and the city of Baltimore. A hearing was held early in 1952 regarding the city's suit against Watner and the NFL, the idea being to acquire another franchise rather than to win a cash settlement. As respected Baltimore attorney William D. Macmillan, representing the city, said, "Fans can't come out to the stadium to watch us count a cash settlement. It's a team we're after" (Steadman 1958, 62). The assets of the 1950 Colts had been scattered in a hundred different directions. Some equipment, other than the helmets sold to Green Bay, was stored in Watner's warehouse. The neon sign outside the Colts' Howard Street office was taken to a junkyard. A landlord's auction was held at the Colt office to reclaim $250 in back rent.

George Preston Marshall once again saw the opportunity to recapture the Baltimore fans for his Redskins, but Baltimore was having no part of it. He was regarded as Public Enemy Number 2 behind Watner as the man most responsible for Baltimore's ouster from the NFL.

Pressure from Baltimore's legal challenge to the NFL was having an effect. Commissioner Bert Bell invited Baltimore interests to the league meeting in January 1952, and let them try to convince New York Yanks owner Ted Collins, the manager of singer Kate Smith, to move his team to Baltimore for the 1952 season. After saying he would consider the Baltimore proposal, Collins sold the team to Dallas interests. The Yanks became the Texans, and one of the more tragicomic episodes in the annals of the NFL was about to unfold. What few if any realized, was that despite Baltimore's setback in not getting the Yanks, the seeds of what would become a championship team in Baltimore by the end of the decade were being sown. It turned out to be one of sports' great bedtime stories.

Despite being in a football-happy state, the Texans bombed in Dallas. Poor promotions, poor club operations, limited personnel, and the fans' unfamiliarity with the NFL were all factors. While fans flocked to high school and college games, they all but ignored the professionals. The Texans weren't exactly bereft of talent. They had Claude "Buddy" Young, a crowd-pleasing runner, along with future Hall of Famers Gino Marchetti and Art Donovan. Plus Dickie Hoerner and Tom Keane who were part of a carload of 11 players obtained from the Rams for rookie linebacker Les Richter. Young later remembered quarterback Bob Celeri, the second-year man from California, as "almost uncoachable. He was the first quarterback I knew who liked to do his own thing, like throw on fourth and 20."

Thank goodness the Texans had a coach with a sense of humor. Jimmy Phelan was a whimsical Irishman who didn't take life very seriously. Says Donovan, "We had a great time in spite of everything, mostly because of Phelan. He had a great line of bull and it was a picnic just being around him. One time we were working out on a field near the Rose Bowl, preparing for the Rams, and we ran off a couple of plays without fouling up. Jimmy was so happy he stopped practice, loaded us all on the bus and took us to the race track. Jimmy loved the ponies." Donovan was Phelan's favorite; Artie could do no wrong. "Phelan went to Mass every morning," says Donovan. "I'd be dragging in around six o'clock and he'd be waiting for me with a cab to take me to church. He cared about the game," Artie continued, "and if he thought you were laying down, he wouldn't stand for it. But football had passed him by. He was the only coach I knew who hated practice more than the players did."

The Texans thought they would fill the Cotton Bowl for their opener on September 28, 1952, against the New York Giants. The Giants featured former SMU greats Kyle Rote and Fred Benners, but only 17,000 turned out to see New York win 24-6. That would be the largest home crowd of the season. After three more home losses to San Francisco, Green Bay, and Los Angeles and total home attendance in four games of only 50,000, Dallas owners Giles and Connell Miller handed the club back to the league. They had lost an estimated $225,000, including the $100,000 to acquire the franchise from Collins. For the rest of the season, the Texans played as a road team under the direction of the league office.

The only win of the season occurred on Thanksgiving Day, November 27, at the Akron Rubber Bowl against the powerful Chicago Bears. NFL commissioner Bert Bell had hoped to play the game in Baltimore, but the traditional high school rivalries, Calvert Hall–Loyola in the morning and City-Poly in the afternoon, took precedence. The morning of the game in Akron, more than 14,800 watched a traditional high school game in the morning, but only 3,000 came out for the Bears-Texans in the afternoon. The final was 27-23 and Art Donovan recalls that in his pregame pep talk, Phelan suggested that since the crowd was so small, "we're going to dispense with the formal introductions over the PA system and go up into the stands and personally shake hands with each fan." Bears coach George Halas was giddy going into the game because his team had upset the eventual 1952 champion Lions the week before. "Halas nearly croaked," Donovan said in remembering the upset. In no other game that season did the Texans come within 17 points of even a tie.

The Texans' last game in Dallas was against the Rams in a driving rainstorm. The only fans to brave the elements gathered under the overhang of the stadium roof. Los Angeles won 27-6. The day the franchise folded, Phelan canceled practice so the players could race to the bank before their paychecks bounced. Nicknamed the NFL's "Lost Battalion," the Texans ended up playing their remaining games on the road and using Hershey, Pennsylvania, as their home base for workouts.

Items such as game programs, press guides, pennants, and pins are tough to locate because the team was in Dallas for such a short time. The Texans' press guide was edited by publicity director Hamilton "Tex" Maule, who went on to fame as *Sports Illustrated*'s top pro football writer. In the front office was former Colt business manager Al Ennis. Phelan's backfield coach was former Colt head coach Cecil Isbell. Team colors were navy blue, silver, and white, which became the colors in Baltimore, replacing the old green and silver. On the Texans' roster, besides Young, Donovan, and Marchetti, were familiar Colt players of the future: Sisto Averno, Joe Campanella, Dan Edwards, Ken Jackson, George Taliaferro, Tom Keane, Zollie Toth, and Brad Ecklund. Also on the roster was future Baltimore high school coach, future Colt assistant, and future Giants general manager George Young, a Little All-American from Bucknell.

In just eight years the Dallas Cowboys would debut and build up a huge fan following not only in Dallas but across the country. But in 1952, Dallas just wasn't ready for pro football. Commissioner Bell, worried about how the league was going to handle the court case in Baltimore, finally discovered an option. Now that the Texans had failed in Dallas and were a ward of the league, the solution to the problem was simple: give Baltimore the Texans. Two problems would then be solved. It had already cost the league $60,000 to keep the Texans afloat. There was a caveat to the transfer, however. Bell, at an Advertising Club luncheon on December 3, 1952, declared that the Texans would come to Baltimore only if the city bought 15,000 season tickets within six weeks. It's doubtful that Bell had any other alternative but Baltimore in which to place the Texans (perhaps Buffalo), but what he did was call Baltimore's bluff and help whoever the new owners would be to get off to a solid start. Auto dealer Bruce Livie was recruited to head the ticket sale program and it was a huge success. Daily graphs showing the ticket drive's progress were published in the newspapers. Despite the Christmas holidays, the 15,000 seats, plus 755 more, were bought up in a little over four weeks and over $300,000 was in the till. Not bad for a football team that had won only one game the year before. So the "orphaned" Dallas Texans were left on the white marble stoops of Baltimore, much like abandoned foundlings.

Now the task was to find a new owner, general manager, coach, and other personnel needed to run the team. Bell had a preference on who the owner should be. It was his old summertime neighbor in Margate, New Jersey, Carroll Rosenbloom. The two had first met at the University of Pennsylvania in 1927 when Bell was an assistant coach and Rosenbloom a halfback on the team. Rosenbloom, after graduation, had worked in his father's shirt company in Baltimore. Despite being the owner's son, he worked his way up through the ranks and at the tender age of 33, thanks to his success in menswear and other manufacturing ventures, decided to retire. When World War II began, Rosenbloom rejoined the business and devoted the majority of his attention to the Blue Ridge Manufacturing Co., which turned out denim used for military work uniforms. Under Rosenbloom's direction the plant became a multimillion dollar operation.

It isn't true that the franchise was left on Rosenbloom's doorstep in a wicker basket, but it certainly came close. When Bell first approached Rosenbloom about owning a team in 1951, his blandishments fell on deaf ears: Rosenbloom wasn't interested. Bell was persistent and kept working on Rosenbloom, but to no avail. Other names, such as Arthur Godfrey, Louis Wolfson, Sid Luckman, John B. Kelly (father of Grace), Bill Veeck, Jack Dempsey, Gene Tunney, and original owner Bob Rodenberg were mentioned as possibilities. Rumor had it that Rosenbloom's brothers were advising him not to get involved because of what happened to Watner.

Finally, on January 10, 1953, Rosenbloom agreed to assume ownership, with 51 percent control. He headed a group that included William Hilgenberg, Zanvyl Krieger, Thomas Mullan, and Bruce Livie, who constituted the other 49 percent. The purchase price was $200,000, with $25,000 up front. Rosenbloom's initial investment was only $13,000. Just four years later the franchise would be valued at one million dollars.

Although unfamiliar with the techniques of running a pro sports franchise, Rosenbloom, more than any other owner, made himself essential to his team's success. He took a genuine interest in his players and, with checkbook in hand, offered them help through bonuses and loans that he often forgave. It all added to the family atmosphere that set the Colts apart.

The next step was finding a general manager, and once again Bert

Bell came up with a winner. Don Kellett, then directing operations at WFIL-TV in Philadelphia and a former three-sport star at Penn as well as professional baseball player (he had nine at bats in the major leagues with the Boston Red Sox), was offered the job and accepted.

One of the enticements to get Kellett to take the job was the promise of a 25 percent share of the Colts' profits. Kellett was multifaceted, having coached several sports on the college level as well as having done the play-by-play for pro and college football and basketball broadcasts in the Philadelphia area. It was one of the greatest hires in Baltimore sports history, as Kellett brought class, experience, and a personal touch to the job. His engaging personality, along with his executive ability, compensated for his lack of expertise in football and made him the ideal man to help make Baltimore an NFL success.

Bell was batting two-for-two with Rosenbloom and Kellett, and now he had to come up with a coach. He settled on former pro running back Keith Molesworth, who had played for George Halas and the Bears in the Bronko Nagurski era as well as playing several seasons of professional baseball that included a stint with the International League Baltimore Orioles in 1934 and 1936. Football, though, was Molesworth's forte. He had played quarterback with the old Portsmouth Spartans in 1929 and 1930 and, after a year with the Ironton Tanks, joined the Bears, where he played for seven seasons. Molesworth then went to the Naval Academy as backfield coach. He also coached plebe baseball and basketball and remained in Annapolis until 1946. After that it was on to Hawaii to coach the Honolulu Warriors for three years, and then back to the states, where he coached the Richmond Rebels of the Eastern Football League to two championships. After spending the 1952 season as an assistant in Pittsburgh with the Steelers, Molesworth joined the Colts. Kellett was very familiar with Molesworth. In 1937 they had been the double-play combination of the Syracuse Chiefs, Molesworth at shortstop and Kellett at second base.

Twenty of the former Dallas Texans, including assistant coach Alex Agase, who switched back to being a player, came to Baltimore with the franchise. Only 13 made the team and five years later, when the Colts won the championship, only four remained: Art Spinney, Arthur Donovan, Gino Marchetti, and Ken Jackson. Phelan had a desire to come to Baltimore as general manager (his choice for head coach would have been none other than Cecil Isbell), but he was passed over by Bell.

There was some discussion about abandoning the nickname "Colts" and adopting something new for the city's rebirth in pro football. A meeting of the directors was held and after a brief debate it was decided that the name Colts was intertwined with Baltimore football and should continue. Gone, though, were the green and silver of the old team, and in their place were the colors of the Texans, blue, silver, and white. Sam Banks was the new public relations director and Herb Wright was back as ticket manager. A season book for six box seats cost $25, while reserved seats in the grandstand cost $19.80 for the season. The Colts band, kept together in 1951 and 1952 by leader Bob Cissin performing at parades and civic gatherings, was ready to return to playing at Colts games.

The 1953 Colts press guide had the familiar blue and silver colt with helmet and ball, designed by Hugh Haynie, a staff cartoonist for the Greensboro, North Carolina *Daily News.* There were in-depth bios of Rosenbloom, Kellett, Molesworth, and his assistants, previews of the league and each team and thumbnail sketches of all the players. There were Gunther beer ads inside the front and back covers, as well as on the back cover. There was no question as to who was the team's top sponsor.

Kellett operated out of a lone room at the Lord Baltimore Hotel when he first arrived. Soon offices were shifted to 2013 North Charles Street. The old rowhouse office is still there, in a decaying area flanked by a methadone drug treatment center, barbershop, and streetcorner drug hustlers.

Kellett had to build the organization from scratch. After an initial setback of failing to sign the team's top two draft picks (Oklahoma's Billy Vessels and Purdue's Bernie Flowers, both of whom opted to play in Canada), Kellett swung a big deal with Cleveland on March 25 involving 15 players. The Colts sent Don Colo, Tom Catlin, future Colt coach Mike McCormack, Hershel Forester, and John Petibon to the Browns for Bert Rechichar, Ed Sharkey, Stu Sheetz, Don Shula, Art Spinney, Carl Taseff, Harry Agganis, Gern Nagler, Dick Batten, and Elmer Willhoite. It was one of the biggest deals in sports history. Only Rechichar, Shula, Spinney, and Taseff were successful in Baltimore, while all five players sent to Cleveland became integral parts of their championship teams. Tragically, Agganis, the "Golden Greek" from Boston University, died suddenly from a viral infection in 1955 while playing for the Boston Red Sox.

Besides having inadequate offices, the Colts were also hampered by the construction going on at Memorial Stadium. They would have to play their games while workmen were literally sitting on scaffolding laying brick.

Yet it was full speed ahead when Molesworth gathered 60 players at their training camp in Westminster. Buddy Young and the "T 'n' T" twins, Zollie Toth and George Taliaferro, were counted on in the running back department. Quarterback wasn't as set with journeymen Tom Dublinski and Gene Mackrides, along with Baltimore's own Bobby Williams and rookie Bobby Kilfoyle. Unfortunately, Williams was called into the Navy and Kellett would later pick up quarterback Fred Enke of Arizona on waivers for $100 from Philadelphia.

The first time the 1953 Colts took the field was on August 6 in the Colts Night intrasquad scrimmage at Memorial Stadium. The Blues played the Whites. After five exhibition games in places like Lubbock, Texas, Norfolk, Virginia, and St. Louis, the Colts played their first home exhibition against the Redskins on September 20 and won 9-3 before 22,800 fans, as Buck McPhail drilled three field goals through the uprights.

In the season opener the following Sunday at Memorial Stadium against the Bears, the Colts made their debut a memorable one by beating Chicago 13-9. Bert Rechichar stole the show by intercepting a George Blanda pass and running 39 yards for a touchdown; he then followed with an NFL-record 56-yard field goal, surpassing Detroit's Glenn Presnell, who booted a 54-yarder at Green Bay in 1934. Rechichar's record would stand until 1970 when New Orleans' Tom Dempsey kicked a 63-yarder.

opposite page

The Colts are back! The fans' first peek at their new blue-and-white clad heroes was at the Colts Night game in early August.

The first game program showed an offensive depth chart that had Gino Marchetti playing left tackle on offense, next to old Colt favorite Dick Barwegen, who returned from the Bears in a July trade. Another defensive star of the future, Joe Campanella, was at right tackle on offense. On the cover of the first program was a painting by Victor Kalin that showed an exuberant crowd rooting on their team. Program covers for that first season back in the NFL were both colorful and varied, with no particular theme. Famed illustrator Lon Keller, the Norman Rockwell of sports artists, made his Colt debut with the October 3 program for the game against the Lions. The cover showed a generic player punting, with an overhead view of a packed stadium behind him and a series of yellow lines emanating from the kicker. Larry Tisdale painted the October 25 program cover for the Washington game, a light-hearted look at a couple floating on a leaf over a stadium. Respected New York cartoonist Willard Mullin drew the

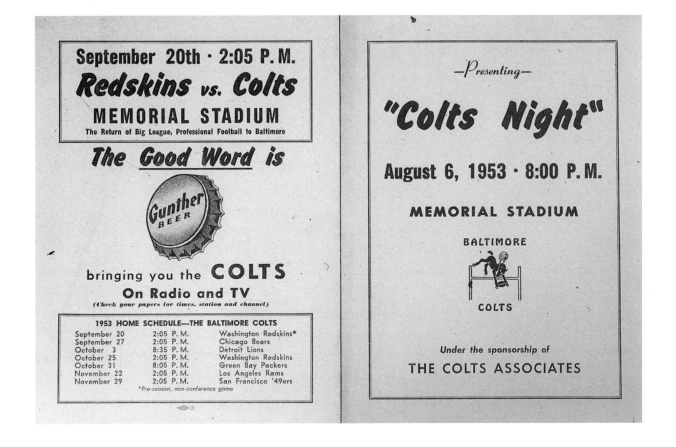

program cover for the final home game against the 49ers on November 29. An old-time player without a helmet was shown bolting from a pack of bewildered modern-day players, on his way to a touchdown.

Except for the intro page written by public relations director Sammy Banks that previewed each game, the program stayed the same from week to week. In fact there were Colt players, such as Gern Nagler, Charlie Robinson, and George Rooks, pictured in every program who didn't make the team or were traded. In the final program, Banks paid tribute to George Taliaferro, who switched from halfback to quarterback the week before in a 21-13 loss to the Rams. "He ran brilliantly, passed adequately and punted in grand style." Advertisements included the Mayfair Theatre on Howard near Franklin, showing "The Last Posse" with John Derek and Wanda Hendrix, the Blue Room on the corner of Mount Royal and Charles, featuring an All Girl Revue, and Harley's Sandwiches at 211 McMechen Street and his "Jazz in Baltimore" show on WITH radio.

The Colts, because of their Dallas origins, were assigned to the Western Division, even though they were farther east than most other teams in the league. They wore pretty much the same uniforms as they had in Dallas, with dark blue helmets. There were a pair of white horseshoes added to the back of the helmets to indicate the team's new nickname; this little flourish was the brainchild of PR man Banks. The Colts thus joined the Rams and Eagles as the only NFL teams with logos on their helmets. They wore the same sideline capes they had used in Dallas, with a tailor sewing a "Colts" patch over the word "Texans."

After losing in the second week to the defending champion Lions, the Colts beat the Bears again, this time in Chicago, 16-14, on Buddy Young's diving end-zone catch of Fred Enke's pass. After another loss at Green Bay, 37-14, close to 5,000 fans met the team with the band playing at the airport upon their return, causing several veteran players to walk down the ramp with tears in their eyes. The following week the hated Redskins were beaten 27-17, and the upstart Colts had a 3-2 record. Then came seven straight losses, including a 45-2 shellacking at Los Angeles, for a final record of 3-9.

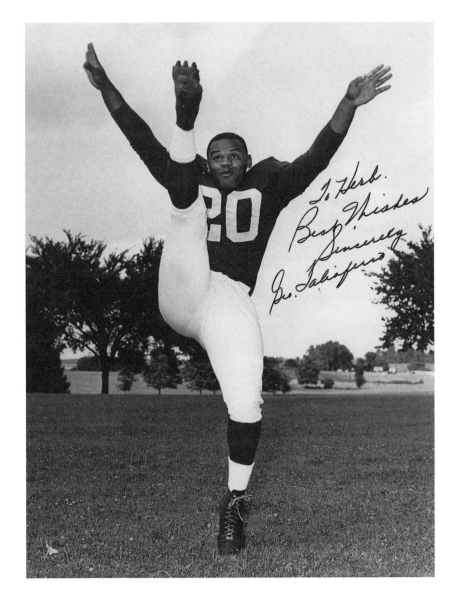

George Taliaferro could do it all. Offense, defense, and kick.

Lack of depth and some crippling injuries took their toll in this inaugural season. One of those injuries occurred in the seventh game at Philadelphia when, after Buddy Young had run the opening kick-off back 104 yards for a quick score, Enke suffered a severe shoulder separation and ended up going back to harvesting cotton in Casa Grande, Arizona. That's when Taliaferro was thrust into the breach. Attendance was encouraging considering the construction work that

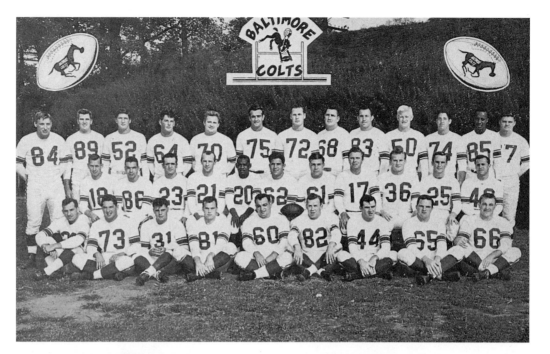

BUDDY YOUNG
COLTS

SISTO AVERNO
COLTS

TED MARCHIBRODA
STEELERS

limited stadium capacity to under 30,000. For the year they drew 168,014, an average of 26,000. Young was voted the team's most popular player in a poll of the fans.

The Bowman Gum trading card set shrank from 144 cards to 96 in 1953, but a handful of Colts were included. Sisto Averno, George Taliaferro, Buddy Young, 14th-round draft pick Frank Continetti (who failed to make the team), Gern Nagler, and Tom Dublinski were featured, although Nagler and Dublinski were also sent packing before the season began. Perhaps the Colts' best player, Art Donovan, was missing, even though he would star in the Pro Bowl game. Dick Barwegen, Tom Keane, and Taliaferro were also picked for the Pro Bowl.

Young, Taliaferro, and Mel Embree were all pacesetters on the Colts, becoming the first black players to remain for a full season. Art Fletcher had played in a couple of games in 1950, but was only on the roster a brief time. The 1953 team picture is a classy, oversized black-and-white photo in which Buddy Young is strangely missing.

On the field, progress had been made in 1953. Some astute trades, drafting, and free-agent signings had resulted in two more wins than in 1952 and this was something to build upon. Rosenbloom had been bitten by the pro football bug and was now totally immersed in the team. In December 1953 Rosenbloom relieved Molesworth of his coaching duties and kicked him upstairs to the front office as chief talent scout. The owner instructed Molesworth to develop the finest scouting operation in the league.

And so the search for a new coach was on. A coach with NFL experience was preferred; Navy's Eddie Erdelatz was the only college coach considered. Others on the list of candidates were Buck Shaw and Red Strader of the 49ers, and Steve Owen of the Giants. The team's first choice was Cleveland assistant Blanton Collier, but his allegiance to Paul Brown was so strong that he asked to be removed from consideration. Just a month later, Collier, who in 1963 would replace Paul Brown in Cleveland, left the Browns to coach at the University of Kentucky.

At this point a Browns executive, Dave Jones, told Rosenbloom about another assistant on Brown's staff, a relative unknown named

opposite page

The Colts proudly pose for their 1953 team photo.

Buddy Young and Sisto Averno were part of the 1953 Bowman trading card set. Future Colt coach Ted Marchibroda, cherubic face and all, appeared in the 1953 Bowman set as a rookie quarterback in Pittsburgh.

Wilbur C. "Weeb" Ewbank. Brown wasn't happy about Ewbank talking to Baltimore; he had already lost one assistant in Collier and didn't
want to lose another. He viewed it as tantamount to desertion, since
he and Ewbank went back several decades to their 1920s college
playing days at Miami University in Oxford, Ohio.

Weeb, however, couldn't let an opportunity to coach an up-and-
coming team like the Colts get away. He accepted the Baltimore offer
and a new era was about to begin. When Weeb took over he uttered
an amazingly accurate prediction: "We'll give you a champion," he
promised the rabid Colt fans, "in five years." Ewbank came pretty
close; because of "sudden-death" overtime in the 1958 title game win
over the Giants, it took them an extra 8 minutes and 15 seconds.

As a chief aide to the legendary Paul Brown for five years, as well
as his lifelong friend, Weeb brought many of Brown's innovations to
Baltimore. "Order and system" became the Colts' slogan. After a stint
with Brown's staff at Great Lakes Naval Training Center during the
war, Ewbank had made his head coaching mark at Washington University in St. Louis; there he built the program from scratch and went
14-4 in two seasons before joining the Browns staff in 1949.

Weeb's new assistants included "Red" Cominsky, Russ Winner,
Charlie Winner, and Joe Thomas, this last another Great Lakes alum
who would one day serve as Bob Irsay's general manager in Baltimore
and preside over the dismantling of one of the game's storied teams.
Weeb also brought in a new trainer, Eddie Block, whom he called
"the best trainer in the business." Block, nicknamed the "little doc-
tor," had served as Ewbank's trainer at Washington University. He
had also been wounded while serving with a tank outfit during the
war and was awarded the Purple Heart. One of 10 children, Eddie was
a bachelor who adopted the entire Colt team as his sons. Frequently,
Block, who had a huge heart, arranged for convalescing players to
visit the Kernan Children's Hospital. Ironically, some 24 years later,
a Courage Award named after Eddie would involve the recipients in
paying a visit to the St. Vincent's home for abused children.

Unlike Brown, who was considered cold, dictatorial, and distant
by his players, Ewbank brought a personal touch to coaching. He
would scold his players, but never bully or embarrass them. From

these humble beginnings he would go on to coach two of the most memorable games in pro football history, the 1958 "Greatest Game Ever Played" and the Jets' upset win over the Colts in Super Bowl III.

The 1954 Colts had some holes to fill. As Weeb said in an interview many years later, "We had maybe 11 players when I got here. It wasn't much of a nucleus." Alex Agase and Brad Ecklund retired, and Barney Poole, Danny Edwards, and the still speedy Young were getting up in age. There was also a question about whether Enke could come back. Weeb returned Gino Marchetti and Joe Campanella to defense and moved Art Spinney from defensive end to offensive guard. Zollie Toth was back at fullback after a double fracture of the jaw in '53. Other newcomers included Cotton Davidson, a quarterback from Baylor, Ordell Braase, a tackle from South Dakota, and military service returnee Jim Mutscheller of Notre Dame. Ewbank envisioned fullback John Huzvar at 6' 4", 252 pounds of power, as another Marion Motley who had starred at Cleveland.

Weeb planned to install a Browns offense in Baltimore. According to Banks' press guide, "The scrappy little mentor can call upon a startlingly impressive ability to diagnose an opponent's attack quickly. Possessor of almost a photographic mind, Ewbank can spot weaknesses in his own club as well as the opposition with little more than a glance at a strip of film or a quick review of a scouting chart. He is a precise systematist." Of the 62-man roster, only two players were older than 28, and they were 31-year-old Dick Barwegen and 30-year old Barney Poole.

Weeb was a chip off Paul Brown's block. Players like Don Shula, Bill Pellington, Carl Taseff, and Bert Rechichar, who had played for Brown in Cleveland, said Weeb's training camp procedures and playbook were exactly the same as those the Browns used. In studying game films, Ewbank realized that the Colts' blue helmet didn't lend itself to easy visibility on film, so he had them change to a white helmet with horseshoes on the back of each side. After the Colts were bombed 48-0 in their opener against the Rams, Weeb ordered plastic face masks installed on all the helmets.

The Colts had an excellent preseason in 1954, winning four of five

The 1954 press guide had a familiar look.

The annual "kick off" banquet program was cleverly shaped like a football.

opposite page

Carl Taseff prepares to tackle Green Bay's Breezy Reid in a 7-6 loss at Memorial Stadium, as Bill Pellington, number 65 on the ground, is blocked out of the play. Reid knew better than to run around the other side, where number 75, Gino Marchetti, was waiting.

Early Colt hero Claude "Buddy" Young runs in the fog at Memorial Stadium. Note the scaffolding in the background.

games, including a 49-14 thumping of the Redskins at Memorial Stadium, but in the regular season they once again finished with a 3-9 record. In the second game they beat the Giants 20-14 before 27,088 to even their record at 1-1. Seven consecutive losses followed before they scored wins over the 49ers and Rams. Hard luck Zollie Toth, who had missed the entire 1953 season because of a fractured jaw sustained in a preseason game with Washington, played the second half of the 17-13 upset of the 49ers with his nose broken and blood streaming down his face. Gary Kerkorian, obtained from the Rams by Kellett for a 10th-round draft pick, ended up as the starting quarterback, with Davidson backing him up. Enke threw only 28 passes and then retired for good. Six of the seven players on the offensive line, including Art Spinney and Alex Sandusky at guard, Buzz Nutter at center, and Jack Bighead, a full-blooded Indian, at end, had never played their positions in the NFL. Buddy Young led the rushers with 311 yards, eight more than his roommate Zollie Toth. Danny Edwards caught 40 passes to lead the receivers, and Shula and Tom Keane tied with five interceptions. Young made the Pro Bowl on offense, while Art Donovan and Gino Marchetti, part of the Ferocious Five on defense that included Don Joyce, Tom Finnin, and Joe Campanella, also made the Pro Bowl.

Game programs in 1954 were similar to those of 1953, in that there was no central theme to the covers. Illustrator Lon Keller, whose covers were used by several pro and college teams, saw his work grace the covers of several Colt programs in '54. An artist who signed his name "C. Beall," painted the November 21 program cover for the Bears game. It portrayed a young boy in football regalia posing in front of his mirror while holding a ball. Pennants of the Colts and Bears were on the wall.

The year 1954 saw the usual Colt souvenirs: pennants, buttons, publicity photos, and bubble-gum cards. Season ticket holders were sent Christmas cards with the team picture. Topps was still a couple of years away from producing NFL trading cards, while Bowman was in its last years of producing baseball and football sets. Bowman put out another attractive set in 1954, upping their output to 128 cards. The fronts were full-color closeups or posed action shots, with a pen-

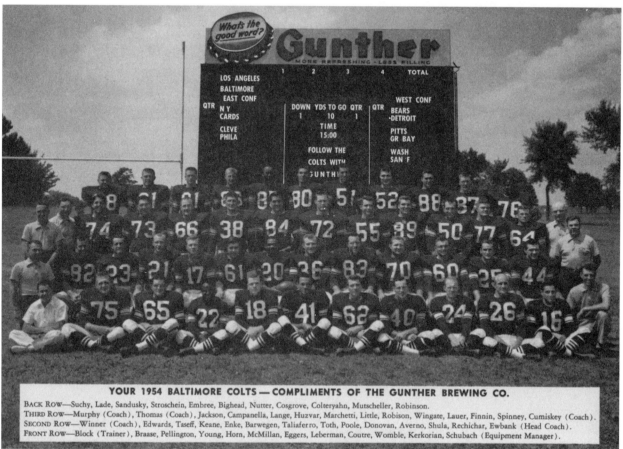

YOUR 1954 BALTIMORE COLTS — COMPLIMENTS OF THE GUNTHER BREWING CO.

BACK ROW—Suchy, Lade, Sandusky, Stroschein, Embree, Bighead, Nutter, Cosgrove, Colteryahn, Mutscheller, Robinson.
THIRD ROW—Murphy (Coach), Thomas (Coach), Jackson, Campanella, Lange, Huzvar, Marchetti, Little, Robison, Wingate, Lauer, Finnin, Spinney, Cumiskey (Coach).
SECOND ROW—Winner (Coach), Edwards, Taseff, Keane, Enke, Barwegen, Taliaferro, Toth, Poole, Donovan, Averno, Shula, Rechichar, Ewbank (Head Coach).
FRONT ROW—Block (Trainer), Braase, Pellington, Young, Horn, McMillan, Eggers, Leberman, Coutre, Womble, Kerkorian, Schubach (Equipment Manager).

nant-shaped trailer at the bottom with the name of the player and his team logo. There were several Colts in the set, including John Huzvar, Fred Enke, Bert Rechichar, Buddy Young, George Taliaferro, Bill Lange, Tom Keane, Ken Jackson, Tom Finnin, and Art Spinney.

The Gunther Brewing Company was heavily involved in Colt sponsorship in those early years, and for the first time in 1954 issued a 7 × 9 color team picture that was taken in training camp in Westminster. The Colts are decked out in their blue jerseys with three white stripes around the arms. Gino Marchetti had abandoned number 75 and was wearing his more familiar 89. Don Shula was wearing number 25. All together there were 44 players in the photo, but only 33 survived the cut. Players such as Tom Cosgrove, Larry Coutre, Barney Poole, and Morgan State's Charley Robinson were gone by the opener. Robinson was in the team photo and in the final preseason program as number 76; a week later in the opener, Don Joyce was wearing that number. Superimposed behind the players in the photo is the Memorial Stadium Gunther scoreboard. On the back was a listing of the stations in the Colts' radio and television network. WCAO was the flagship of the seven-station radio network, which had a station in Redskin territory on Washington's WTOP. WAAM, the forerunner of WJZ-TV, headed up the three-station television network.

Colt players didn't make much money in those pre–network TV days, but that didn't stop them from having a lot of fun. And if fun was being had on the Colts, Arthur Donovan was usually part of it. One of Artie's favorite pastimes was eating contests. In one training camp contest, Artie promoted, not himself, but Gino Marchetti, against fellow defensive lineman Don Joyce, an off-season wrestler with an enormous appetite. The Colt players ponied up almost $500 in wagers to see who could consume the most chicken. Marchetti devoured 26 pieces of chicken, but was outclassed by the insatiable Joyce: "Joyce was eating it all," said Artie. "Thirty-six pieces of chicken, plus peas and mashed potatoes. I think he even ate the bones. When the match was over, he poured himself a glass of iced tea. Then he reached into his pocket and poured two packets of saccharin into the tea. He looked up and explained, 'I got to watch my weight.'"

opposite page

Program art had a look of nostalgia in 1954.

The 1954 team picture was a full-color effort shot in Westminster with the Gunther scoreboard superimposed in the background.

Artie symbolized those early Colt teams. He had come out of Boston College as the "other tackle." Ernie Stautner was more publicized and when Stautner was enshrined into the Hall of Fame in Canton, Ohio, in 1969, a year after Donovan, it gave Boston College a unique distinction. No college had ever produced two Hall of Famers playing the same position, in this case defensive tackle, from the same team. Young Arthur's grandfather, Mike Donovan, was the middleweight boxing champion of the world and taught pugilism at the New York Athletic Club for several decades. His father was the famed fight referee Arthur Donovan, who was in the ring for 18 world heavyweight title fights. After serving in the Marines in World War II, Artie came back home to play football. He had a round, cherubic face that in 1951 needed 39 stitches to repair damages from two separate accidents: a slash across the cheek from the spikes of an unidentified shoe and a cut over one eye from Deacon Dan Towler's elbow.

Artie's weakness was food. He ballooned to 309 pounds in 1954, and the Colts inserted a caveat in his contract that said he'd be fined $50 for every five pounds over 265. From that point on the threat of the fine caused Artie to maintain his weight at 265. In his induction speech at Canton in 1968, Donovan talked about an opposing player he couldn't whip. "I know one person who has to be laughing when he reads that I made the Hall of Fame. That was a guard named Bruno Banducci of the San Francisco 49ers who blocked me all over the field. What a great lineman." The 1954 Colt program referred to Artie's tree limb arms, which powerfully fought off the charge of blockers. "He 'chucks' opponents readily, is hard to knock off his feet and diagnoses plays like a revenue agent ferreting out a band of 'moonshiners.'"

Nineteen fifty-five was a pivotal year in the proud history of the Colts. When historians look back to the keys that brought the Colts from a second-division team to the heights of NFL success, they invariably turn to 1955 and, more specifically, that year's draft; an incredible 12 drafted rookies made the 33-man squad. Not many teams

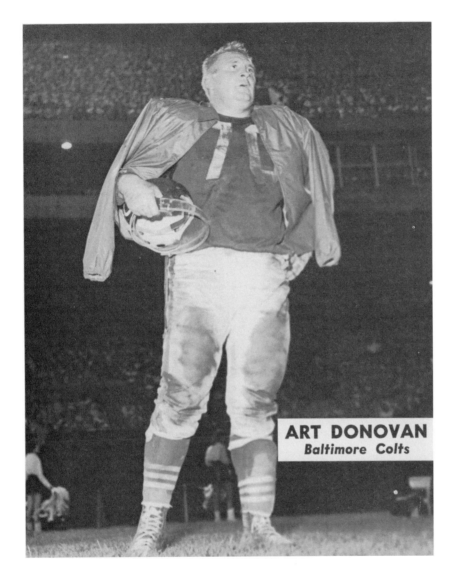

"The Gladiator," Art Donovan.

spent much money for scouting departments in those days. Legend
has it that some clubs would go through the Street and Smith college
annual to pick their players. Molesworth was far more sophisticated
than that, relying on the many coaching contacts he had made in most
of the collegiate conferences as he formulated a draft-day game plan.
After the Colts played the 49ers in San Francisco to end the 1954
regular season, assistant coach Joe Thomas, a bachelor, volunteered
to spend the holidays in California and scout the Rose Bowl teams

and the East-West practices. Soon after, Thomas left to take a better-paying job with the Rams, but told the Colt brass to pick Heisman Trophy winner Alan Ameche and either Oregon quarterback George Shaw or Notre Dame signal caller Ralph Guglielmi. The Colts' first choice was going to be the second pick in the entire draft. Plus, that year they were awarded a bonus choice that was given to each team on a revolving basis.

Heading for the draft meeting in New York, the Colt brass was disappointed to learn the player they wanted to take, quarterback Bobby Freeman of Auburn, had signed with the Winnipeg Blue Bombers of the Canadian League. They next focused on Georgia Tech linebacker Larry Morris, but Thomas, in his final days with the Colts, adamantly argued for his favorites and the Morris hunt was abandoned.

The "bonus choice" was a gimmick that had been suggested by George Halas and adopted years before to give teams that were consistent contenders a chance to get a name player. By getting the bonus choice in 1955, Baltimore got the first two picks of the draft. It ended up being a bonanza for the Colts. Having scored fewer points (131) than any other team in the league in '54, they were looking to bolster their offense. They led off by picking Shaw with the bonus pick and then opted for Ameche. The 49ers immediately offered ten players for Shaw and Detroit offered six for Ameche but the Colts wisely turned them down. Baltimore had to sweat out Shaw's possible signing of a professional baseball contract, but he opted to play football for the Colts. Also in the draft, which numbered an incredible 29 rounds, the Colts chose Dick Szymanski of Notre Dame with the second pick, running back L. G. Dupre with the third selection, and offensive lineman George Preas with the fifth. Add in Raymond Berry of SMU, a 20th-round pick the year before who had by then graduated and you've got a banner crop of talent. All of these players became integral parts of the Colts championship teams.

Sportswriter John Steadman joined the Colts in 1955 as the assistant to Don Kellett and Sam Banks' replacement as publicity director. National Bohemian beer replaced Gunther as the chief sponsor and Chuck Thompson, Bailey Goss, and Ernie Harwell became

opposite page

The Colt Roundup was another way fans could get information on the Colts.

The *Baltimore American,* not yet merged with the *News-Post,* featured a full-page sepia supplement on the Colts.

the broadcast team. Steadman began a new feature for season ticket holders in 1955. It was a four-page publication called *The Colt Roundup* that featured stories on the players, photos, and columns from Kellett and Steadman. Several other teams also had this kind of newsy team publication. They were another link between the fans and the team and became collectors' items in their own right.

The 1955 Colts still had some holes to fill. Quarterback Cotton Davidson was called to military duty, end Dan Edwards left for the Canadian League, and Dick Barwegen and John Huzvar retired. Buddy Young was back at halfback, along with Royce Womble and George Taliaferro. Gary Kerkorian would be challenged by Shaw at quarterback and the Ferocious Five (Donovan, Finnin, Marchetti, Joyce, and Campanella) were the strength of the defense, with Bill Pellington and Doug Eggers at linebacker.

For the first time the Colts had a chance to finish above .500 and they started with a bang when they beat the Bears 23-17 before over

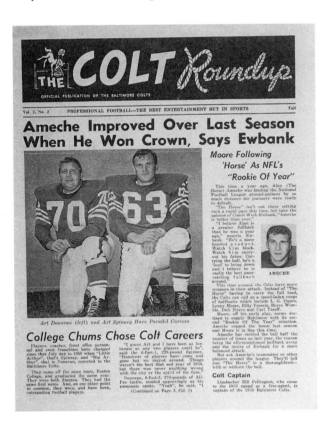

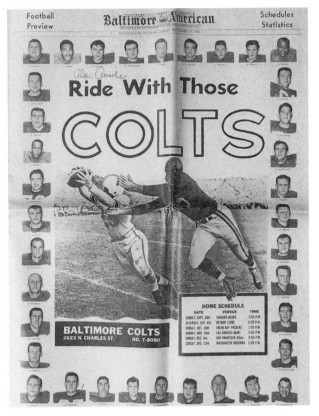

"The Horse" pets his
namesake.

opposite page

Quarterback George Shaw was
the Colts' "bonus choice" in
the 1955 draft.

Jim Mutscheller was a hard-
nosed tight end from Notre
Dame.

36,000 at Memorial Stadium. The first time Alan "The Horse"
Ameche touched the football, he rambled 79 yards for a touchdown
en route to a 194-yard rushing debut. With Shaw at quarterback, the
Colts followed with a 28-13 win over the Lions before over 40,000
at the Stadium, Ameche gaining 152 yards on 21 carries, and then a
24-20 win in Milwaukee against the Packers. The next week they lost
in Chicago 38-10, but over 7,000 rabid fans turned out to welcome

the team home at Friendship (now Baltimore-Wasington International) Airport. Roads to the airport were jammed, the terminal building was packed solid, and authorities had to work hard to keep people from pouring out onto the runways. Baltimore was rapidly becoming Colt-crazy.

They managed just two more wins the rest of the way, however, plus a 17-17 tie with the Rams to finish with a 5-6-1 record. With Memorial Stadium now completed the Colts drew over 51,000, a pro record in Baltimore, for a 14-13 loss to the rival Redskins on October 23.

Ameche rushed for 961 yards and scored nine touchdowns in winning the NFL rushing title as a rookie. Shaw passed for 1,586 yards and ten touchdowns. Mutscheller caught 33 passes for seven touchdowns to lead the pass catchers. The Colts had five players in the Pro

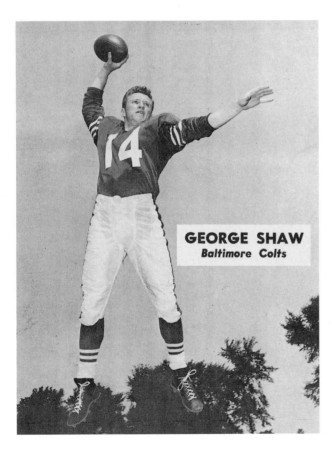

GEORGE SHAW
Baltimore Colts

JIM MUTSCHELLER
Baltimore Colts

Bowl: Dick Szymanski and Alan Ameche on offense, and Art Donovan, Gino Marchetti, and Bert Rechichar on defense.

Artist Lon Keller was once again utilized for the covers of the Colt programs in 1955. His cover on the Colts-Lions program of October 1, 1955, is a classic. A young boy, wearing a football helmet and looking particularly unhappy, is being forced to practice the piano when undoubtedly his pals are out on the vacant corner-lot gridiron playing football. Willard Mullin painted the cover of the Redskins-Colts game of October 23; it depicted a free-for-all of players piling on to recover a fumble with the referee at the bottom of the heap.

The 1955 Bowman gum football set was the last printed by the Philadelphia-based company, which beginning in 1948 had issued the classiest football cards ever produced. There were 160 cards in the 1955 set, which pictured each player outlined in a white glow. Colts in the set were Alan Ameche, Bert Rechichar, Buddy Young, Carl Taseff, Art Spinney, Doug Eggers, Royce Womble, L. G. Dupre, and Zollie Toth. Topps, which bought out Bowman to establish a card monopoly, had been producing baseball cards since 1951. In 1955, they issued a 100-card set of Topps All-Americans before producing their first NFL set in 1956.

If 1955 laid the foundation for the championship Colts of 1958 and 1959, then 1956 helped complete the project, if for no other reason than a crew-cut reject from the Pittsburgh Steelers coming to town. Johnny Unitas, a Pittsburgh native out of St. Justin High School who had played his college football at unheralded Louisville (having been turned down by his top two choices, Notre Dame and Indiana), had been a ninth-round draft pick of the Steelers in 1955. For some inexplicable reason, the Steeler coaches, led by head coach Walt Kiesling, ignored Unitas and favored Jim Finks, Ted Marchibroda, and Vic Eaton. After not seeing any action in five exhibition games, Johnny was released right before the season, too late to catch on with another team. While getting a couple of construction jobs, he kept his hand in football by quarterbacking the Bloomfield Rams, a semipro team in Pittsburgh, for $6.00 a game. Then, early in 1956, Don Kellett made the famous 80-cent phone call from Baltimore to Pittsburgh that would change pro football history. Kellett asked Unitas

opposite page

The 1955 Bowman cards had the players framed in a white glow, similar to the 1956 Topps set.

to come to Baltimore in May to work out for Coach Ewbank. If he did okay, he'd be invited to training camp and if he made the team he'd receive a salary of $7,000. Both Kellett and Ewbank had different versions of why they called Johnny. Kellett said he was going over the waiver lists early in 1956 and saw the name Unitas. He said the Colts had been interested in him as a late round choice in 1955 but Pittsburgh beat them to the punch. Ewbank said the waiver story was a hoax. What really happened, said Weeb, was that a fan who had watched Unitas throw passes for the Bloomfield Rams contacted the Colts and said he deserved a chance to play; Weeb already knew about Unitas because of his friendship with Louisville coach Frank Camp.

The Colts didn't have movie equipment in those days, so they took a series of still photos of Johnny in practice. The workout was held on a field next to the Clifton Park swimming pool that wasn't marked off in football dimensions, but was large enough for Unitas and some other free agents to show their talents. "We took pictures

of John under center," remembered Ewbank, "and again when he set up and right at the last, when he followed through. That was the thing we noticed right away, the way he followed through. It was exceptional. The pictures showed it clearly. His arm went through so far that he turned his hand over like a pitcher throwing a screwball. You saw the back of his hand. With this tremendous follow-through, he'd snag his fingernails on the back of a guy's shirt and jam his fingers, like one of his own linemen. You knew right away, though, that he was special."

Johnny impressed the coaches in the May workout and was invited to training camp. Meanwhile the 1956 college draft had brought the Colts running back Lenny Moore from Penn State, the eighth selection in the entire draft and, "the greatest back I ever coached," according to Nittany Lion coach Rip Engel.

The first look the rabid Colt fans had of Unitas and Moore was at the annual intrasquad game at Memorial Stadium on August 6, 1956. Johnny had never seen so many people in one place before, as 38,447 enthusiastic Colt rooters came to see the Blues play the Whites on a Monday night. Since Shaw's backup, Gary Kerkorian, was holding out and concentrating more on law school, Unitas was getting plenty of work in camp and was making the most of it. He completed 14 passes for 288 yards and three touchdowns in the intrasquad game, which ended in a 20-20 tie. One of his passes was a 53-yard completion to Raymond Berry and another a 46-yard TD pass to Dean Renfro.

George Shaw was still the number-one quarterback, however, and he led the Colts to a 28-21 win over the Bears in the season opener, hitting 14 out of his first 15 passes and tossing touchdowns to Moore and Royce Womble. Losses followed to the Lions and Packers, and then, in a return match with the Bears in Chicago, Shaw suffered a knee injury after being tackled by Fred Williams, and Unitas was thrust into action.

Unlike a Hollywood script in which an understudy is pushed out on the stage to save the show, it was not a memorable beginning. On his first attempt, Johnny tossed an interception to J. C. Caroline that was returned 59 yards for a touchdown and he botched two hand-offs that resulted in fumbles, leading to two more Chicago scores.

opposite page

Johnny Unitas' first appearance at Memorial Stadium was on "Colt Night," in the annual preseason scrimmage.

Young Johnny Unitas proudly holds his Colt helmet. Could he be contemplating the glory that awaits?

The Bears won big, 58-27. As a postscript to the back-to-back losses to the Packers in Milwaukee and the Bears in Chicago, Carl Taseff had a Colt record 90-yard punt return against Green Bay for a touchdown, and then a week later had a 96-yard touchdown return on a blocked field goal, also a Colt record. Unsure of Unitas' ability, Kellett ran up a fair-sized phone bill persuading Kerkorian, out on the Pacific Coast, to come back and finish out the season.

While there was concern among the fans, Ewbank didn't panic over Unitas' inauspicious debut. "The boy wasn't ready mentally," said Weeb. "He hadn't expected to play and he came off the bench ice cold. He hadn't worked out with the first-string backfield often enough to have their moves and timing down right and he was bumping into them as much as they were bumping into him. I still think he can help us."

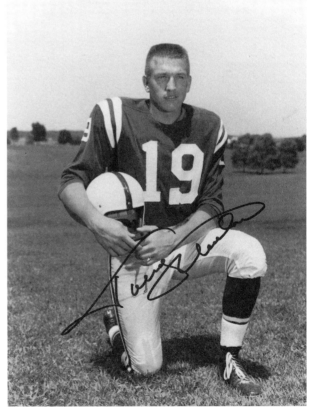

OCTOBER 28, 1956

— ★ —

BALTIMORE MEMORIAL STADIUM

COLTS

PACKERS

Green Bay was next at Memorial Stadium and Johnny worked all week in practice with the starting unit. The result was a 28-21 win in which he hit 8 of 16 passes for 100 yards and two touchdowns. Moore ran for 185 yards, including dazzling touchdown runs of 72 and 79 yards. The following week the Colts beat the Browns in Cleveland for their first win ever against Cleveland dating back to the All America Conference days. Lenny Moore's spectacular 70-yard touchdown run broke a 7-7 tie and the Colts went on to win 21-7 in perhaps their biggest win ever up to that point. After the game, a disgusted Paul Brown refused to shake hands with his longtime friend Ewbank.

Unitas was 2-for-2 in the victory column as a starter, but the next week, despite a whopping 324 yards passing, Johnny and the Colts tasted defeat in Detroit, 27-3. Back home the next week against the Rams on a freezing day that alternated between wet snow and cold rain, the Colts blasted the Rams 56-21. It was the game in which Unitas "arrived" as a quarterback. Wrote *News-Post* sports editor Roger Pippen:

> Back in 1950 when the Rams were strong and our Colts weak, Los Angeles gave our team unmerciful shellackings, 70-27 and 70-21. They laughed at our Colts, sneered at them, jumped on them when they were down. The lust of victory gave the Rams a fiendish delight which has no place in any sport. Only two Colts remain from that team that the Rams ravaged so brutally, Art Donovan and Art Spinney, and you can imagine how much they enjoyed the game. There were many heroes but three stood out. Alan Ameche, the human tornado at fullback, was wonderful, a whirling dervish with 162 yards gained in 20 carries. So was Johnny Unitas, who clicked on 18 out of 24 passes for 293 yards and three touchdowns, the best individual performance by any quarterback in the league this year. Johnny had the Rams in a fog as thick and disagreeable as their famous Los Angeles smog. Billy Vessels, getting his first real chance to run with the ball, gained 80 yards on nine attempts and scored three touchdowns. He caught two passes for 50 yards and his blocking was equally as good. Unitas, Vessels and Ameche are the toast of this city and state today. For at least this one day they were the best players in the league at their respective positions.

opposite page

Johnny Unitas' first start as a Colt was against Green Bay.

Lenny Moore, an exciting
rookie from Penn State, leaves
a defender grasping air in a
game against the Bears.

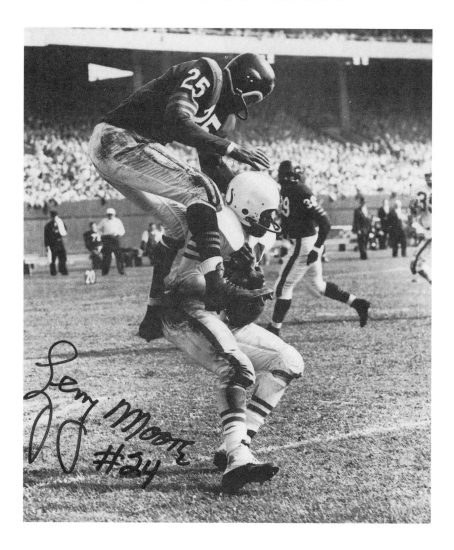

Said Ewbank about Unitas: "We knew Johnny would be the guy
sooner or later, but it turned into sooner rather than later because of
Shaw's injury."

When it came to Vessels, the Colts showed persistence. They
drafted him in 1953, but he opted to play in Canada. Then came two
years in the Army before the Colts finally signed the Heisman Trophy
winner in 1956. The Colts, with Ameche and Vessels, were the only
team that sported two Heisman trophy winners in its backfield.

The Colts couldn't sustain the winning pace, however, as three
straight losses followed before a 19-17 win over Washington to end

the season; this win went a long way toward saving Ewbank's job, as rumors were rife that Weeb was in jeopardy. Unitas tossed a 53-yard touchdown pass with 15 seconds left for the win. Weeb stayed. And Unitas stayed, while Kerkorian, who threw exactly two passes all season, went back to law school.

Unitas finished up his first season with 110 completions in 198 attempts for 1,498 yards and 55.6 percentage, the best ever achieved by a rookie in the 38-year history of the NFL. For the second straight year the Colts had the league's rookie of the year, as Lenny Moore followed Alan Ameche, gaining 649 yards on just 86 carries, an average of 7.5 yards a carry. Like Ameche the year before, Moore's longest run was a 79-yarder and like "the Horse," Lenny scored nine touchdowns.

There was another newcomer on that 1956 team who arrived with far less fanfare but became one of the all-time great Colts. Gene "Big Daddy" Lipscomb, a grad of Miller High School in Detroit and having played two seasons with the Marines at Camp Pendleton, was picked up on waivers from the Rams. At 6' 6" and 285 pounds "Big Daddy" was a giant of a man. He never knew who his father was and he lived in a furnished room with his mother in Detroit. One night, when he was 11, a policeman came to the room and told him his mother had been murdered, stabbed 47 times at a bus stop by a man she knew. He moved in with his grandfather and as a teenager worked all night at a steel mill before going to school in the morning. He never went to college, joining the Marines instead.

After failing with the Rams, "Big Daddy" would go on to become a three-time all-pro with the Colts. With his size and sweeping defensive style, he captured the fans' affection. Insecurity plagued Lipscomb in his private life, however, and he would tell Unitas that he had been scared all his life. "You wouldn't know it to look at me, but I have been." He was traded to the Steelers in 1961 and, two years later, died from a heroin overdose in Baltimore at the age of 33, a tragedy that his teammates and friends find surprising to this day. Unitas, for one, was skeptical that "Big Daddy" took the heroin willingly. "For one thing, he was right-handed and yet the needle marks

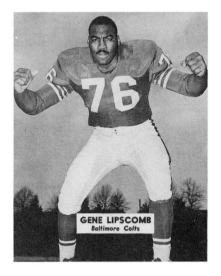

Gene "Big Daddy" Lipscomb was an awesome physical specimen.

were on his right arm. For another, he was like Jim Parker. They hated needles like poison. We'd have to back him in a corner to take a tetanus shot."

In the early 1950s Colts press guides, Gino Marchetti's bio said he worked in a California restaurant in the off-season and hoped to have his own place some day. Those prophetic words were about to come true in abundance for Marchetti in 1956; in fact, they became the height of understatement. Owner Carroll Rosenbloom took a real interest in the welfare of his players and helped many set up their own businesses. Colts middle guard Joe Campanella, who retired after the 1957 season at the age of 27, was eyeing his future beyond football since he already had three children. An old Ohio State teammate, Lou Fischer, had been toying with the idea of getting into the restaurant business with some of his former teammates. He contacted Joe and together they opened a small hamburger place in July 1956. The logical next step was to bring in another investor who would be recognizable to customers in the Baltimore area. That's when Alan Ameche, with much trepidation, got involved and the first "Ameche's" opened. Soon Marchetti would add his name and efforts to the business and the four partners would incorporate under the name "Gino's."

Rosenbloom said it took him five years to convince Marchetti to join Ameche and Campanella in the fast-food business. "He wanted to go back to Antioch, California, and work with his brothers in the family gas station," remembered Rosenbloom. "I told him he could make all the money he wanted in Baltimore because they loved him so. He finally agreed and became a rich man."

Campanella would later leave Gino's and open the Rustler Steak House chain in 1964, only to sell the five restaurants and return to Gino's a year later. Ameche's featured the special "35" sauce that was served on the famous "Powerhouse" and "Kingfish" sandwiches, among others. There were soon Ameche's Drive-In Restaurants at Ritchie Highway and 5th Avenue in Glen Burnie, 5800 Reisterstown Road, and Loch Raven Boulevard at Taylor Avenue. "Meetcha at

opposite page

He was apprehensive at first, but Gino Marchetti would strike it rich in the fast food business.

Both Gino's and Ameche's teamed up with Colonel Sanders and Kentucky Fried Chicken.

Ameche's" became a popular catchphrase in Baltimore. Alan also became a sportscaster, and was heard every Friday at 6:15 P.M. with "Ameche's Powerhouse Sports News and Views" on WBAL. Gino's 15-cent hamburger restaurants were all over the region. He would later team with Colonel Sanders and Kentucky Fried Chicken, and by the time Gino and Alan sold their businesses in the 1970s they were millionaires many times over. "At one time, between the Rustlers, Kentucky Fried Chickens, and Gino's, we had close to 500 outlets," remembers Gino. "We were all over the East and as far west as California."

Campanella, the catalyst behind the business operation, tragically collapsed and died of a heart attack in February 1967, while playing handball with Don Shula and Bill Arnsparger at the Downtown Athletic Club. He died in Shula's arms at the age of 36, less than three months after succeeding the retiring Kellett as Colts general manager. The death of Campanella at such a young age, leaving his wife Nan and seven young children, was a shock of enormous proportions. Said Gino Marchetti at his friend's funeral: "If I live to be 100, I'll never meet a better friend. He showed me the right directions to go: in business, and spiritually by bringing me back to the church. He meant to me what air means to the body. If you want to know what a real man is like, well, man he was!"

Like so many of the enduring linemen of the 1950s, Gino had fought in a war and gone to college on the G.I. Bill. He was born to immigrant parents who saw no purpose in playing games where people hurt each other. In reluctantly letting Gino play football, his father warned him, "Gino, whatever you do, stay out of the other boys' way so they no hurt you." His father so disliked football that he never watched his son play in high school or college. He finally relented for the 1958 title game, watching it on television; Gino ended up breaking his leg.

Gino had left high school and enlisted in the Army on his 18th birthday, and eventually won medals while fighting with the Sixty-ninth Infantry on the Siegfried Line during the Battle of the Bulge. He came back, finished school, and went on to star for Joe Kuharich at the University of San Francisco.

opposite page

Gino Marchetti seems to be flicking away this Detroit Lion running back the way King Kong swatted a plane out of the air above the Empire State building.

In his early years with the Colts, Gino had the reputation of skirting the rules to get in a few extra licks. That ended one day when he tackled Detroit's Doak Walker and rubbed the heel of his hand into Doak's nose while he lay on the ground. Gino was waiting for Walker to retaliate, but Doak just stared at him. "I knew exactly what he was thinking," remembers Gino. "How could a big guy like me, with probably 80 pounds and six inches on him, have to resort to a mean, low-down trick like that. That look of disgust reformed me." After that, Gino became a law and order man, functioning as a policeman who dished out justice when opposing players took cheap shots at his teammates. When Gino retired after the 1964 season, Kuharich, who had gone on to a long NFL coaching career, called him "the most valu-

The Colt programs of 1956 again featured different cover artists.

able man ever to play his position." Said San Francisco's Leo Nomellini: "He was just the best defensive end there ever was. He had the look of death in his eyes. It's a good thing his parents brought him up right" (Herskowitz 1990, 66).

Different cover artists were used for the 1956 Colt programs, with Lon Keller's work appearing on the majority of them. Inside there were full-page pinup photos of the players and write-ups on the team, as well as sections on the radio-TV broadcasters and newspapermen who covered the team. The 1956 Topps set of 120 cards was

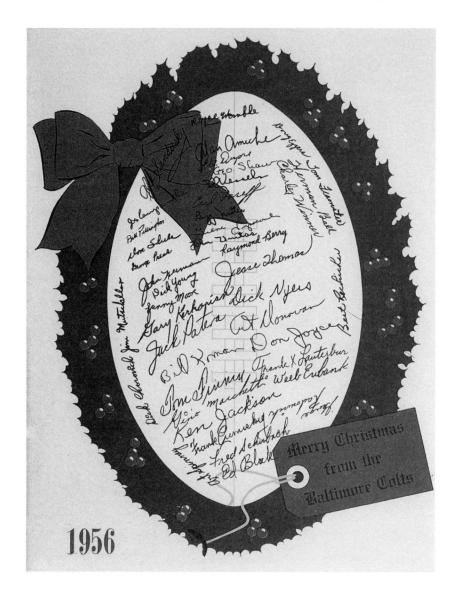

For a couple of seasons the Colts used this December program cover to wish their fans a Merry Christmas.

their first to feature NFL players and the first to have team cards. There were several Colts in the colorful set, which resembled the 1955 final Bowman set: Alan Ameche, Joe Campanella, Arthur Donovan, Lenny Moore, Jim Mutscheller, Bert Rechichar, Buddy Young (who had retired after the 1955 season), George Shaw, and Billy Vessels.

In 1957, the Colts went into the next to the last game of the season with a chance to win a championship. It was the breakthrough season they were hoping for. It was also the first year that the Colt

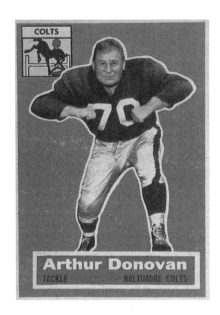

Arthur Donovan
TACKLE   BALTIMORE COLTS

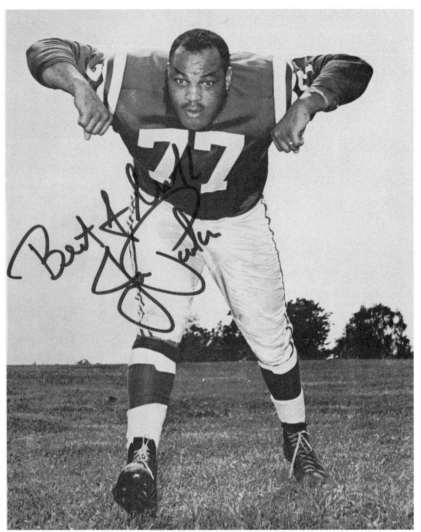

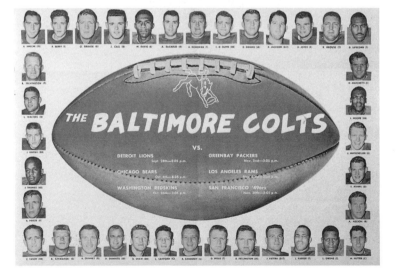

THE BALTIMORE COLTS

VS.

DETROIT LIONS   GREENBAY PACKERS

CHICAGO BEARS   LOS ANGELES RAMS

WASHINGTON REDSKINS   SAN FRANCISCO '49ers

horseshoe was moved to the side of the helmet from the back, and the last year the team wore jerseys with stripes around the arms rather than the shoulders. It was not until the second to the last game, a 17-13 loss in San Francisco, that their chances at the championship were finally extinguished.

Through astute drafting and picking up retreads like Unitas, Lipscomb, Bill Pellington, Milt Davis, and Buzz Nutter, the Colts were becoming a team to be reckoned with. The 1957 draft had brought another future Hall of Famer in Ohio State lineman Jim Parker. Don Shinnick, Jackie Simpson, and Andy Nelson also came in the draft. Nelson, an 11th round choice out of Memphis State, had played quarterback in college, but became a ferocious tackler on the Colt defense. Art Donovan called Nelson the toughest man on the team. Said teammate Art DeCarlo, "You have to like to hit people to play defense. Andy thrived on it. He loved to hit people and was as good as anybody who ever played the game in that respect."

Although he had been signed only a year earlier, Billy Vessels was gone by 1957. Ewbank, for some reason, played Vessels sparingly and almost seemed to resent his presence. Rather than becoming embroiled in controversy, the man whom Dick Szymanksi called the greatest natural talent he ever saw retired at the age of 25.

It was evident as the 1957 season began that Shaw was now second-string and would never get his job back. Unitas threw for 241 yards and four touchdowns in the opening 34-14 win over Detroit that sent the crowd of 40,112 into a frenzy. L. G. Dupre, Raymond Berry, Jim Mutscheller, and Lenny Moore caught the TD passes, while the Colt defense, anchored by Marchetti, Donovan, Don Joyce, Lipscomb, and Jack Patera, held the Lions to only 23 yards rushing. They followed with a 21-10 win over the Bears before over 46,000, and there was already talk of a championship.

One obstacle the Colts had to overcome to become a champion was a tendency to lose on the road. Entering the 1957 season the Colts were only 4-26 away from home, but in the season's first road game they went a long way toward erasing the memory of that dismal record by scoring 38 second-half points in Milwaukee to crush the Packers 45-17. Over 5,000 fans, led by their number one fan, Hurst

opposite page

Nine Colts made the roster of the 1956 Topps football trading card set, Topps' first venture into NFL cards.

Jim Parker went from All-American status at Ohio State to becoming one of the premier offensive linemen in NFL history with the Colts.

The Colts issued a placemat with player photos and the schedule in 1957.

"Loudy" Loudenslager, who would hook up his primitive record player and string a long extension cord to play the Colt fight song, awaited the 3-0 Colts upon their return. Altogether, "Loudy" would welcome the Colts at the airport over 300 times throughout the years.

More and more fans were "For the Colts" as the team evolved into a solid contender.

opposite page

The Colts photo albums were popular fan collectibles from 1957 through 1961.

The following week in Detroit, Unitas fired four touchdown passes and the Colts led 27-3 in the third period, but the Lions, who would go on to the NFL title in 1957, capitalized on five Baltimore fumbles, including three in the last five minutes, to steal the game 31-27. That loss sent them reeling to two more defeats before they regrouped to beat the Redskins, Bears, 49ers, and Rams for a 7-3 record. In the 21-19 win over the Redskins, Unitas hit Berry an incredible 12 times for 224 yards and a touchdown. Johnny carried in the third touchdown himself for the winning score.

Over 50,000 turned out to see the Colts beat San Francisco, 27-21; many have called this the most satisfying win up until that point in Colt history. Unitas fired three touchdown passes in the 31-14 win over the Rams. The 7-3 Colts were now building a national following as the Cinderella team of 1957. Up by a game on the 49ers and Lions, who were both 6-4, the Colts' last two games were on the road in San Francisco and Los Angeles. In the first one, a spectacular 82-yard touchdown pass to Lenny Moore gave the Colts a 13-9 lead in the second half before the 49ers rallied to win 17-13 on John Brodie's touchdown pass to "The King," Hugh McElhenny. The Colts insisted McElhenny pushed off on Milt Davis allowing him to get open, but no flag was thrown.

Although deflated by the previous week's loss, the Colts led the Rams 7-3 before Norm Van Brocklin threw four touchdown passes as Los Angeles closed out the Colts season with a 37-21 defeat, despite a 92-yard kickoff return for a touchdown by Moore. The 7-5 record was the best in Colts history; attendance was 279,888 for the six home games. Unitas was awarded the Jim Thorpe Trophy as the best player in the league, and was picked for his first Pro Bowl, joining teammates Art Donovan, Gino Marchetti, Alan Ameche, Bert Rechichar, and Jim Mutscheller.

Johnny U. also made his bubble-gum trading card debut in the 154-card 1957 Topps set. The cards are in a horizontal format with a close-up shot on the left and a posed action shot on the right. Card number 138, showing a smiling, crew-cut Unitas along with a shot of him tossing a white football, is now one of the most sought-after football cards of all, retailing for over $800 in mint condition. On the back it says that Johnny is one of the best "on the run" passers in the league. Other Colts in the set are Gino Marchetti, Art Spinney, Billy Vessels (who only played the 1956 season in Baltimore), Bert Rechichar, Alan Ameche, Art Donovan, Carl Taseff, Royce Womble, Raymond Berry, Jim Mutscheller, now second-string George Shaw, and Lenny Moore.

John Steadman, in his final year as publicity director before succeeding Roger Pippen as sports editor of the *News-Post,* unveiled a new *Colt Pictorial Yearbook* in 1957, a photo album of player and action photos. The Picture Album cover was an oversized blowup of the press guide cover with the coaching staff and players pictured one to a page, except at the end where there were four players (many of

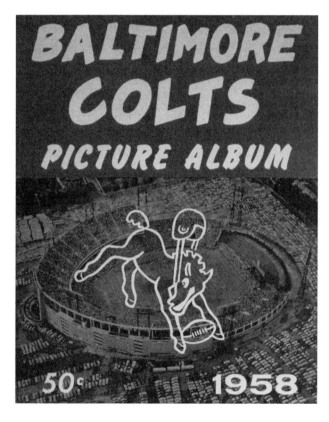

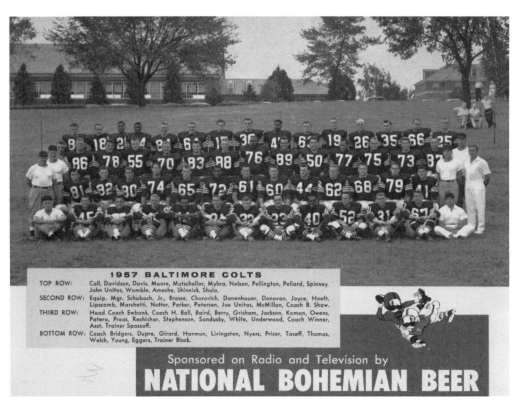

1957 BALTIMORE COLTS

TOP ROW: Coll, Davidson, Davis, Moore, Mutscheller, Myhra, Nelson, Pellington, Pollard, Spinney, John Unitas, Womble, Ameche, Shinnick, Shula.

SECOND ROW: Equip. Mgr. Schubach, Jr., Brasse, Chorovich, Danenhauer, Donovan, Joyce, Hoeft, Lipscomb, Marchetti, Nutter, Parker, Petersen, Joe Unitas, McMillan, Coach B. Shaw.

THIRD ROW: Head Coach Ewbank, Coach H. Ball, Baird, Berry, Grisham, Jackson, Koman, Owens, Patera, Preas, Rechichar, Stephenson, Sandusky, White, Underwood, Coach Winner, Asst. Trainer Spassoff.

BOTTOM ROW: Coach Bridgers, Dupre, Girard, Harmon, Livingston, Nyers, Pricer, Taseff, Thomas, Welch, Young, Eggers, Trainer Block.

Sponsored on Radio and Television by

NATIONAL BOHEMIAN BEER

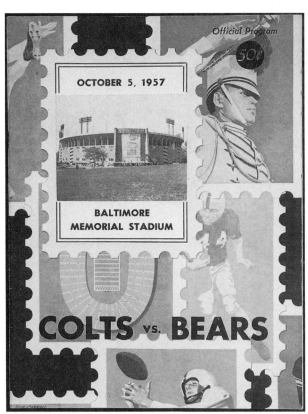

Official Program

50¢

OCTOBER 5, 1957

BALTIMORE
MEMORIAL STADIUM

COLTS vs. **BEARS**

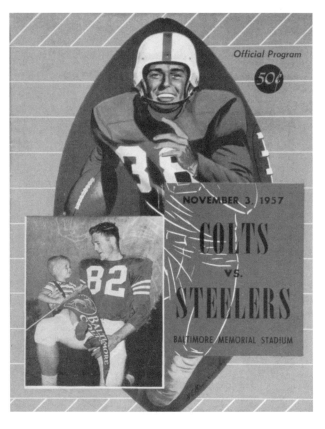

Official Program

50¢

NOVEMBER 3, 1957

COLTS
vs.
STEELERS

BALTIMORE MEMORIAL STADIUM

them young players or backups) to a page. There were also photos of the cheerleaders, majorettes, and band. On the back cover was a National Boh ad that featured a football contest with an Esther Williams swimming pool as first prize, and other prizes that included a 1958 Dodge Lancer, a 19-foot Owens Speedboat, two trips to Havana (Fidel was not yet head of state), and five Zenith 21-inch TV sets.

Game programs in 1957 again featured different cover artists, led by the prolific Lon Keller. Still 50 cents, the program was loaded with player photos and write-ups. An ad on one page showed Lenny Moore, adorned with number 42, advertising his WSID radio show, and then on the opposite page wearing number 36, Bill Pellington's number, in a one-page posed action shot.

The career of Raymond Berry may have been an even bigger Cinderella story than Johnny Unitas'. Said Ewbank: "Usually a coach cannot afford a first impression. Raymond had one leg shorter than another, he wore contact lenses, and he needed a back support. For him to come through, with the great dedication he had, why, he made coaching a joy. He'd eat up anything you said, try everything. Raymond made himself a great receiver, but he was so frail, you shuddered every time he got hit." When he retired after the 1967 season, Berry had caught more passes than anyone in NFL history (631), for 9,275 yards and 68 touchdowns. He was a 20th-round draft pick, a gangly, spindly 6'2", 185, who without glasses or contacts could read nothing more than the "E" on the eye chart, and he became simply the best pass receiver of his time. Berry proved that God-given ability wasn't always a requirement; endless work and sheer strength of will could also play a part. Even Unitas, who was no hell-raiser, admired the self-discipline of the scholarly son of a football coach from Paris, Texas.

Berry arrived the year before Unitas and caught only 13 passes his rookie year. In his second training camp, he felt his days were numbered. "I got the drift right away—my neck was on the line all the time. I put pressure on myself and lost every bit of confidence I ever had. I was afraid for anybody to throw me the ball. That fear is very real. I kept thinking I was going to mess up." Once Raymond began getting comfortable with Unitas, he willed the fear of failure

Raymond Berry became
known for his excellent hands
and precise pass patterns.

out of his system. The two of them became as delicately attuned to
each other's moves as an experienced dance team.

Like Ted Williams in baseball, Berry had uncanny instincts when
it came to football. After his playing days, when he joined the staff
of the Dallas Cowboys at their Thousand Oaks, California, training
camp he complained for three days that something was wrong with
the field. Finally, he borrowed some highway engineering tape, mea-
sured the width himself and found that the field, which the Cowboys
had trained on for six years, was one and a half yards too narrow.

When Weeb Ewbank was hired as head coach in 1954 he predicted the Colts would win a championship in five years. What a prophet the "Little Round Man" turned out to be! The 1958 Colts had come close in 1957 and now, a thoroughly mature team indoctrinated in Ewbank's system, they were ready to break through.

With John Steadman returning to sportswriting, Herb Wright switched from his ticket department duties to take over as publicity director and Harry Hulmes was appointed business manager. The 1958 press guide showed an aerial view of Memorial Stadium with the Colt logo superimposed over it. Who would imagine the thrills that were on the verge of reality on 33rd Street the next two seasons? The modest Unitas was developing into a superstar. By this time every fan in the country knew about his rejection by the Steelers and emergence with the Colts. With his crew-cut hair, boyish good looks, and almost shy demeanor, Johnny became a national cover boy for *Sports Illustrated, Sport Magazine,* and many football annuals. It was New York writer Jimmy Breslin who did the first major story on Unitas in *The Saturday Evening Post.* The basic story line centered on a kid who wasn't born with a silver spoon in his mouth and who overcame adversity at all levels to reach the heights of greatness.

For the first time since 1950, the Colts produced their own program covers with a central theme in 1958. Veteran *Baltimore Sun* cartoonist Jim Hartzell, creator of the Oriole bird logo, drew the covers. He had a playful but powerful Colt throwing off a Redskin for the Washington game; a David-like Colt using a slingshot to slay a huge Goliath for the Giant game; and, for the Packer game, the Colt shipping a frightened player back to Green Bay, as he sat on the box examining the freight rates. A new feature, "Calling on the Colts Alumni," debuted. Several former Colts were highlighted in each program as they recounted their memories of playing in Baltimore and what they had been up to since their playing days.

After a 2-3-1 preseason in which both victories were registered over the Giants, in Baltimore and Louisville, the Colts opened with a 28-15 win over the defending champion Lions before 48,377, the biggest opening day crowd in Colt history. Unitas was superb, com-

pleting 23 passes for 250 yards, including two touchdown tosses to his favorite target, Raymond Berry, who caught 10 passes in all. The Colt defense was equally superb, with Big Daddy Lipscomb and company holding Bobby Layne in check.

Five more wins followed, beginning with a 51-38 win over the Bears before 52,622 on a Saturday night in Baltimore. Lenny Moore scored four touchdowns, two of them on 77- and 33-yard passes from Unitas. Next the Colts beat the Lions again, this time on the road, 40-14, and then came back home to whip the Redskins 35-10 before a record 54,403; Lenny Lyles ran a kickoff back 101 yards for a touchdown in the latter victory.

The value of George Shaw came to the forefront the following week (November 2), when the Colts registered the first shutout in their history, a 56-0 shellacking of the Packers in a steady, driving rain. Unitas suffered three broken ribs and a collapsed lung on a quarterback sneak after a late hit by Johnny Symank, and Shaw came in and completed 10 of 13 for three touchdowns.

Sitting at 6-0, the Colts lost their first game of the season, ironically (in view of later events) in New York on the following Sunday, November 9, before over 71,000 cheering Giant fans. The Giants won 24-21, despite three touchdown passes from Shaw. Unitas watched the game from his hospital bed in Baltimore. Giants quarterback Charley Conerly said afterwards that the Giants "outgutted" the Colts. The Colt players were outraged at the quote and would use it as a rallying cry when they met the Giants again in six weeks for all the marbles.

The Colts rebounded with a well-executed 17-0 win over the Bears at Wrigley Field, the first time the Bears had been shut out at home in 149 games, dating back to 1946. Unitas, wearing a special steel and foam rubber harness, returned to action the following week at home against the Rams and on the first play from scrimmage fired a 58-yard touchdown pass to Lenny Moore. A crowd of 57,577 frenzied fans watched their Colts triumph 34-7. If Johnny U. was hurting, he never let on, despite being pursued in all-out fashion by the Ram defense. He didn't hurry a single pass and didn't throw any interceptions. Unitas left the game to a thundering ovation with a cut

opposite page

Sunpapers cartoonist Jim Hartzell drew the covers of the 1958 game programs.

Raymond Berry exhibited a certain artistry as he made one impossible catch after another.

over his right eye and blood coming from a torn lip. The fans loved Johnny not only for his skill, but for his guts.

There were three games left, and the 8-1 Colts needed only to remember the year before to know how important those games would be. There was one game left in Baltimore, against the 49ers, and the last two were out west in Los Angeles and San Francisco. On a raw, cloudy Sunday after Thanksgiving, with temperatures ranging from 16 degrees to a high of 27, the Colts played one of the most memorable games in their history. The crowd of 57,557 had watched their Colts fall behind 27-7 at halftime to the 49ers. They, along with the players, were in shock. Ewbank, showing no panic, scrawled "4

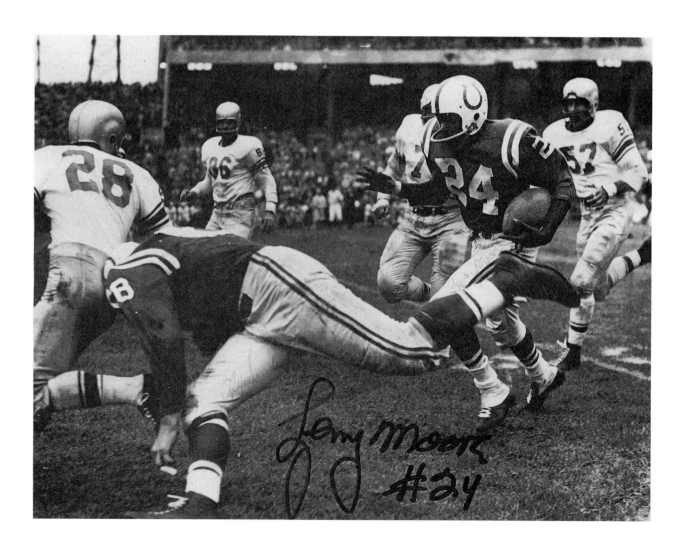

TD's" on the blackboard, and told the defense that they would have to keep the 49ers off the scoreboard. His team would oblige Ewbank by scoring 28 unanswered points, including 21 in the last quarter. Lenny Moore fueled the comeback with an electrifying, spinning, zigging and zagging, 73-yard touchdown run to tie the score and Steve Myhra added the point after to put the Colts in front for good. Lenny came out of the game shortly after that brilliant run, although he wanted to stay in because he felt the Colts could have scored even more points. As it was they picked off five 49er passes, two by Andy Nelson and two by Ray Brown, and won 35-27 to clinch the Western Division championship. A Unitas-to-Berry touchdown pass sealed the victory; it was Johnny's 23rd consecutive game with a touchdown pass, matching the league record set in 1941 and 1942 by former Colt coach Cecil Isbell.

The Colts would meet the winner of the December 21 Giants-Browns playoff game, which was won by New York 10-0; the Giant defense held the immortal Jimmy Brown to only eight yards rushing on seven carries. Meanwhile, the Colts, with many of the regulars resting, had lost to the Rams and 49ers on the West Coast to finish with a 9-3 regular season record.

The Giants, after shutting out the Browns in the playoff the week before, hosted the Colts on a gray, damp day at Yankee Stadium for the championship of the pro football world. It was just three days after Christmas, and a festive air surrounded the game. Unlike the Giants, who had had to expend every ounce of their energy to win four tough games in a row just to take the conference title, the Colts were rested and healthy. The only injured regular was center-linebacker Dick Szymanski, who was back in his Toledo, Ohio, home recuperating from knee surgery. Of the 64,185 fans in attendance, 12,000 had made the trip from Baltimore.

In the locker room before the game, Weeb Ewbank didn't talk football. He talked from his heart, recounting how 14 players on the Colts 35-man roster had been rejects from other teams, given up on as not having the ability to play in the NFL. Among those were Unitas and Donovan, two eventual Hall of Famers. Weeb, himself a future Hall of Famer, even mentioned himself, a second choice behind

opposite page

Lenny Moore was emerging as one of the NFL's most electrifying runners and pass catchers by 1958.

Blanton Collier for the Colts job. Add in Charley Conerly's "we out-gutted them" comment in the newspapers and the Colts were sky-high.

After trailing 3-0 early, Baltimore scored two touchdowns on an Ameche run and a Unitas-to-Berry 15-yard pass and led 14-3 at half-time. The Giants' offense, with Frank Gifford fumbling twice, had sputtered. The Colts drove to the 2 yard line and a first and goal early in the third quarter. A touchdown could have put the game away, but the Colts failed to punch it in as the Giants defense rose up to stop them. Three plays later, Conerly fired a deep pass to Kyle Rote, who raced to the Colt 25 before he was hit by Andy Nelson. The ball bounced free, and Giants back Alex Webster, trailing the play, picked it up while racing at top speed. He got to the 1 before being pushed out of bounds by Carl Taseff. Mel Triplett scored on the next play and the Baltimore lead had been cut to 14-10. The momentum had suddenly swung to the Giants. Early in the fourth quarter, Conerly hit tight end Bob Schnelker for two big gains and then passed to Gifford, who ran it in from 15 yards out to give the Giants a 17-14 lead.

It was getting late, the sky was growing darker and time was running out. Once more the Giant defense stiffened, throwing Unitas for 21 yards in losses and forcing the Colts to kick. All the Giants needed to do was get a couple of first downs and run out the clock. From their own 40 and with the clock ticking inside four minutes, the Giants faced a third and four. Gifford got the call and went off the right side behind blocker Jack Stroud. Marchetti quickly closed the hole, stopping Gifford a foot shy of the first down. As the Colts wrestled Gifford to the ground, Lipscomb fell across Gino's ankle, breaking it in two places.

While Gino was being carried off on a stretcher, Giants coach Jim Lee Howell debated whether to punt or go for the first down. Deciding to trust his great defense, he let Don Chandler punt to Carl Taseff at the Colt 14.

What Howell neglected to figure in his decision was the courage and resolve of the stoop-shouldered, crew-cut kid from Pittsburgh, Johnny Unitas. With less then two minutes left and without even bothering to huddle, Unitas threw seven straight passes, three of them to Raymond Berry, totaling 62 yards. The third Berry catch brought the ball to the 13 yard line. Raymond had outfaked defensive back Carl Karilivacz and streaked toward the sideline; Unitas led him perfectly. There were only 20 seconds to go on the game clock and Steve Myhra got the call to kick a field goal. The noise was deafening and tension gripped the huge stadium. Two tired teams, their uniforms dirtied by the grime and mud of a late December day, lined up opposite each other for the biggest play of the game. The ball was snapped by Nutter to Shaw, the holder, who said that "when the ball reached my hands it felt like a heavy hunk of ice." Myhra, successful on only 7 of 14 field goals during the year, booted the ball through to tie the game 17-17 with just seven seconds left in regulation.

The rule to institute sudden-death overtime in championship games had been enacted in 1947 to ensure that there would be one champion at the end of the year. Since this was the first time that a title game had gone into overtime, many were unsure what would happen next. Several players, including Mutscheller and others on the Colts, thought the game was over. Referee Ron Gibbs and his crew knew what to do, however. After a three-minute waiting period, there was a coin flip at the center of the field. Unitas, standing in for the fallen Marchetti (who had prevailed upon the stretcher bearers to pause at the mouth of the tunnel so he could watch Myhra tie the game), called "tails." It was the only wrong call Unitas made all day, as the coin came up "heads." The Giants would receive the kick and if they scored, the game would be over.

The Giants couldn't capitalize on their advantage, however, taking three cracks at the Colt defense without making a first down. Don Chandler punted to the Baltimore 21. There began a series of 13 plays that would live in football history: a drive so magnificent it would set a standard for perfection that has rarely been duplicated. L. G. Dupre ran around end for ten yards to get things started. After an unsuccessful long bomb downfield to Moore in which Johnny tried to end it all, Dupre ran for three more. Next, on third and seven from the 33, Unitas threw to Ameche, who barely gained the first down. After a short Dupre run, Johnny faded to pass but was flattened by Dick Modzelewski for an eight-yard loss. On third and 15, Unitas

December 28, 1958, became the most significant date in Baltimore sports history.

wanted to pass to Moore, but Lenny was double-teamed. So instead, Johnny sidestepped, twisted, and spotted Berry, who had come open. Johnny had tried to wave Berry into a deep pattern, but Raymond was too busy with his fakes to notice, so Unitas hit him with a bullet pass instead. Berry was tackled at the Giants' 43: another first down.

Johnny noticed, as he went to center for the eighth play of the series, that linebacker Sam Huff had dropped back a few short steps, apparently expecting to defend against a pass. Johnny wisely checked off at the line of scrimmage and sent Ameche plowing through the middle that Huff had vacated. "The Horse" rambled 23 yards to the 20 before Jimmy Patton and Carl Karilivacz brought him down.

The Giants were determined not to let Moore beat them, so they continued to double-team Lenny, who became a decoy. After no gain on a Dupre run, Unitas went for the kill. He quickly hit Berry on a slant pattern at the 10 and Raymond carried Patton to the 8 before he went down. Now it was goal to go, game to go, and championship to go.

At about this time, the cable to the national television broadcast was accidentally unplugged and TV screens around the country went black. At the same time there was a pause in the action, as an inebriated spectator came out on the field and ran up the middle for 80 yards, with police in pursuit. Miraculously, just as soon as the fan disappeared from the field, the TV picture returned. It's often been said that an NBC executive ordered a staffer to disrupt the game until the picture could be restored.

Unitas trotted toward the bench during the stoppage for a quick consultation with Ewbank. "Goal to go, John," said the coach. "Keep it on the ground now. Three plays ought to be enough, but we'll have the field goal left for the fourth." Unitas nodded and returned to the huddle.

When play resumed, Johnny handed to Ameche for a one-yard gain. Certainly the Colts were well within range of a field goal, but Unitas was thinking touchdown, and rather than hand off again, he crossed up everybody by passing to Mutscheller in the right flat. It looked for a second like he might score, but the field was icy and Mutscheller stepped out of bounds at the 1. The coup de grace was a play called "16 power," a handoff to Ameche on the right side. With Mutscheller blocking Cliff Livingston, George Preas cutting down Jim Katcavage, and Lenny Moore blocking Emlen Tunnell, Ameche scored without being touched. The Colts were the world champions and most of the 12,000 fans from Baltimore poured onto the field to celebrate. The Colts band was playing and the goalposts were torn down. It had taken 8 minutes and 15 seconds of sudden-death overtime.

Immediately the game was called the "greatest ever played." The final score was 23-17 Baltimore. "Who outgutted who?" Big Daddy wanted to know. About risking an interception by throwing to Mutscheller at such a crucial time, Unitas said,

The National Brewing Co. issued a commemorative recording of the exciting windup to the 1958 "sudden death" game.

> When I talked with Weeb on the sideline, he told me to stay on the ground for three plays and to try a field goal on fourth down. But when Ameche carried on the first down I could see they were packing the middle of the line. Cliff Livingston was the only man they had on the right side of the field and he was playing Mutscheller head to head. I figured if Jim went right out to the corner, he'd have a step or two on Livingston, and I'd have a good target with Jim leaning out toward the sideline and Livingston unable to get at him from that side. There was only one man out there and he was in no position to intercept it. Plus I overthrew Jim on the out-of-bounds side. If I hadn't thrown it so far outside, we'd have had the touchdown right there. When you know what you're doing, [not trying to be immodest] they're not intercepted.

For the game, Unitas threw 40 passes, completing 26 for 349 yards and a touchdown. Berry caught 12 passes for 178 yards and a touchdown. Moore caught six for 101 yards. No Giant receiver caught more than three passes, as Conerly finished 10 of 14 for 187 yards.

Marchetti and the medical staff had been in the locker room not knowing what was happening on the field. Only when the players burst in smiling did he know who had won. Eleven years of fighting adversity, dating back to the All-America Conference days in 1947, had been overcome. Said Tunnell about Unitas afterwards: "Everything we expected him to do, and what you absolutely believed he would do, he didn't do. He did exactly the opposite. Those of us who have been around knew we had been beaten by a better man" (Steadman 1997, 149). Unitas was awarded the first Chevrolet Corvette presented by *Sport Magazine* to the oustanding player in the championship game. Ed Sullivan wanted Unitas on his TV show that night, but the shy quarterback declined and Alan Ameche filled the breach. Said Ewbank afterwards: "I had been involved with a championship team in 1950 as an assistant in Cleveland, which was a thrill, but that wasn't my team. Being the head coach and winning this championship is my greatest thrill. As the head coach, this is my team." About Unitas' gambling approach to playcalling, Weeb added, "For me to send in plays like they do in Cleveland would have been an insult to Johnny. He's a great signal caller, he knows the game and he knows what he's doing."

More than 30,000 fans jammed Friendship Airport to welcome the Colts home. All the airport parking spaces were gobbled up and cars were lined bumper to bumper on all approaching roads. Some people abandoned their cars and walked to the airport. Two buses met the team and the traveling party on the tarmac, and by the time they had made their way to the airport exit they were engulfed by fans. The buses sat for over an hour with fans on top and standing on the bumpers, making it impossible for the drivers to see. Finally, the buses eased out the back way and with a police escort made their way back to Baltimore. Several kids remained on the buses and were eventually plucked off by police, whose nerves by this time were frazzled. The worried youngsters calmed down after Unitas and linebacker Leo Sanford got off to shake their hands. It was a day and a night that nobody in Baltimore will ever forget.

The winning shares gave each player an extra $4,718.77, a huge amount in those frugal times. It was more than Arthur Donovan had made in his rookie season in 1950.

On Thursday, November 19, 1998, a forty-year reunion was held at Martin's West to honor the 1958 Colts. Unfortunately, Weeb Ewbank, looking forward to attending the event, passed away suddenly at his Oxford, Ohio, home just two days before. All but a couple of the living Colts were on hand, and each carried a particular memory of his days with the Colts and that "sudden death" game in particular.

Defensive back Milt Davis:

The thing that made the game big was that we were playing in Yankee Stadium, on their turf, in the worst conditions that we had played in all year. Frozen ground, cold conditions, and everything at stake. That's the epitome of playing football. It shows a side of you under pressure. What I tell young people about football is that it's about trust. Trust. It's for all of us. Team sports allow you to trust the person next to you. Individual sports don't have that same kind of bonding. When you have players like we had on that championship team, we bonded. Free agency has all but killed it in today's game.

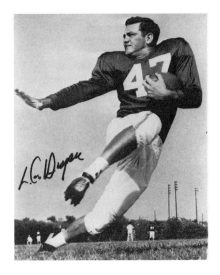

L. G. Dupre was known as "Long Gone" Dupre in Baltimore in recognition of his running ability.

Running back L. G. Dupre:

It broke our hearts the year before to lose the 49er and Ram game at the end because we might have won it three years in a row. My role on the Colts was more of a supporting player. Whenever I got the call, I tried my hardest. We had a great team. One out of a thousand make a pro team and I was so happy to have made the ballclub. I didn't make the big money but the friendships last forever.

Defensive end Don Joyce:

When I first joined the Colts we had had five tackles playing across the defensive line with Gino, myself, Artie, Tom Finnin, and Joe Campanella. I had played quarterback when I entered college at Tulane and then became an end so I had pretty good speed. Gino had great speed and we were all pretty quick. My memory of the '58 game was coming off the field and people throwing paper from the stands and the bunting hanging around was flying in the breeze. It was twilight and the lights were on and just before going down the tunnel I turned and looked one more time. I thought, 'There will never be another moment like this.' I stood there for about two or three minutes. Our line coach John Bridgers came off and I told him to turn around and soak it in. I scouted for 30 years after the '58 game and I can honestly say there will never be anything to duplicate it. We were playing one year at a time, and we weren't making much money. If you had three or four kids, even if you liked it, you almost had to get out unless you had some kind of side job going. Today you make a million dollars a season and can play a long time. We couldn't think long term. I saw guys arrive on crutches, get a shot, play a great game, and then go home again on crutches. I saw it over and over.

Defensive end Gino Marchetti:

If someone told me during my rookie year that people would still be talking about us after 40 years, I'd have never believed them. We belonged to the Baltimore community. We'd go out and speak at banquets and make personal appearances. We didn't make any money but we were out there. I used to say of the 57,000 who came to our games every week, I personally shook hands with every one of them. That made a big difference. If you talked with a fan for two minutes, that fan now knows you. You're not a number, you're a person to them. When I broke my ankle in the late going at Yankee Stadium, I made them put me down on the sideline because I wanted to see the last minute and 30 seconds. After Steve Myhra kicked the field goal, then I had to get off the field. When it was over, Ray Brown came running in and said, 'We won, we're the champs, we're going to get a ring!' The pain in my ankle went away. I used my $4,700 winner's share to put down on a house in Campus Hills.

Gino's most vivid memory surrounding the championship game came after the team had arrived back in Baltimore.

The officials wouldn't let the plane taxi for fear the fans would overrun it, so they parked us a few hundreds yards away. I remember Don Kellett saying the fans came out here to see us so we'll get in the buses and ride through the fans. I was in an ambulance that followed behind the buses and when we entered the crowd they jumped all over the buses, the roofs, the hood. The buses had to stop but our ambulance was able to pull out, and as we drew closer to Baltimore, I saw this lone man standing on the side of the road with his seven- or eight-year-old son. He's shining his flashlight on a sign that said, 'Welcome Home Champs!' I thought that was phenomenal. They were on the side of the road all by themselves. I think about that a lot and I wished I had told the driver to stop so I could have said hello to them. That's how impressed I was with that gesture. Now it's all changed because there is no more loyalty. The players don't have loyalty to the city, the city doesn't have loyalty to the players, the ownership doesn't have any loyalty to the community. I was fortunate to start and end my career with one team, and thankfully it was the Baltimore Colts.

Offensive guard Alex Sandusky:

In all three championship games I played, 1958 and 1959 against the Giants and 1964 against Cleveland, I played opposite Dick Modzelewski. He was a great competitor and became a good friend. I was very tired after that sudden-death game. It was a tough game and we went almost an extra quarter. The timing was right for the Colts to emerge in 1958. We were ready. The city was ready. Weeb did an awful lot for all of us, not just as a football coach. He instilled something in us that we carried through in business and in our family lives. Plus he gave me a chance. I came down here as an end and he made a guard out of me.

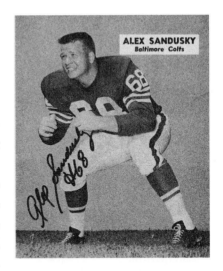

Alex Sandusky came out of little Clarion State Teachers College in Pennsylvania and became a Colt mainstay for 13 seasons.

Giants tackle Dick Modzelewski:

We felt good about coming from behind to take the lead. I remember I sacked Unitas two or three times and in the last situation, it was third and 17 and I'm going for sack number four, and he calls a trap play, a smart play, and Ameche got 23 yards and the rest is history. The Colts went on to score. Early in the game we blocked Myhra's first field goal attempt. Rosey Brown and I pulled our people and Sam Huff got through to block it. Comes time to tie it, Rosey and I should have moved over to our right to pull two different people, and we didn't do it. But I'm glad I was part of it, even on the losing side. I never realized the impact of the game until years later when people referred to it as the greatest. Don't forget, we had to beat the powerful Cleveland Browns three times in one year just to get to the title game. About 1964 with Cleveland, I had to get traded in order to beat the Colts.

Defensive back Johnny Sample:

I was a rookie in 1958 and Carl Taseff and Milt Davis were the starting cornerbacks. I don't know whether it was fortunate or unfortu-

Johnny Sample was a rookie
defensive back in 1958.

opposite page

By 1958 tickets to Colts home
games had become much
sought after.

nate for me but Milt got hurt in the last part of regulation and I had
to step in and play the sudden death. The one thing that went
through my mind as, after we lost the coin toss, the defense trotted
onto the field, was that my mother and father were up in the stands
watching and the Giants are going to complete a long touchdown
over me and win the game and I'm going to feel so bad. The three
plays they ran lasted two hours to me. I was so happy when they had
to punt the ball and we went off the field. Then we could watch the
offense at work, and John Unitas has never, ever, played better in his
life, and no quarterback has ever played as well as he did in that sudden-death period. He did things that were unbelievable. On one
third and 11 play, Raymond Berry ran a 12-yard hook pattern. Andy
Robustelli was reaching over Jim Parker and nearly grabbed John.
John took his left arm and knocked Robustelli's arm and threw a
completion for a first down. Greatest play in the game and very few
people talk about it. John had no fear. That was the greatest thing
about him. He had great confidence in his game and what his teammates could do. In my book he's the greatest quarterback to ever
play. I don't care, you can name Elway, Marino, any of them. And I
love Joe Namath. We played on the 1968 Jets who upset the Colts
in Super Bowl III. I tell him, 'Unitas is the greatest quarterback to
ever play.'

Then there's Weeb. Together we played in three of the most
memorable games in pro football history, the '58 Sudden Death, the
Super Bowl in which we beat the Colts, and the 1968 "Heidi" game
in which NBC pulled the plug on our game with Oakland when the
Jets pulled a miracle comeback.

You have to realize that when you play football, your next play
could be your last. So a lot of guys today want to get the money first
and foremost. They want to get paid. They think about winning the
championship secondarily. When we played in 1958 we all thought
about winning the championship first, because nobody was making
any money anyway. I was making $8,000 in 1958 and I got a check
for $4,700 for winning the title. I was so happy I didn't know what
to do. My mother and I counted the money on a bed for about four
hours. None of us, my father included, had ever seen that much
money at one time.

Wide receiver Raymond Berry:

> One thing the 40th reunion accomplishes is it makes me realize how
> fortunate I was to play in Baltimore. You live long enough and you
> realize the odds on certain things happening in life and to think you
> could ever play for the Colts at the best time you could possibly be
> here on a team like this and playing a game like that is hard to be-
> lieve even today. We should have put the game away in the third
> quarter, but the Giant defense rose. All of a sudden we found our-
> selves losing with two minutes left. None of us had ever heard about
> overtime and I'm surprised the officials knew how to handle it. I was
> impressed. When we lost the toss in the extra period, we didn't get
> down because we felt we were going to win the ballgame, so I don't
> think it occurred to us that by losing the toss, we could have lost the
> ballgame. When you stop and think about the last two drives in
> which Johnny drove us the length of the field twice, once to tie and
> the other to win, that says something. In the overtime he hit me on

one sideline pass, but in the drive to tie, every pass he completed to me was an inside route. It goes with his thinking of doing something opposite of what the defense thinks you're going to do. He hit me three straight times on inside plays.

I've coached the modern player and I do believe the way the NFL is going now is hurting itself. It has a system that destroys team continuity and puts all the focus on money. I'm glad I played when I did because the focus was on football teams and football players. The fans are the ones that benefited.

Johnny Unitas:

This was a special team. I grew up with these guys and spent an awful lot of time with them, sleeping together, eating together, playing together, drinking together, everything you could possibly do. We've lost eight guys off the team, including Weeb, and that's sad. As far as the closing drive in overtime and the sudden death, it was just part of what we did to be successful. We worked all year on situations like that, every week working on the two-minute drill. It would depend on what the opposition did defensively that would determine what we felt would work. We just didn't pull it out of a hat. On the trap to Ameche, I checked off. We had been hitting Raymond on the quick slant against Harland Svare, and Sam Huff was usually up tight in the middle. When we hit a couple of passes on Svare, Sam drifted back to try and help and when he did that it gave George Preas a chance to come across and get him. I knew Modzelewski was coming hard so it was just a matter of changing the play at the line of scrimmage, and Alan got 23 yards.

On the pass to Mutscheller to the one in the overtime, the way they lined the defense up gave us the opportunity to hit Jimmy right away, because the linebacker took an inside position and so did Emlen Tunnell, so there was nobody out there to cover him. On his first step he was open and all I had to be concerned about was Linden Crow, and he had to go with Lenny. He wasn't going to let Lenny run free so I just read him. If he went with Lenny, I'd pop a pass to Jimmy and if he comes up on Jimmy, I'd just hit Lenny.

opposite page

The Colts logo donned a crown and the words "World Champs" adorned the Colts' pennants after championships in 1958 and 1959.

The *Baltimore News-Post* sold more copies the day after the "sudden-death" game than any paper since the end of World War II.

Offensive tackle Jim Parker:

> I was opposite Andy Robustelli in both 1958 and 1959 and the name alone is enough to kill you. Robustelli, Robustelli, that's all I'd hear. It threw some fear in me but I went up there with the attitude to win the game and that's what we did. Everybody on our team had a winning attitude, not to accept second place. The greatest memory of the game I have is when Alan Ameche ran in for the winning touchdown on the other side of the line. When I saw him in the end zone, I went berserk. I was the happiest person in the world.

Johnny Unitas was suddenly the hottest property in pro football. Next to Mickey Mantle and Willie Mays, he was the biggest name in sports. Local Baltimore businesses were getting in line trying to get him to endorse their products. To his credit, he didn't let the adulation go to his head.

Defending a championship successfully had been accomplished only four times in NFL history. In 1959 the Colts embarked on the challenge of becoming the fifth. After a 4-2 preseason in which they blanked the College All-Stars 29-0 and the Giants 28-3, the Colts won their fifth straight home opener, 21-9 over Detroit, after trailing the Lions 3-0 at halftime.

They weren't as fortunate the following week against the Bears, losing 26-21 despite three fourth-quarter touchdown passes from Unitas. The Colts were convinced the Bears had stolen their signals, since when Unitas would check off at the line of scrimmage, the Bears invariably shifted to the right defense. Wins came against the Lions, Bears, and Packers, followed by consecutive losses to Cleveland, 38-31, in which Jimmy Brown scored five touchdowns for the Browns, and the Redskins, 27-24.

After this, however, the Colts reeled off five straight wins to finish the regular season as they had the year before, with a 9-3 record. For the first time ever, after 11 straight defeats dating back to 1947, they beat the 49ers at Kezar Stadium, 34-14, as the defense picked off six passes. The next week they rallied for 21 fourth-quarter points to knock off the Rams, 45-26; the scoring was capped by Carl Taseff, who picked up a missed field goal and returned it 99 yards for a

The Colts had great ability, but a little rabbit's foot on a souvenir button didn't hurt.

This rare pennant reproduced the *Sunpaper* front page after the 1959 title game win.

touchdown. Unitas was superb in the must win at San Francisco, completing 21 of 36 passes for 273 yards. He threw three touchdown passes, eclipsing Sid Luckman's NFL record of 28 in a season. His string of touchdown passes in consecutive games had now reached an amazing 36. The three TD passes Johnny tossed against the Rams gave him 32 for the year and made him the first NFL quarterback to throw for over 30 touchdowns in a 12-game season.

Once again the Colts were in the title game and once more it was against the Giants; this time, however, it would be in Baltimore, the only time the Colts ever hosted a championship game. Two days after Christmas, on an unseasonably warm December afternoon in Baltimore, the Colts became the fifth team in NFL history to win back-to-back championships. There were 57,545 fans crammed into "the world's largest outdoor insane asylum," as Chicago sportswriter Cooper Rollow aptly named it, on 33rd Street to watch the Colts defend their championship. Even though the players were mainly the same as they had been the year before, the 1959 game didn't come close to duplicating the atmosphere or the emotion of 1958's heart-stopper. One reason was the domination of the Colts. Just six plays into the game Unitas hit Lenny Moore for a 59-yard touchdown. The Colts led 7-6 at halftime, the only Giants points coming on two Pat Summerall field goals.

Unitas came out firing in the second half, throwing touchdown passes to Lenny Moore and Jerry Richardson. He also ran for a TD

WORLD CHAMPION

COLTS
VS
PACKERS

WORLD CHAMPIONS 1958

OFFICIAL
50¢
PROGRAM

SUNDAY OCTOBER 25, 1959   BALTIMORE MEMORIAL STADIUM

himself, around the right side from four yards out. Meanwhile, the Colt defense was shutting the door on Conerly. Andy Nelson picked off one pass and Johnny Sample intercepted two, returning one of them for a 42-yard touchdown and a 28-9 advantage. Sample's last interception set up a Myhra field goal to complete the Baltimore scoring. The Giants didn't score a touchdown until 32 seconds remained in the game; the final score: Colts 31, Giants 16.

Unitas completed 18 of 29 passes for 264 yards and two touchdowns. The Colt defense had a spectacular game, setting up 17 of their 24 points in the wild and wooly fourth quarter. Said the dejected Sam Huff, who was completely throttled by Colts center Buzz Nutter, "The Colts deserved to win. Their defense is definitely improved and their offense unquestionably is the best in the league. Unitas is great. Nobody around even compares with him" (Fitzgerald 1961, 126). For the second straight year Unitas received a Chevrolet Corvette from *Sport Magazine* as the MVP of the championship game. Frank Gifford referred to Johnny as "The Burglar. He stands out there and picks your pocket, just like a burglar. Plus he has the guts of a burglar" (Fitzgerald 1961, 137).

Unitas had a remarkable season in 1959. Shaw had been traded to New York in the preseason; halfback Ray Brown was listed as the backup and defensive back Andy Nelson was on the depth chart as third-string. The Colts took a tremendous gamble that Johnny would stay healthy, and it paid off. Unitas completed 193 of 367 passes for 2,899 yards and 32 touchdowns. The only other passes thrown the entire year were one by Brown and two by Lenny Moore.

One of Unitas' first endorsement contracts happened quite by accident after the 1959 title game. In the locker room afterwards he was photographed in a celebratory mood, waving a bottle in his hand and being hoisted by teammates Steve Myhra and Carl Taseff. The photo was transmitted to over 500 newspapers nationwide. It sparked a flood of letters wondering what Johnny was drinking, and condemning his choice if it was beer. It looked like a beer bottle even though it was plain old ginger ale. When blowups of the offending picture showed that the bottle was Nehi Ginger Ale, William C. Franklin, president of the Baltimore bottling company that produced the bev-

opposite page

Artist Jim Shanks illustrated the 1959 Colt program covers.

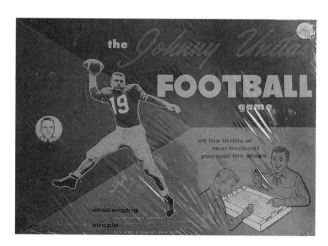

erage, gave Unitas one of his first major endorsement contracts. Johnny also signed a deal with the Marlboro Shirt Company to endorse the firm's line and make a series of appearances around the country.

Winning back-to-back championships produced what easily became the "golden age" of Colt collectibles. There were programs, ticket stubs, pennants, pins, souvenir pottery, beer advertisements, comic books, statues, records, and many more. Both title game programs are much sought after, with the 1958 edition ranking at the top of the list. That program has an artist's view of a game in progress at Yankee Stadium on a sunny day. The same cover was used on the program for the regular-season game between the Colts and Giants on November 9. In excellent to mint condition the title game program is worth over $300.

The 1959 championship game program in Baltimore, which also sold for 50 cents, culminated a season-long series of covers painted by artist Jim Shanks. The blue-and-white-clad Colt lineman is shown burying a Goliath-type Giant in the turf against a bright orange background. As had Hartzell the year before, Shanks painted covers in which a Colt player or an actual colt was doing a number on the opposition's mascot. The Colts would produce their own programs through the 1964 season, after which the league itself began issuing programs. The Colts resisted this "NFL Illustrated" innovation, but the league had taken over for good. Game programs would never again be the same; the idiosyncrasies of each city's program traditions were gone.

It was apparent from paging through the Colt game programs in 1959 that several Colts were endorsing products or working as spokesmen for different Baltimore businesses. Raymond Berry, Alan Ameche, Art Donovan, and John Unitas were in a Baltimore Federal Savings ad, Gino's and Ameche's drive-ins shared a full-page ad, Unitas was pitching footballs for Crown Gold Gasoline, and the Farboil Company, makers of paints and plastics, announced that Johnny would work for them between seasons. Berry was the central figure in a Baltimore Gas and Electric ad, while Don Joyce was about to chomp on a Becker pretzel. L.G. Dupre was in sales and public re-

opposite page

Endorsements came Johnny Unitas' way after back-to-back championships. Crown Gasoline was just one of many.

Johnny had his own football board game.

Johnny could drill passes on the gridiron and drill holes with DeWalt power tools.

lations for Eastern "Overall" Uniform Rental Service. Clearly, the Colt players were capitalizing on their world champion status.

Until 1958, press passes had always been made of thick paper with a string attached. The Colts changed that in 1958 by issuing a beautiful enamel pin that was worn in lieu of the pass. The 1958 pin was shaped like a football with a blue border that said "Baltimore Colts Press—1958." In the middle was the Colt insignia in white with gold lettering. In 1959 the colors were reversed, with a white outside border and a blue inside with the Colt logo in gold. In 1960, the pin was round, with a Colt helmet and the words "Baltimore Colts, '58 and '59 World Champions" around the rim. In 1961, the pin had a three-dimensional colt with helmet and ball jumping over a crossbar. In 1962 and 1963 the pins were once again shaped like footballs, with the protruding Colt logo on each. The 1964 pin was shaped like a horseshoe with the three-dimensional Colt logo in gold. The pin tradition continued throughout the 1960s, stopping in 1969.

In 1958, National Beer put out the smaller color team photo-postcard as well as a giant, color team picture with an easel back that was made for bars and taverns. National also released a collectible 45-rpm record of the "sudden death" game, narrated by Chuck Thompson and featuring the play-by-play of Bob Wolff. The back cover of the record jacket had the team photo in a red, white, and blue motif. National even debuted a brand of light beer called "The Colt," with the Colt insignia above the National Bohemian label. Several Baltimore department stores, among them Stewarts, Hutzlers, and Hochschild Kohn, distributed ceramic ashtrays, plates, and mugs with newspaper headlines emblazoned on the white pottery. There were also championship drinking glasses with the scores of the games in 1958 and 1959.

In the early 1960s, Bobbing Head dolls made their debut. The Colt nodder stood on a blue wooden base and wore a blue jersey with a double zero on it. Others followed with a white base and then a more elaborate gold base with a larger figure wearing a face bar. These sold for $1.00 each and now can go for over $100 in top condition.

In the late 1950s, the Hartland Plastics Company of Hartland, Wisconsin, began putting out a series of cowboy heroes from movies

opposite page

Several area department stores issued souvenir ceramic pottery, everything from glasses and mugs to ash trays.

Colt nodders debuted in the early 1960s and sold for 50 cents each. The black version is extremely rare and valued at several hundred dollars.

The Colts began issuing the press quality pins for game admittance in 1958. The pins were produced through the 1969 season.

opposite page

Topps controlled the trading card industry and in exchange for catalog gifts, players would grant Topps usage of their photos.

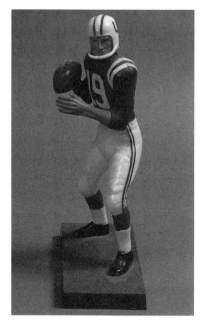

The Hartland Plastics statue of Johnny Unitas originally sold for $1.98. You could take away the decimal point and call it an even $200 if you found one today.

and television. The statues were so popular that they decided to dabble in sports and produced 17 baseball players, from Hank Aaron and Mickey Mantle to Babe Ruth and Ted Williams. In 1960, Hartland issued a generic set of NFL running backs and linemen. They made just two statues depicting actual players: Jon Arnett of the Los Angeles Rams and Johnny Unitas of the Baltimore Colts. Johnny is depicted wearing his blue number 19 jersey and is looking to throw, standing on a green base with his signature in gold etched into the base next to the team name, "Colts." The statue, which originally sold for $1.98, is worth over $200 today.

Several years later, in 1965, the Aurora plastic model company produced a series of "Great Moments in Sport" model kits. Willie Mays, Jimmy Brown, Jerry West, Babe Ruth, Jack Dempsey, and Johnny Unitas made up the set. In a beautiful cover painting on the box top, Johnny is about to throw a pass against the Rams at jam-packed Memorial Stadium, with Buzz Nutter and Jim Parker blocking for him. The kit included Unitas, a blocker, and a red-dogging linebacker. The value of an unassembled model in the original box is now over $100.

In 1962, the Colts came out with a new 25-cent comic book, similar to the first one in 1950. This time the cover was blue and white, with the Colt mascot proudly prancing. There were flashbacks on Colt history, going back to that long ago season of 1950, as well as artists' renderings and write-ups of Rosenbloom and Kellett, Weeb Ewbank and his coaching staff, and the players. The comic was produced by longtime Colt backer Ralph Elsmo, one of the original Colt Associates in 1947. It was written and edited by Colt publicity director Harry Hulmes.

Besides all the souvenir items available to the fans, owner Carroll Rosenbloom gave out presents every year to the Colt players, their wives, and the media. In 1958, he gave each player a set of four dinner plates, with the Colt insignia in the center, the score of the 1958 championship game, and facsimile signatures of the team members decorating the plate. In 1959, he complemented the plate with a tea service comprised of cups and saucers, a creamer, and a sugar bowl. The cups had the score of the 1959 title game burned into

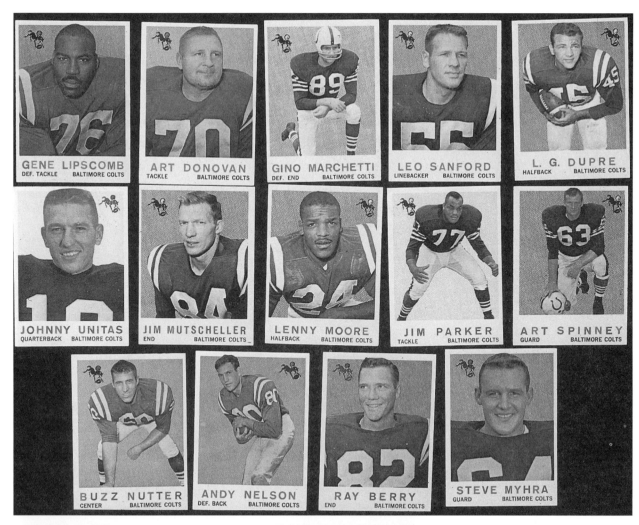

GENE LIPSCOMB
DEF. TACKLE BALTIMORE COLTS

ART DONOVAN
TACKLE BALTIMORE COLTS

GINO MARCHETTI
DEF. END BALTIMORE COLTS

LEO SANFORD
LINEBACKER BALTIMORE COLTS

L. G. DUPRE
HALFBACK BALTIMORE COLTS

JOHNNY UNITAS
QUARTERBACK BALTIMORE COLTS

JIM MUTSCHELLER
END BALTIMORE COLTS

LENNY MOORE
HALFBACK BALTIMORE COLTS

JIM PARKER
TACKLE BALTIMORE COLTS

ART SPINNEY
GUARD BALTIMORE COLTS

BUZZ NUTTER
CENTER BALTIMORE COLTS

ANDY NELSON
DEF. BACK BALTIMORE COLTS

RAY BERRY
END BALTIMORE COLTS

STEVE MYHRA
GUARD BALTIMORE COLTS

Colts owner Carroll Rosenbloom made a practice every holiday season of giving elaborate gifts to players, media, and friends of the team. In 1958 the boss made presents of autographed plates bearing the team logo and the inscription, "1958 World Champions"; the following year he gave away similar cups, saucers, creamers, and sugar bowls.

them; the logo and signatures were displayed on all of the pieces. These are magnificent memories of the Colt glory days and practically impossible to find today. Another unusual gift was a woman's compact and mirror, with a pewter-type finish that had the logo and signatures on the top and bottom. Throw in the team-issued player photos, Colt Action Pictorials, and Topps gum cards that had Unitas number one in the set from 1959 through 1963 and you've got a treasure trove of Colt memorabilia. These, indeed, were the halcyon days of the Colts on and off the field.

FOUR

The Sixties:
The Bridesmaid Decade

The 1959 Colts had eight All-Pros and they sent nine players to the Pro Bowl (Hall of Fame–bound Arthur Donovan, whose career was winding down, didn't get selected). They were a star-laden team. Although eight regulars were at least 30 years of age, the Colts looked strong enough to win several more championships. Yet they didn't win a third straight in 1960, finishing with a 6-6 record. The key reason was injuries.

The injuries that didn't crop up when the Colts were winning titles in 1958 and 1959 broke out in almost epidemic fashion in 1960. Key men in the attack were either shelved completely or rendered ineffective while trying to remain in action. Still, at times the Colts were brilliant, blasting the Bears 42-7 in the second game of the season; the defense picked off seven passes, setting the offense up for easy scores. They got off to a 6-2 start, which included a 38-24 win over Green Bay on November 6 that avenged an earlier loss, and in which Unitas threw the 100th touchdown pass of his meteoric NFL career.

The season's turning point happened on November 13 at Chicago's Wrigley Field. The Colts won a brutal hard-fought battle with the Bears 24-20, but the victory didn't come without a price. With the Colts down by three points and just 19 seconds to go, Unitas was leveled by the Bear defense. He was bleeding from a cut above the eye and his nose was torn and swollen. It took an officials' time-out and almost five minutes of medical attention to patch Johnny back up. The Bears, just 19 seconds from victory, waited in

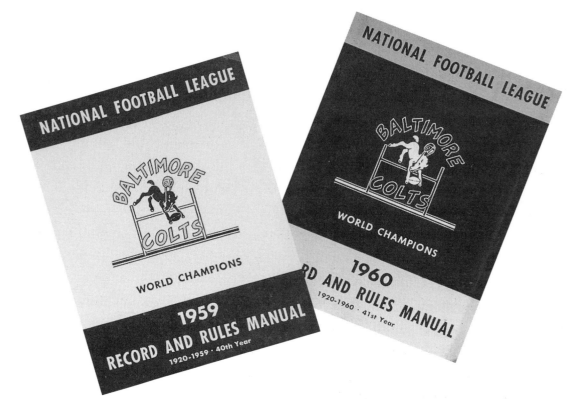

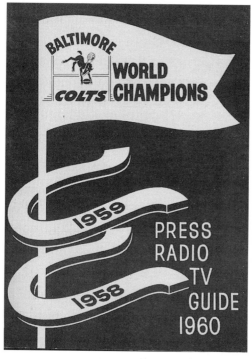

anticipation for the game to resume. From the Chicago 39 yard line, the battered and bleeding quarterback took the snap, faded back and looked for Lenny Moore. He threw, Moore caught and then ran it in for the winning touchdown, stunning the Bears. It was an incredible display of courage from Unitas. His veteran teammates, such as Donovan, Marchetti, and Spinney, said afterwards it was the most brutal game, from a punishment standpoint, that they had ever been involved in.

The Colts were 6-2 at this point with designs on a third straight championship, but the Bears game so sapped them that they didn't win again the rest of the year. They lost four straight, as did the Bears. Against the Rams in Los Angeles on December 11, the Colts lost 10-3 with Unitas' record string of at least one touchdown pass snapped at 47 straight games. He did become the first passer to ever throw for over 3,000 yards in a 12-game season. Injuries took their toll on Mutscheller and Berry. Berry, just a token performer over the last four games, still led the league in receiving with 74 catches despite catching just three passes in the last two games. He totaled 1,298 yards on those catches and then underwent off-season knee surgery.

In 1961 Unitas was bothered with a hand injury that affected how he gripped the ball, and although his completion percentage was up, his touchdowns declined from 25 to 16. He sustained the injury in a preseason game against Dallas. The Colts won four of their last five games in '61 to finish with an 8-6 record, good for only third place in the Western Conference behind Green Bay and Detroit. Retirements rocked the Colts in 1961. A torn Achilles tendon from the year before sent Alan Ameche into a premature retirement at the age of 28. Art Spinney, Milt Davis, Art DeCarlo, and Ray Brown also called it quits. Big Daddy Lipscomb and Buzz Nutter were traded to Pittsburgh for Jimmy Orr.

One of the Colts' most effective weapons in 1961 was the field-goal kicking of Steve Myhra. Myhra kicked 21 in all, including a 39-yarder in the opener to beat the Rams and a 52-yarder on the last play of the game to beat the Vikings 34-33. Three weeks later he beat the Lions, 17-14, with a field goal with eight seconds left. One of the sea-

opposite page

The NFL paid tribute to the champions of 1958 and 1959 by adorning the league's annual guide with the Colt colors and logo.

Spalding made a Johnny Unitas football that was ideal for autographing.

The 1960 press guide showed a pair of winning horseshoes.

Colt press guide, 1961.

Colts defensive back Wendell Harris runs back a San Francisco fumble as Monty Stickles makes the tackle. Longtime Colt linebacker Bill Pellington, number 36, tried to come to Harris's aid.

opposite page

Art Donovan called it quits before the 1962 season. Draped in his cape, an emotional Donovan walks off the Memorial Stadium field for the last time amid a thunderous standing ovation.

son's oddities was that Raymond Berry caught more passes than ever before (75), but none for a touchdown.

Nineteen sixty-two produced another .500 record, 7-7, with four of the losses at home. Lenny Moore was lost in the final exhibition game when he fractured his kneecap while landing on the hard ground of Forbes Field in Pittsburgh. Lenny still led the team in rushing, but with only 470 yards. Orr caught 55 passes, 11 of them for touchdowns. How frustrating was it? In one game in Green Bay, the Colts outgained the Packers 380 yards to 116, recorded 19 first downs to 8 for Green Bay, and had the ball 30 more plays, 79 to 49, but still lost, 17-13. One of the high spots in the year was a 36-14 win at Cleveland in which the Colt defense held Jimmy Brown to only 11 yards on 14 carries. R. C. Owens became the first player believed to block a field goal at his own crossbar. The "Alley-Oop" man, made famous by his leaping catches from Y. A. Tittle in San Francisco, jumped high and deflected a 40-yarder by Washington's Bob Khayat in a 34-21 Colts win. Jim Parker became one of the few players to be named All-Pro at two positions, guard and tackle, in the same season.

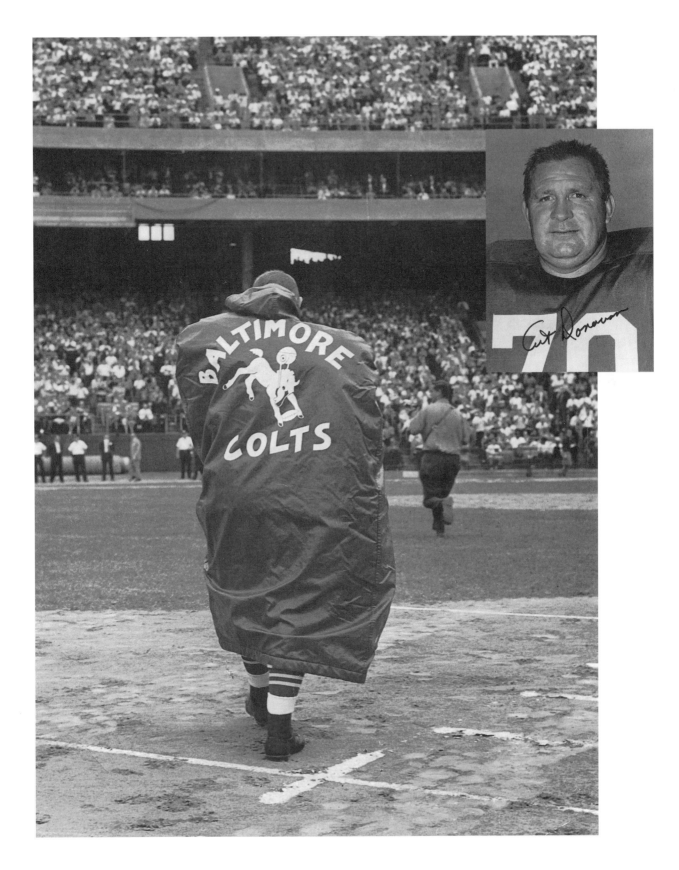

Arthur Donovan went to training camp in 1962 and realized at the outset that Ewbank had no plans for the 37-year-old on the defensive line. After a meeting with Kellett, Artie reluctantly decided to retire and ceremonies were held before the 1962 opener with the Rams. More than any other Colt, Donovan symbolized the rags to riches rise from a team nobody wanted in 1950 to one of the most successful franchises in any sport. He truly loved football, he truly loved Baltimore, and he truly loved the Colts. And the feeling was mutual. He was the gentle giant, a man of warmth and wit, the team's "Falstaff," reveling in a joke, even when it was on himself, which it often was. For his size, which was close to 300 pounds, Artie was amazingly quick. In his prime he rushed the passer, read the keys, closed off the middle, split the double-team blocks, and followed the flow of play. He was all-NFL four straight years and played in five straight Pro Bowls.

At first Artie refused to wear his uniform for the retirement ceremony but eventually bowed to the wishes of the ceremony organizers and appeared in full regalia, including shoulder pads. After some speeches and gifts, including a new Cadillac, Artie opened his heart with a sincere acceptance as he struggled to control his emotions. Tears fell down the big man's cheeks as he remembered his mother. "There's a lady up in Heaven who wants to thank all the people of Baltimore for being so good to her boy, a kid from the Bronx." Then the ex-Marine donned his cape and walked off the field to a standing ovation from over 54,000 sobbing fans and players on both teams. Owner Carroll Rosenbloom declared the number "70" would never again be worn by any Colt. Less than six years later, the Pro Football Hall of Fame enshrined Artie as the first Colt player to be singled out for the game's greatest honor.

After three straight disappointing seasons, Rosenbloom decided to make a coaching change, feeling Ewbank had lost control of the team. Weeb was fired after the 1962 season, having compiled a record of 59 wins, 52 losses, one tie, and two NFL championships. He had brought critical organization and continuity to the franchise when it

opposite page

Weeb Ewbank's 1962 coaching staff. *Left to right:* Herman Ball, John Sandusky, Weeb, Don McCafferty, and Charlie Winner.

Don Shula, backed by coaches Chuck Noll, Bill Arnsparger, Dick Bielski, chief scout Ed Rutledge, John Sandusky, and Don McCafferty.

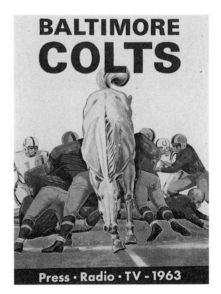

Colt press guide, 1963.

opposite page

Along with Cleveland's Jim Brown, Johnny Unitas was the biggest star in the league in 1964.

Two Colt immortals, Gino Marchetti and Bill Pellington, retired after the 1964 season and were honored before the final home game. Fans were given souvenir buttons of Gino the Giant and the Iron Horse.

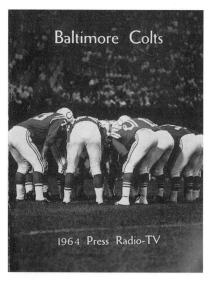

Colt press guide, 1964.

had been most needed. Weeb didn't stay unemployed long; he was hired by the New York Jets of the AFL.

On January 8, 1963, Don Shula was named to succeed Ewbank. The former Colt was only 33 years old and was serving as an assistant in Detroit. Shula had been a student of the game during his playing days in Baltimore, often coaching the coaches and calling the defensive signals. No one could have envisioned in 1962 that over the course of his long career, Shula would become the winningest coach in NFL annals, eclipsing George Halas and winning 347 games. His seven-year record in Baltimore was a glittering 74-22-4, but he was never able to win a championship.

Shula's inaugural season was much like Weeb's last, injuries again taking their toll. The team went 8-6, winning five of their last six. Berry missed several games with a shoulder injury and Lenny Moore had a head injury. Tom Matte proved he could play, leading the team in both rushing and receiving, and a pair of rookies, Bob Vogel and John Mackey, stood out. Johnny Unitas had a banner year, concluding the season with eight team records and an NFL-record 237 completions, besting Sonny Jurgenson of the 1961 Eagles by two. Yet 8-6 was good for just third in the conference. Mackey, who forged a Hall of Fame career in Baltimore, came to the Colts with little fanfare. "At Syracuse I played for a team that didn't throw the ball, so when I came to Baltimore I was handicapped because I didn't know how to run pass patterns. Unitas and Raymond Berry stayed after practice and worked with me. It was a matter of learning, and with that kind of comfort zone it made the learning all the easier."

The next year, 1964, saw the Colts return to glory. After losing to Minnesota to start the season, Shula's Colts reeled off 11 consecutive victories, including shutout wins over the Bears and Lions. They finished with a 12-2 record and scored a club record 428 points. The winning streak began with a 21-20 win in Green Bay in week two as Unitas tossed a 52-yard touchdown pass to Moore and a 40-yarder to Mackey.

Two more Colts were accorded farewell honors. On December 13, 1964, before the final game of the regular season, defensive end Gino Marchetti, dubbed the greatest defensive end in NFL history,

COLTS   REDSKINS

BALTIMORE MEMORIAL STADIUM   DECEMBER 13, 1964   FIFTY CENTS   SEE PAGE THREE

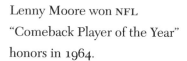

Lenny Moore won NFL "Comeback Player of the Year" honors in 1964.

and longtime linebacker Bill Pellington were honored. Both graced the cover of the game program, the last one produced by the club before the Colts agreed to let the league take over program production the following year. A special commemorative button in blue and white featured photos of both Marchetti and Pellington. The button also had the date and the word "Booster" across the front. Both Gino and Pellington were accorded All-Pro honors, Gino as a first-teamer and Pellington on the second team. Lenny Moore had a career year in 1964, scoring 20 touchdowns and winning "Comeback Player of the Year" as well as All-Pro honors (this coming after the Colts had shopped him around before the season, finding no takers).

The Colts were heavily favored to whip the Browns in the NFL title game in Cleveland on December 27. After a scoreless first half, quarterback Frank Ryan began hooking up with receiver Gary Collins, and the Browns scored 17 third-quarter points en route to a shocking 27-0 win. Ryan threw scoring passes of 18, 42, and 51 yards, all to the former University of Maryland All-American Collins, who beat Bobby Boyd each time. The Browns outgained the Colts 339 yards to 171. Jimmy Brown rushed for 114 yards on 27 carries, as Cleveland largely controlled the ball. Brown graced the cover of the championship game program; he was shown running with the ball in a dazzling color photo.

Although the Colt pictorial yearbook ceased after the 1961 season, yearbooks were produced for the Colts in both 1963 and 1964; however, neither was edited by the club. Local entrepreneur Tom Gorman, with help from broadcaster Vince Bagli, issued a 10th anniversary yearbook in 1963. The book mixed photos and text and chronicled the first ten years of the franchise from its return to the NFL. The cover featured a blue and white picture of the Colt helmet and the familiar team insignia. Other yearbook *Our '64 Colts* came out after the regular season; it recapped the 12-2 year and previewed the championship game in Cleveland. This publication was also edited and produced by Tom Gorman. Its cover was a gorgeous shot of Johnny Unitas throwing a pass with Jim Parker protecting him. Besides providing an account of the season from training camp to the last game, the book also had feature articles on Raymond Berry, Lenny Moore, Ordell Braase, Alex Hawkins, Unitas, Gino, and Bill Pellington. Johnny was in an ad pitching Jarman Pontiac, while Ordell was enjoying a great Baltimore favorite, Frostie Root Beer, in another advertisement.

The frustration of not winning a championship in 1964 carried over to 1965, but this time it was an official's call in the last game of the year that would cost the Colts dearly. Baltimore finished with a 10-3-1 record, tying Green Bay for the Western Conference cham-

Colts press guide, 1965.

opposite page

Tom Matte brought boyish zest
and a world of ability with him
from Ohio State.

pionship and forcing a play-off. The season was a study in courage for
the Colts and tested Shula's coaching wisdom to the hilt. With a 9-1-
1 record, the Colts were in successive weeks stripped of both quarterbacks, Johnny Unitas and Gary Cuozzo, through severe injuries.

Unitas had been on his way to another spectacular season.
Against the Lions in early October at home, he hit 18 of 24 passes for
319 yards and three touchdowns in a 31-7 win. Against the 49ers in
Kezar Stadium on October 31 he outdueled John Brodie by con-
necting on 23 of 34 passes for 324 yards and four touchdowns and a
34-28 victory.

Unitas first went down with a back injury in Chicago on November 7. Cuozzo rode to the rescue and quarterbacked the following week in a 41-21 win at Minnesota, in which he threw for a club record five touchdowns. Unitas was back the following week and pitched the Colts to a win over the Eagles and a Thanksgiving tie in Detroit before disaster struck against the Bears. With 4:42 left in the first half, Unitas severely injured his knee while passing, tearing up ligaments and damaging cartilage. Surgery was performed the next day and Johnny was lost for the season. Things turned even more grim when Cuozzo separated his shoulder the following week against Green Bay before over 60,000 fans at Memorial Stadium. The Packers prevailed 42-27, as Paul Hornung scored five touchdowns. Now Cuozzo was also lost for the year and Shula was without a quarterback for the critical last game against the Rams in Los Angeles.

Tom Matte had been a split-T quarterback at Ohio State, but rarely threw the ball in Woody Hayes' "three yards and a cloud of dust" system of ball control. In desperation, Shula turned to Matte, heretofore strictly a running back in the pros, to be his quarterback. The coach limited Matte to mostly basic running plays, while equipping him with a wristband that would remind him of the play calls. Wearing the portable cue cards, which became a famous part of NFL lore and were eventually housed in the Pro Football Hall of Fame, Matte ran the ball 16 times from the quarterback slot, gaining 99 yards, handling the ball flawlessly, and setting up the winning field goal, a 50-yarder by Lou Michaels, in a 20-17 win. Veteran signal caller Ed Brown, who had arrived just the day before for backup support, tossed a 68-yard scoring strike to John Mackey.

This win meant the Colts and Packers had finished with identical records. There would be a playoff in Green Bay on the day after Christmas, and the gritty Matte would once again be the quarterback. The Colts scored just 21 seconds into the game when Don Shinnick picked up a fumble and ran it 25 yards for a touchdown. Packer quarterback Bart Starr exited early with an injury and Zeke Bratkowski took over the Packer offense. The game became a defensive struggle. The Colts, with Matte going all the way at quarterback, led 10-7 with 1:58 to play. A victory over the powerful Packers in Green Bay without a regular quarterback would be a colossal achievement.

The Colts didn't need help as much as they did some good luck.

The cheerleaders got a chance to strut in the 1966 press guide.

With time running out, the Packers attempted a field goal from the 27 yard line. Don Chandler, who had been on the losing side with the Giants in 1958 and 1959, booted the ball and immediately grimaced as it looked as though the ball was slicing to the right, higher than the upright. The kick was obviously wide, but official Jim Tunney, who went on to a long career as an NFL official, signaled that it was good, and thus the score was tied. Unbeknownst to Tunney, Chandler had turned away in despair and was shocked to discover that the kick had been called good. The Colts were outraged, but the call stood. Then at 13:39 of overtime, Chandler hit another field goal to win the game 13-10.

Slow-motion replays of the game film proved that the tying kick had been off to the right. A frame-by-frame photo sequence, printed in the Baltimore newspapers, provided further graphic evidence. Packer fans in the end zone, including the city editor of the *Green Bay Press-Gazette*, said that they were shocked that the kick had been ruled a field goal.

Instant replay calls were still many years away in 1965. All that happened was that the league decided in future games to place two officials under the goalposts on field goal attempts, instead of one, and to raise the uprights 10 feet (the so-called "Baltimore Extensions"). While the Colts went home a loser after a courageous effort, Vince Lombardi's Packers went on to beat the Browns 23-12 on a muddy Lambeau Field in Green Bay to win the NFL championship.

There were some significant developments after the 1965 season. In March 1966, Keith Molesworth, the Colts' first coach upon their return to the NFL in 1953 and personnel director since 1954, died of a heart ailment. Then in July, a merger was announced between the NFL and AFL that would take effect in 1970. At the end of the 1966 season, a championship game between the two league winners would be held.

The 1966 season was much like 1965's. The Colts got off to a 7-2 start that included five straight wins and were tied with Green Bay, when Unitas injured his throwing arm against the Falcons in a 19-7 win. Johnny continued to play, but he wasn't the same and the

Colts went into an offensive tailspin. The following week against Detroit, Unitas threw five interceptions before Cuozzo relieved him.
The Colts lost three of four before the finale, when Unitas exploded
for 339 yards passing and four TD passes in a 30-14 win over San
Francisco. The final record of 9-5 was good for second place, three
games behind the Packers, who went on to whip the Chiefs 35-10 in
the first AFL-NFL championship game in Los Angeles. There were
more off-the-field woes for the Colts, as newly named general manager–vice president Joe Campanella died unexpectedly of a heart attack in February 1967, at the age of 36. Publicity director Harry
Hulmes was named to replace him.

In 1967 the Colts compiled an 11-1-2 record and still did not
make the playoffs! With the addition of Atlanta and New Orleans the
two conferences were broken into four, with the Colts, along with the
Rams, 49ers, and Falcons, in the Coastal. The Colts had a sensational
year; with a healthy Unitas at the helm they amassed 5,008 yards, the
best in football, and established a club record for fewest points allowed by the defense (195). Both Los Angeles and Baltimore finished
with glittering 11-1-2 records, by far the best in either the NFL or
AFL. Since postseason dates leading to the AFL-NFL championship
were carved in stone, there was no date available for a playoff; a tie-
breaker system was used instead. Under this arrangement, the team
scoring more points in their head-to-head matchups would be declared the winner. The Colts and Rams tied 24-24 in their first meeting, while the Rams bombed the Colts in the season finale 34-10; thus
the Rams advanced while the Colts stayed home.

The highlight of the 1967 season was an incredible comeback win
over the Colts' nemesis, the Green Bay Packers. Over 60,000 fans
squeezed into Memorial Stadium on November 5; for 58 minutes the
Colts appeared to be a beaten team, trailing 10-0 with just over two
minutes remaining. Then Unitas whipped a TD pass to Alex Hawkins,
but Lou Michaels missed the extra point. Lou redeemed himself,
however, with a beautiful onside kick that was recovered by rookie
Rick Volk. After missing on two passes, Unitas tossed the winning
touchdown to Willie Richardson for a 13-10 Colt victory. Unitas had
a spectacular season, throwing for 3,428 yards and 20 touchdowns; in

Willie Richardson made a little
extra "bread" pitching the
virtues of Blue Ribbon bread.

Lenny Moore called it quits after the 1967 season. His like will never be seen again in the National Football League.

one game against Atlanta he passed for 401 yards. Shula shared NFL Coach-of-the-Year honors with George Allen of the Rams, but it remained an almost unbearably disappointing season for Shula and the Colts.

Three future pro football Hall of Famers and all-time Colt greats, Raymond Berry, Lenny Moore, and Jim Parker, announced their retirement after the 1967 season. Berry spent 13 seasons as a Colt, catching more passes (631) for more yards (9,275) than any other receiver in history. He brought a scientific approach to the art of pass receiving, and his hard work reaped huge rewards. In high school Berry played for his dad in Paris, Texas, but he didn't start until his senior year. In his years at SMU he caught only 33 passes for one touchdown. Yet he was still drafted as a future prospect by the Colts. Berry, by actual count, developed 88 maneuvers for getting around defenders. He also practiced daily at recovering his own fumbles; this was a wasted exercise, since he fumbled only once in the 631 times he handled the ball.

Moore, nicknamed "Spats" because of his white-taped cleats, scored 113 touchdowns during his 12 seasons and amassed more than 11,000 yards rushing and receiving. Lenny, quite simply, was the most exciting and explosive player ever to play the game.

The giant Parker turned in 11 outstanding seasons, eight of them as an All-Pro, and ranked as the top offensive lineman of his or any other time. Parker handled both the tackle and guard positions in All-Pro fashion; in 1973, he would become the first man who played solely as an offensive lineman to be elected to the Pro Football Hall of Fame. Rather than stick around and play on a team that was Super Bowl–bound, Parker stepped down. "I can't help the team and I won't deprive 40 guys of their big chance," he said. The jersey numerals of Berry (82), Moore (24), and Parker (77) were permanently retired, joining those of Art Donovan and Gino Marchetti.

Another venerable Colt institution, the Council of Colts Corrals, celebrated its 11th birthday in 1967. There were over 20 Corrals, including one in Hagerstown and one in the Maryland state penitentiary. The Corrals often traveled to road games, honored players, raised money for charity, and promoted the game of pro football throughout the region. They even held a yearly convention in Ocean City. To show their loyalty, the Corrals, like the Colts band, stayed together all through the dark days when pro football had abandoned Baltimore. They resurfaced as the Ravens Roosts when the Ravens began play in 1996.

One of the more unique Colt items of memorabilia was produced for the 1967 season: an oversized colorful book of action photos that were perforated and ready to be punched out and assembled. The punch-outs were the brainchild of local radio personality Ken Jackson, whose company was named "Johnny Pro." The Johnny Pro Kick Off punch-out album featured 42 different players, including Hall of Famers Unitas, Berry, Moore, Parker, and Mackey, in posed action shots. There were also players who never made it, such as Jim Detwiler, Bob Wade, and Norman Davis. Wade went on to make an impact in basketball, coaching the Dunbar Poets and then the Maryland Terrapins. Jackson took the punch-out concept to other sports, issu-

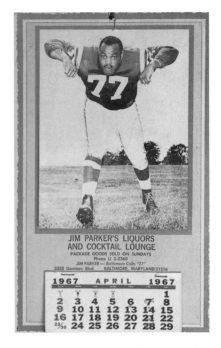

Named the greatest lineman of the league's first 50 years, Jim Parker retired to work full-time at his liquor business.

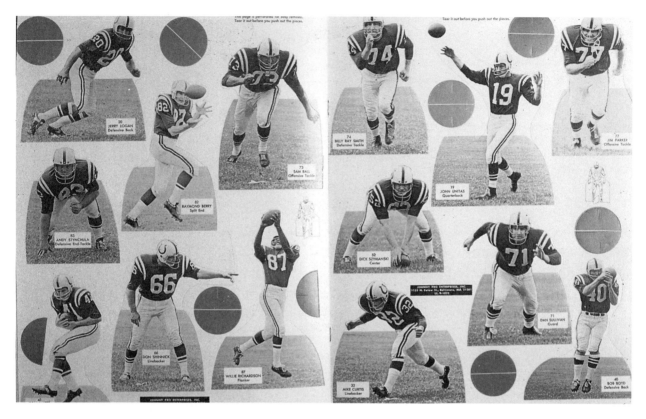

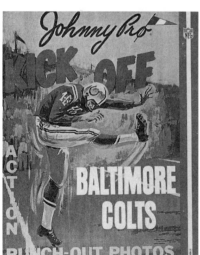

ing sets on the Orioles, Bullets, and Phillies. The Colts were his first effort, and the album with the players still intact is worth a tidy sum.

After so many near misses and heartbreaks, the Colts, from Shula on down, were wondering if things would ever turn their way. In 1968 they did. The season began in grand style with Art Donovan's election to the Pro Football Hall of Fame. Donovan, one of the most popular players in NFL annals, the perpetual butt of jokes who would feign anger, throw out some Marine invectives while threatening to punch someone, only to break out in a grin, was inducted along with Cliff Battles, Elroy "Crazylegs" Hirsch, Wayne Millner, Marion Motley, Charley Trippi, and Alex Wojciechowicz (who had been Artie's boyhood hero back in the Bronx).

Despite just 32 passing attempts and 11 completions from Johnny Unitas all year, the Colts tore up the league in 1968. They compiled a 13-1 record, their only loss coming against Cleveland on October

20, 30-20, as Unitas attempted to play and completed just one of 11 passes. In one four-game stretch, against the Cardinals, Vikings, Falcons, and Packers, the Colt defense didn't surrender a touchdown. Not since the 1937 Giants had a defense been as strong or as stingy.

Unitas had torn the ligaments inside his right elbow in the final exhibition game against Dallas and was lost for virtually the entire season. Earl Morrall, who had joined the Colts in a trade with the Giants just two weeks before, filled the breach and had a career year. "I'm thankful for the chance to play with the Colts," said the journeyman Morrall, who had previously played with the 49ers, Lions, Steelers, and Giants before joining the Colts. "It's a team with no cliques, no showboating, no individuals clamoring for glory—just everybody acting as one unit, with one common goal." Morrall admits he was not eager to play in Baltimore because he expected to just be occupying a seat on the bench. "I told Shula there was no reason to come. I was in my 13th year. I'd sit on the bench and they'd bring in a young quarterback the next year to replace me. Shula told me about Johnny's previous arm problems, plus the fact I'd have to beat out Jim Ward as the backup. That little zinger from Shula got my competitive juices flowing. When he said he couldn't guarantee me a spot, I told him I'd be down. Shula was a master at working on an athlete's pride."

The 34-year-old Morrall quarterbacked wins over all four of his previous teams, winning the NFL passing title as well as the league's Most Valuable Player award. Although he lacked mobility, Morrall had a good if not great arm, was smart, mixed plays well with an emphasis on play action, and was a solid leader.

The 13-1 record was the best in club history and the Colts were being hailed as one of the league's all-time powerhouses. In giving up just 144 points the entire year, the Colts rang up three shutouts (after having only six in their history prior to 1968).

In the first round of the play-offs, the Colts led Minnesota 21-0 after three quarters and held off the Vikings 24-14 before over 60,000 in Baltimore. A 49-yard Morrall to Mackey touchdown pass and a 60-yard fumble return for a touchdown by Mike Curtis keyed the win. Next came the always tough Browns for the NFL championship. The Colts avenged their only regular season loss and got some solace for

A unique Colt punch-out book was created and marketed in 1967. Colt players could be punched out and stood up like paper dolls.

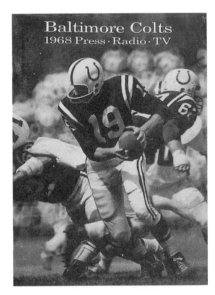

Johnny Unitas graced the 1968 press guide cover, but most of Johnny's season was spent on the injured list.

THE SUN MAGAZINE

The *Sun* had high hopes for the 1968 Colts.

the 1964 championship loss in Cleveland by blanking the Browns 34-0 before over 80,000 in the cavernous Municipal Stadium on Lake Erie. Tom Matte, a native Clevelander, scored three touchdowns, while NFL rushing leader Leroy Kelly was held to only 27 yards.

Next came the meeting with the AFL champion New York Jets, in what was now officially called the Super Bowl. Kansas City owner Lamar Hunt had come up with the new name after watching his kids play with what was called a "Super Ball." It sounded hokey at first and the league was hoping for something better, but the name stuck. New York was coached by former Colt coach Weeb Ewbank and had Joe Namath calling the signals. Shula, of course, had replaced Ewbank as coach in Baltimore and it was Weeb who had released Shula as a player in 1957. So the matchup of the two coaches was rife with human interest.

Shula faced a bit of a dilemma with his quarterback situation. Unitas had worked his way back and was 95 percent healthy; on the other hand, Morrall had gotten the team this far and was the league's MVP. The coach decided to go with Morrall, to the delight of the up-start Jets. In fact, former Colt and now Jet Johnny Sample was pray-ing that Unitas wouldn't start and rejoiced when he heard it would be Morrall. "I told my teammates about what Unitas could do, especially under fire. I knew we'd be in trouble if he started," said Sample, on the occasion of the 20th anniversary reunion game between the Jets and Colts at Memorial Stadium in 1989. "He scared me. In fact, I'm looking across at him now and he still scares me." Sample says that the Jets, to a man, all felt the Colts were beatable. "We had to stop looking at film on the Wednesday before the game because we were getting so overconfident. We were a young team. I was probably the oldest guy on the team. Yet on film we could spot their zone defense and Joe knew he could pick it apart."

In the pregame hype before the January 12, 1969, game at the Orange Bowl in Miami, Namath, nicknamed "Broadway Joe" for his flamboyant lifestyle, reacted to the skeptics who picked the Colts to win in a cakewalk by boldly predicting a Jets victory at a dinner held in the days leading up to the game. "I guarantee it," said Namath, em-phatically. He later said after looking at game films of the Colts that he was almost giddy because he felt so confident. In rating Morrall, he said there were at least four quarterbacks in the AFL who were better, including himself. Ewbank, who liked his players to keep their mouths shut, in the tradition of his mentor Paul Brown, was exas-perated over Joe Willy's boast. Namath assured Weeb that the Jets would win. The Colts, meanwhile, looked with disdain at the Jets and were supremely confident, probably overconfident, that they would make the bragging Namath eat his words.

Of course, everyone with even a casual interest in football knows what happened that day. The Jets, 16½ point underdogs, shocked the Colts 16-7. The Colts simply didn't come ready to play. They made numerous mistakes and failed to capitalize on many opportunities. In

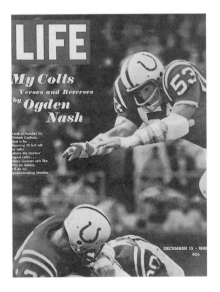

Baltimore-born poet and pundit Ogden Nash told about his love for the Colts in *Life* magazine.

the first half alone, the Colts drove the opening kickoff to the Jet 20, recovered a Jet fumble on the New York 12, saw Matte run 58 yards to the Jet 12, and had Jimmy Orr open in the end zone on a flea-flicker play, but had no points to show for any of it. As badly as they had played in the first half, the Colts still only trailed 7-0 at halftime; the Jets' score came as Matt Snell capped an 80-yard drive with a four-yard run. New York's game plan was to run away from linebacker Mike Curtis and right at the older side of the Colts' defense—Ordell Braase, who would retire after the game, Lenny Lyles, and 12-year veteran Don Shinnick.

The biggest play of the game occurred late in the first half when the Colts faced a second and nine at the Jet 41. Morrall handed to Tom Matte (who had a great game with a 58-yard run and 116 yards total). Matte pitched the ball back to Morrall for the old flea-flicker. Morrall looked downfield for his target, Jimmy Orr, but couldn't see him. Perhaps a marching band, which was assembling behind the end zone in preparation for halftime, had camouflaged his receiver. Be that as it may, Orr was standing in the end zone wide open, flailing his arms, but Morrall couldn't find him. Instead, he passed down the middle to fullback Jerry Hill. The Jets had Hill well covered, however, and Jim Hudson intercepted the pass.

The Colts had muffed an earlier chance to score when they recovered a George Sauer fumble on the New York 12. Morrall's pass intended for Tom Mitchell in the end zone was tipped by linebacker Al Atkinson and intercepted by Randy Beverly. At the same time, the Jets weren't exactly crushing the Colts; their only second-half points were three Jim Turner field goals.

Shula stuck with Morrall, the man who had helped them to a 16-1 record, and it was probably an ill-fated decision. Then, too, the fact that the Colts had the ball for four plays in the third period didn't help matters. Finally, with 13:26 remaining in the game, the legendary Unitas trotted on the field. Johnny got the Colts to the Jet 25 before a pass intended for Orr in the end zone was picked off by Beverly. The next time the rusty Unitas saw action, he directed a well-executed 80-yard drive that was capped by a Jerry Hill one-yard plunge, and the Colts were on the board. Could Unitas work another mira-

National beer produced a record album commemorating the 1968 season. Wisely, there was no mention of the Super Bowl.

cle? No, this time it wasn't to be, as time was running out and the Jets were milking the clock. Still, there were some anxious moments for New York. Remembers Sample: "I don't care if Unitas was hurt or not. I told the guys in the huddle, don't let up because this guy can play. He's cunning, he's smart, and he's gutty. He got the only touchdown they scored." Final score: Jets 16, Colts 7. Unitas, at game's end, was not happy and blamed Shula's ego and stubbornness for not putting him in sooner. The Colts had done everything but put points on the board; afterwards they had to go to Rosenbloom's pre-planned "victory" party, which turned into a solemn wake.

Namath, in looking back at the game, said he didn't get nervous until he looked up and saw 6:11 left in the game. "Prior to that, the normal nervousness was there and the adrenaline was pumping. At the 6:11 mark I got frightened. It was the longest 6:11 of any athletic contest I had ever been involved in." The game, of course, rocketed Namath into superstar class. "It's been a lasting memory. I'm thrilled, because every day of my life someone brings up Super Bowl III and it brings a smile to my face."

Next to the Colts' sudden-death victory in 1958, the 1969 Super Bowl was the most important game in pro football history. Amazingly, Ewbank was the victorious coach in both. The Jets' win gave the AFL legitimacy, just as the merger with the NFL was about to take effect. Rosenbloom was embarrassed by the loss, blaming Shula for giving him the dubious honor of being the first NFL owner to lose to the AFL. Colt tight end John Mackey may have summed it up best when he said in a recent interview, "We went into the game overconfident and when we realized that we had a tough game on our hands, it brought on panic because we couldn't believe we were losing to an AFL club. Then we couldn't get anything going. The best team I ever played on lost the Super Bowl and the worst team won it. The lesson is if you keep your feet on the ground you have a better chance of winning."

Super Bowl III souvenirs are much sought after by collectors. The program, the first with the word "Super Bowl" in the title, is a real prize and goes for over $200. The significance of the game adds to the aura of the program, which has a classic painting by Merv

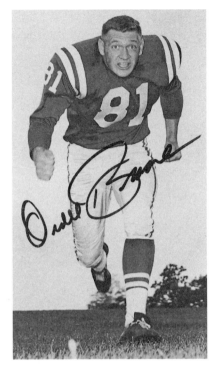

Longtime Colt Ordell Braase, who had first joined the team in 1954 before departing for military service, called it quits after the 1968 season.

Corning depicting Lenny Lyles of the Colts defending against Jets receiver Don Maynard. Ticket stubs, pennants, buttons, and pins are also collectors' items. The press pin for the game was a tie clasp that had a football helmet resting on the outline of the state of Florida. On the pin, it read, "AFL VS NFL, 3rd World Championship, 1969 Miami." The pin is difficult to obtain and has sold for over $700. Both the Colts and the Jets put out record albums commemorating the season, produced by Fleetwood Records in Revere, Massachusetts. The Colts' version, called "Colts Stampede," is sponsored by National beer and narrated by Chuck Thompson, and concludes just before the Super Bowl loss.

The Colts vowed to get back to the Super Bowl as soon as possible, but it wasn't to happen in 1969. In what turned out to be Don Shula's final season in Baltimore, the Colts compiled a respectable 8-5-1 record, with wins over the Rams and Packers, but it wasn't enough, as the Rams won the Coastal Division with an 11-3 record. Ordell Braase, Bobby Boyd, and Dick Szymanski had called it quits. Injuries also took their toll, as tight end John Mackey missed two games and was hampered in several others. Two other receivers, Jimmy Orr and Tom Mitchell (who missed the last six games), were also struck down with injuries. In 1969 only three rookies made the team, including number-two pick Ted Hendricks of Miami, the 6' 7" "Mad Stork," who became an All-Pro in his five years in Baltimore. He would eventually gain admission to the Pro Football Hall of Fame after several years in Oakland. Says Hendricks, "I was very concerned when I came to Baltimore because of all the veterans on the team when I arrived. It was a team of All-Pros. I was too light to play the line at 214 pounds and they didn't know where to put me. Johnny Unitas, Lou Michaels, and Danny Sullivan took me under their wing and brought me along." With his height and quickness, Hendricks helped revolutionize the linebacker spot. He would intercept passes, bat passes down, and rush the quarterback, plus block field goals. His height made it difficult to lob passes over him. "There are people who play for years who don't win," says Hendricks. "I was in my second year as a starting linebacker on a Super Bowl winner. Then I made

The "Mad Stork," Ted Hendricks, began his Hall of Fame career in Baltimore.

All-Pro the next year. What else was left?" Just induction into the Hall of Fame.

Nineteen seventy ended up being both monumental and historical for the Colts. As part of the merger of the two leagues, three of the NFL's most storied teams, the Colts, Browns, and Steelers, were compensated $3 million apiece for switching to the American Football Conference. This meant that the rivalries with Green Bay, Chicago, Minnesota, and the Rams were history, and in their place would be games with Buffalo, the Jets, Miami, and Boston. Not many fans were pleased with the switch, although on the flip side a lowering of the quality of competition compared to the NFC meant that the ride to the postseason would be less difficult for Baltimore. The Colts' press guide, which since 1948 had been issued in a 5 × 6 size, underwent a transformation in 1970; the AFC, in order to have its own identifiable look, produced its press guides in a more vertical 8½ × 3½ format. The 1970 guide had a color action shot of the Unitas-led offense running a play against the Los Angeles Rams.

As it turned out, 1970 brought many more changes; the move to the AFC was just for starters. In early January, Don Klosterman came from the Houston Oilers to replace Harry Hulmes as the Colts general manager. Hulmes soon took a similar job with the New Orleans Saints. Then, just a few weeks later, Shula was gone too. When the Miami Dolphins were unsuccessful in hiring Paul "Bear" Bryant from Alabama, they turned to Shula. Shula went to Steve Rosenbloom, who was in charge of the Colts while his father was on a trip to the Orient. The younger Rosenbloom granted Shula permission to talk with Dolphins owner Joe Robbie and on February 18, Shula called the elder Rosenbloom, by this time in Hawaii, and told him that he was leaving Baltimore to coach Miami. Inwardly Rosenbloom was pleased that Shula was leaving, but when public opinion went overwhelmingly against the Colts for losing such a renowned and respected coach, the owner cried foul and charged the Dolphins with tampering (Steadman 1997). Commissioner Pete Rozelle, in an effort to keep the peace, awarded the Colts a first-round 1971 draft

The 1970 press guide sported a new look.

pick, who turned out to be North Carolina running back Don Mc-
Cauley.

The Colts stayed within the organization in hiring a new coach;
49-year-old Don McCafferty, nicknamed the "Easy Rider" for his un-
ruffled manner, moved up from offensive coordinator. McCafferty,
hired by Weeb Ewbank 11 years earlier, had played his college football at Ohio State for Paul Brown.

John Unitas was embarking on his 15th season in 1970. Six times
an All-Pro and a ten-time Pro Bowler, Johnny had completed more
passes (2,450) for more yards (35,502) and more touchdowns (266)
than any quarterback in NFL history. In tribute to his accomplish-
ments, Unitas was named the starting quarterback on the NFL's 50th
anniversary team. As former Chicago quarterback great Sid Luckman
said of Unitas in the Colts press guide: "Johnny Unitas is the greatest
quarterback to ever play the game—better than me, better than
Sammy Baugh, better than anyone." Joining Unitas on the anniversary team offense was tight end John Mackey; heading the defense
was Gino Marchetti, who was named the league's finest defensive end
over the first 50 years. Raymond Berry, Lenny Moore, Jim Parker,
and Art Donovan made the second team.

On September 20, 1970, the Colts began their new era in the
American Football Conference with a 16-14 win over the Chargers
in San Diego. In a sign of things to come, rookie receiver-kicker Jim
O'Brien booted three field goals, including the game winner with 56
seconds left. The Baltimore defense stopped Lance Alworth's streak
of catching at least one pass in 96 consecutive games.

Coach Don McCafferty's easy-going demeanor belied an imagi-
native side that loved innovation. In fact, the Colts began several
games with a new wrinkle. In their first meeting with the Jets at Shea
Stadium, it was using just one running back and five receivers. The
Colts prevailed over Joe Namath and the Jets 29-22, despite 397 passing yards from Namath. Broadway Joe also tossed six interceptions
among his 62 pass attempts. Against Green Bay, the surprise play was
a 54-yard halfback option pass thrown by Sam Havrilak, who had
lined up as a wide receiver on the opposite side. "It was a play I stole
from my son's playbook at Dulaney High School," said McCafferty.

Johnny Unitas was still at the
helm in 1970, his fifteenth
season in Baltimore.

"I was looking through it one night and copied it down. It worked fine" (quote from record album produced by the author). The Colts buried Don Shula's Dolphins 35-0 before over 60,000 on November 1 as Ron Gardin ran a punt back 80 yards and Jim Duncan scored on a 99-yard kickoff return.

Many experts thought the "bump and run" pass defenses in the AFC would throw off Unitas' timing. Usually quarterbacks throw less to their wide-outs against the bump and run. Unitas didn't even blink an eye over the tactic. He just sent his receivers straight down the field and dumped the ball out in front of them. The defenders' backs were turned so they couldn't see the ball in the air. After Johnny got the defense rattled over the deep passes, he went back to his old turn-ins and square-outs.

Even though Baltimore was now playing in a new conference, there were still a few links to the past. The Colts ground out a 13-10 win over the Packers in Milwaukee and nipped the Bears 21-20 at Memorial Stadium, as Unitas brought his team back from a 17-0 deficit and threw a 54-yard TD pass to John Mackey in the last four minutes to win it. They ran their record to 9-2-1 by beating the Eagles before the 50th successive home sellout crowd. The Colts clinched the AFC East the following week, December 13, in snowy Buffalo, 20-14, after the Bills had taken a 14-0 halftime lead.

Earl Morrall got some solace against the Jets in the final regular season game, throwing for 348 yards and four touchdowns in a 35-20 win. With a final record of 11-2-1, the Colts were pitted against Paul Brown's feisty Cincinnati Bengals in the first round of the AFC play-offs, held the day after Christmas.

It was a cold, windy day in Baltimore and upwards of 9,000 fans decided to stay home. Unitas tossed TD passes to Eddie Hinton and Roy Jefferson in a 17-0 win that put the Colts in the conference championship game against the Oakland Raiders on January 3, 1971. In that one, the passing of Unitas and the running of Norm Bulaich powered the Colts to a 27-17 win before 56,368 fans at Memorial Stadium. Bulaich scored twice and Unitas passed for 245 yards, with a 68-yard scoring strike to Ray Perkins being the big play. George Blanda became, at 43, the oldest quarterback to play in a title game, throwing for 271 yards and two touchdowns. The old warhorse was also intercepted three times.

For the second time in three years the Colts were in the Super Bowl, again at Miami's Orange Bowl, only this time they weren't the favorite. Tom Landry's Dallas Cowboys were 12-4 coming into the game, having beaten the Lions by the unlikely score of 5-0 and San Francisco 17-10 in the postseason. Unlike two years before, when they had taken a rather casual approach to the game, even bringing their wives and families with them, the Colts this time were all business. Unlike the 1969 Super Bowl, in which they were the NFL representative, the Colts were now coming from the AFC.

The game itself was both the sloppiest and one of the most exciting of all the Super Bowls. There were 11 turnovers, moving *New*

York Daily News columnist Dick Young to write the next day, "The thing I can't quite decide is this: Have I just watched one of the greatest football games ever played, or the worst." Wrote Edwin Pope in the *Miami Herald*: "If you like cutthroat football—gut wrenching, fumbling and intercepting and piling on and clipping and plain-out punching—it was a great game."

"The Colts and Cowboys might not have looked like Super Bowl teams. But they were in super combat. They smashed and clawed and tore each other like gang-fighters going for each other's jugulars instead of just the $15,000 first prize. These guys were playing for manhood. That is why, out of all the debates about the total of skills shown in Super Bowl V, there never will be any about this game's grip on the hearts of real football men. It had it."

Colts rookie Jim O'Brien climaxed one of the zaniest title games ever played by lofting a 32-yard field goal through the Orange Bowl uprights with five seconds left in regulation to give Baltimore a 16-13 Super Bowl triumph over the Cowboys. "I was happy I was young," says O'Brien in talking about not feeling the pressure. "Ignorance is bliss."

Dallas nearly put the game away early in the third period when, leading 13-6, they recovered Jim Duncan's fumble on the second-half kickoff and took it to the Colts 2 yard line in five plays. However, the troubled Duane Thomas fumbled on the next play and the Colts dodged a bullet. Rick Volk provided the Colts an opportunity to tie the game midway through the fourth quarter when he intercepted a Craig Morton pass on the Dallas 33 and returned it to the 3. Tom Nowatzke then carried it over and the score was tied at 13-13. Mike Curtis intercepted another Morton pass on the Dallas 41 in the final minute and returned it to the 28. After two Bulaich running plays, O'Brien hit the winning field goal.

Unitas did not have a typical game, being intercepted twice and fumbling once, but he hooked up with John Mackey on a tipped pass early in the second quarter that went for 75 yards and a touchdown. The pass was intended for Eddie Hinton, but was thrown high. Hinton tipped it and Cowboy defensive back Mel Renfro got a finger on the ball before it landed in the arms of Mackey. If Renfro hadn't

opposite page

Collecting all the various Colt schedules over the years became a nearly impossible task.

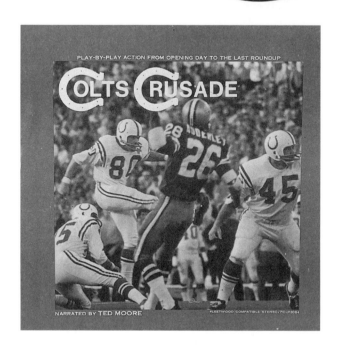

touched the ball, the play would have been called back. Instead it became a freakish 75-yard touchdown. Unitas left later in the period
after a vicious tackle by George Andrie tore his rib cartilage, and
Morrall took over.

Dallas didn't even attempt a pass in the third quarter. Morton had
had arm trouble late in the season and Coach Landry was relying on
the running game. In the fourth quarter, however, Dallas had no
choice but to throw. Morton tried 10 passes, but completed only four
for 27 yards. Three of his passes were intercepted, with Volk's pick-
off setting up the tying touchdown.

By winning Super Bowl V, the Colts got some vindication for the
game two years before. Shula watched this one from the stands with
obvious mixed emotions. McCafferty was being hailed as a coaching
genius. This was to be Baltimore's only Super Bowl champion up till
now. After the game, two more all-time great Colts announced their
retirements: wide receiver Jimmy Orr and defensive tackle Billy Ray
Smith.

The game program from Super Bowl V is one of the tougher to
find on the collecting market. The cover depicts a clay-molded player
running with the football. Another record album was put out after the
Super Bowl win. Narrated by Colt announcer Ted Moore, the album
was called "Colts Crusade" and the cover pictured Jim O'Brien kicking the winning field goal. It was written and produced by this writer
in his first assignment with Fleetwood Records near Boston, after
being discharged from the Army in the fall of 1970.

There was also another interesting Colt collectible during this
era. A magazine called *The Huddle*, begun in 1969 with nine issues,
grew to 12 issues in 1970. It was geared to supplying fans with a program containing both news and feature articles when the Colts were
on the road and their followers were home watching the game on television. It was available through subscription only and was edited by
Tom Gorman, the same guy who produced the Colts' 1963 and 1964
yearbooks. *The Huddle* was a classy publication with full-color covers, but was gone from the scene by 1971.

Things were never the same with Baltimore football after the win
in Super Bowl V. Rosenbloom, despite his elation over winning the

opposite page

Finally, the Colts celebrated a
win in Super Bowl V. Colt fans
could mount a souvenir
beneath their license plates.

Jim O'Brien's winning kick
graced the cover of the
commemorative record album.

Fans who couldn't get enough of their Colts could subscribe to *The Huddle,* which served as a game program for away games.

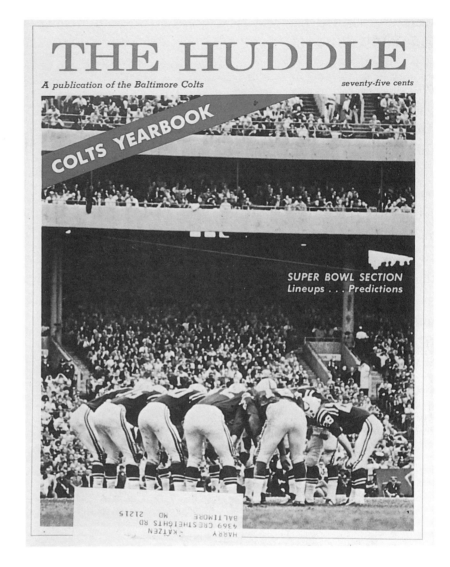

Super Bowl without Don Shula, had become unhappy in Baltimore. By the same token, there were many in Baltimore who were not too happy with Rosenbloom. His ego was huge and he could be a vicious businessman. He and Oriole owner Jerry Hoffberger weren't speaking. He was disenchanted over the city's lack of interest in erecting him a new stadium, and even threatened to move the Colts to Tampa.

Just a month before his 38th birthday, on April 7, 1971, Johnny Unitas ruptured his Achilles tendon while playing paddle-ball with Tom Matte at the Towson YMCA. Surgery was successful and, remarkably, Unitas was back to play in the first regular-season game, a 22-0 shutout of the Jets in which Norm Bulaich ran for a team record 198 yards on 22 carries on a muddy field. Alan Ameche had set the record as a rookie with 194 yards, 16 years before. Unitas ended up playing in every game but one and divided playing time with Morrall. The Colts finished 10-4 in the AFC East, making the playoffs as the wild-card entry with Miami ahead of them at 10-3-1.

Two of Unitas' greatest efforts ever came in wins over Oakland and Miami. Against the Raiders in Oakland on November 28, 1971, Johnny led the Colts to a 38-14 win and then, two weeks later, in a 14-3 win at home against Miami, he was 16 of 19 for 142 yards, and conducted two long scoring drives in which he was flawless. The Colts thus led the Dolphins by a half game, with one game to go against the 5-8 New England Patriots at Memorial Stadium. A victory would mean a division title and hosting the AFC championship in Baltimore. Instead, they lost to Jim Plunkett and the Patriots 21-17. Randy Vataha caught an over-the-head pass for 88 yards from Plunkett, his former Stanford teammate, late in the game that stunned the Baltimore crowd of 57,942. Now the Colts were forced to play on the road as the AFC wild-card entry.

In what was to be their last postseason win as the Baltimore Colts, Unitas went all the way in leading the Colts to a 20-3 victory at Cleveland before over 74,000 in the opening playoff game. Don Nottingham, "The Human Bowling Ball" from nearby Kent State, filled in for the injured Norm Bulaich and rushed for 92 yards and two touchdowns.

The Colts were one game away from a possible Super Bowl repeat. They next faced the Dolphins in Miami and decided to go to Tampa to work out in the week before the game. Tampa had designs on getting the Colts to move there and rolled out the red carpet for the team. It ended up being a distraction, as the Colts traveled to Miami and, playing without injured backs Tom Matte and Norm Bulaich, were blanked 21-0 at the Orange Bowl in the AFC championship game. It was the first time the Colts had been shut out since December 13, 1965, a span of 97 games. Unitas had a solid day, hitting 20 of 36 passes for 224 yards, but was unable to penetrate the end zone. Dick Anderson's 62-yard return for a touchdown in the third quarter that made it 14-0 pretty much sealed the Colts' fate.

Rosenbloom announced after the season that the Colts would leave their Western Maryland training camp after 19 years and train in Tampa, where they would also play three exhibition games. Bumper stickers appeared on Maryland cars that read "Don't TAMPA With Our Colts," reacting to rumors that the Colts were being courted by Tampa. Rosenbloom had feuded with resentful fans and media alike over his insistence that season ticketholders also had to buy tickets to preseason games.

After longtime Rams owner Dan Reeves died of Parkinson's disease in 1971, the glamorous Los Angeles franchise was up for grabs. Rosenbloom dearly wanted to buy the Rams, but he already owned the Colts so it was impossible, unless he involved a third party who could be manipulated like a puppet on a string. That third party ended up being Robert Irsay.

Johnny Unitas' Topps rookie card, 1957.

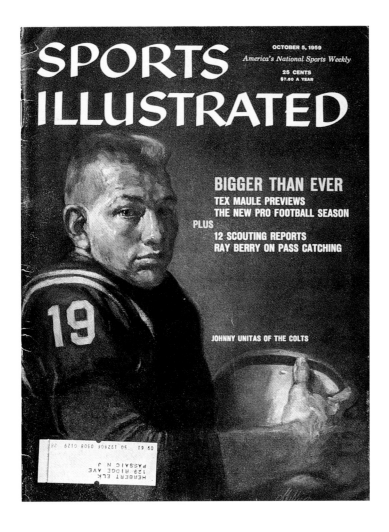

Johnny Unitas and Raymond Berry began getting national acclaim for their heroics in Baltimore.

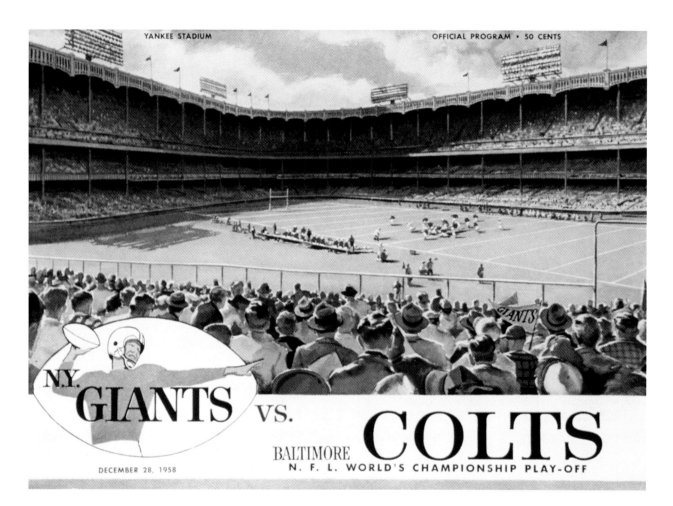

YANKEE STADIUM   OFFICIAL PROGRAM · 50 CENTS

N.Y.
GIANTS vs.

BALTIMORE COLTS
N. F. L. WORLD'S CHAMPIONSHIP PLAY-OFF

DECEMBER 28, 1958

The 1958 "sudden death" program pictured a sunny, fall afternoon
at Yankee Stadium. The December 28 game instead was played in a
winter mix of gray skies and chilly temperatures.

opposite page

The National brewery honored the 1958 champs with a large color team
photo for display in bars and taverns and anywhere Natty Boh was served.
A program, bus ticket, and a pair of game ticket stubs to the 1959 NFL
title game, the only championship game played in Baltimore.

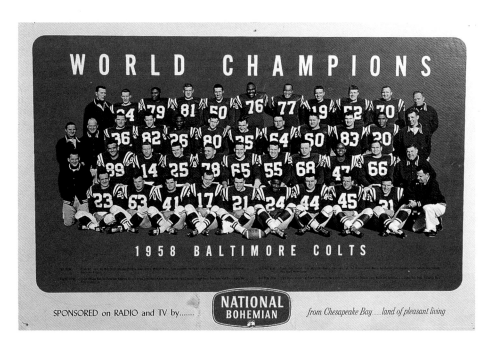

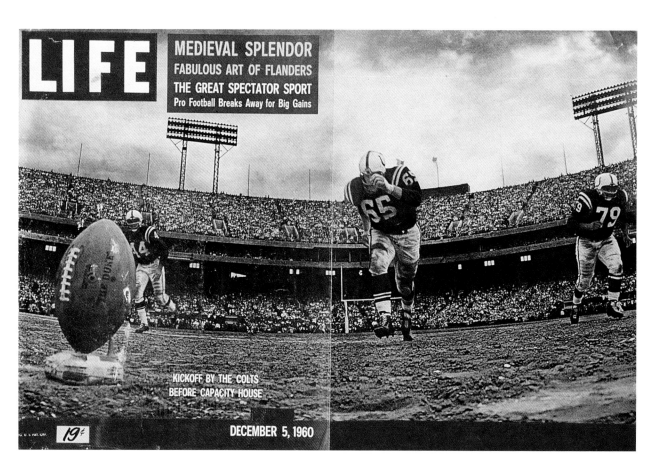

LIFE

MEDIEVAL SPLENDOR
FABULOUS ART OF FLANDERS
THE GREAT SPECTATOR SPORT
Pro Football Breaks Away for Big Gains

KICKOFF BY THE COLTS
BEFORE CAPACITY HOUSE

19¢

DECEMBER 5, 1960

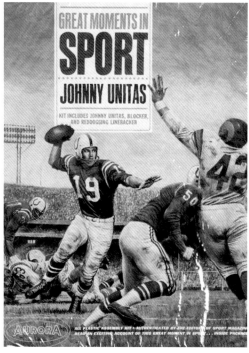

GREAT MOMENTS IN
SPORT
JOHNNY UNITAS

KIT INCLUDES JOHNNY UNITAS, BLOCKER,
AND REDDOGGING LINEBACKER

AURORA

ALL PLASTIC ASSEMBLY KIT • AUTHENTICATED BY THE EDITORS OF SPORT MAGAZINE
READ AN EXCITING ACCOUNT OF THIS GREAT MOMENT IN SPORT . . . . INSIDE PACKAGE

OUR '64 COLTS

A SEASON'S REVIEW FROM TRAINING CAMP TO CHAMPIONSHIP WITH FEATURES ABOUT SHULA . . . MOORE . . .
MARCHETTI . . . PELLINGTON . . . UNITAS . . . "CAPTAIN WHO" . . . BERRY . . . PARKER . . . SANDUSKY . . . BRAASE.

ONE DOLLAR

The familiar Unitas
follow-through on the 1964
yearbook cover.

opposite page

Steve Myhra prepares to kick off with Memorial Stadium as a backdrop in the December 5, 1960, edition of *Life* magazine. The "Golden
Arm" was preserved in plastic in this 1965 model kit. The Colts once
again were featured in their own comic book in 1962.

On the cover of *Sports Illustrated* Tom Matte and the Colts thrashed the Browns in Cleveland to gain the right to play the Jets in Super Bowl III. Need we say more?

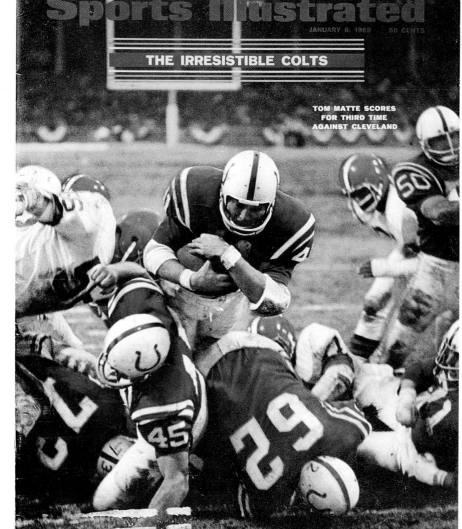

Sports Illustrated

JANUARY 6, 1969   50 CENTS

THE IRRESISTIBLE COLTS

TOM MATTE SCORES
FOR THIRD TIME
AGAINST CLEVELAND

opposite page

The colorful cover of the Super Bowl III program, the first to use the name *Super Bowl*, showed Lenny Lyles defending against the Jets' Don Maynard.

The cover of the Super
Bowl V program.

SUPER BOWL V

Price $1.50

**WORLD PROFESSIONAL FOOTBALL CHAMPIONSHIP
FOR THE VINCE LOMBARDI TROPHY**
Sunday, January 17, 1971 • 2:00 p.m. Orange Bowl, Miami

Nationally known illustrator Jack Harvey painted the cover of the 1974 media guide.

The Colts Silver Anniversary team was honored with an eye-catching poster of the team's all-time greats.

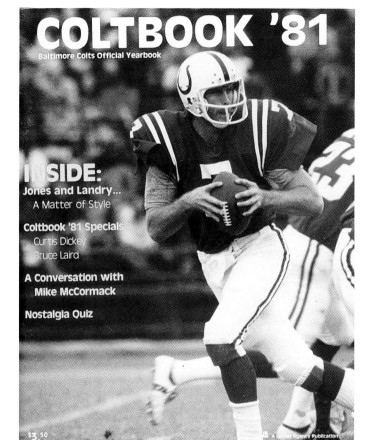

Bert Jones became known as "The Ruston Rifle" because of his hard-throwing passing style.

In 1982 the Colts' season tickets featured a colorful game-action painting of each week's opponent.

opposite page

"The Magnificent Seven," the Colts Hall of Famers, were honored in a beautiful 1979 poster sponsored by the Eastside Athletic Club.

Buttons were often
accompanied by ribbons
and, in this case,
a gridiron star of the
future.

Pennants cost 50¢ but were priceless additions to many a bedroom and
rec room wall.

The Winner distributing company honored Johnny Unitas with his own liquor canister in 1983.

Between 1958 and 1969 the Colts issued pins instead of passes to reporters headed to the press box at Memorial Stadium.

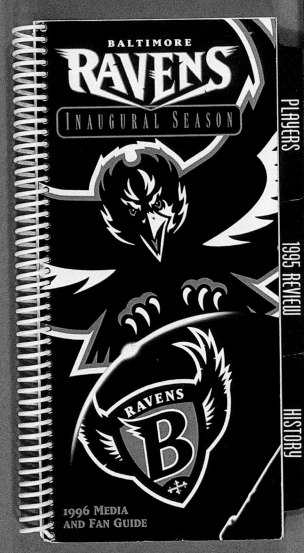

One of the historic first tickets to the Ravens Stadium at Camden Yards.

opposite page

The first two Ravens press guides (1996 and 1997). The first gave fans a close-up view of the new team's logo; the second paid tribute to Memorial Stadium.

The Ravens Stadium and six all-star players graced the cover of the
1999 *Fan and Media Guide*.

FIVE

The Decline and Fall

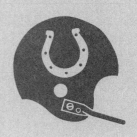

Carroll Rosenbloom was known as an astute businessman; the end run that he quarterbacked, enabling him to leave one coast and end up on the other was his crowning achievement. Never before had football franchises been swapped, but Rosenbloom found his trump card in Robert Irsay. Irsay had made his millions in the air conditioning business in and around his home base of Skokie, Illinois. His company did contracting work for Disney World, Cobo Arena in Detroit, and many buildings constructed on Chicago's Loop. He was a complete unknown in Baltimore, as well as in pro football circles; before long, however, he had put his imprint on a couple of cities.

How did Irsay make his way into the NFL? He was discovered by former Colt assistant Joe Thomas, who helped broker the deal with Rosenbloom. Thomas had risen through the NFL ranks since his days as a Weeb Ewbank assistant in 1954. He had been the first personnel director of the Minnesota Vikings in 1960 and of the Miami Dolphins in 1965, but with the arrival of Shula, found his dream of becoming the general manager of the Dolphins blocked. Dolphin owner Joe Robbie offered him a new three-year contract to stay as personnel chief, but Thomas wanted to be a general manager, and so in 1971 he resigned.

For six months, Thomas kept abreast of the NFL from his Miami home, looking for an opportunity to get control of a team. He read about Rosenbloom's interest in the Rams and called Pete Rozelle, who encouraged Thomas to try and put a group together to buy either the Colts or the Rams. The brother of his heart-bypass surgeon put him in touch with W. H. "Bud" Keland, who had been a minority owner of the Dolphins, and Irsay, who was itching to get into the NFL. Instead of getting a finder's fee, Thomas would get the general manager's job he coveted. At the 11th hour, Keland, who was expected to be the majority owner of the group, backed out, leaving Irsay. Soon Thomas got Rosenbloom and Irsay together and their plan to swap franchises was conceived. Irsay would buy the Rams from the estate of Dan Reeves for the huge sum of $19 million, and then swap them with Rosenbloom for the Colts.

There was never a question of Irsay keeping the Rams. If that had happened, the city of Baltimore might have been spared the punishment that was about to be inflicted by Irsay. Rosenbloom felt at a dead end in Baltimore. The city would not build him a stadium, and when he threatened to build his own stadium in Baltimore County he was rebuffed by Baltimore County executive Dale Anderson, who said the Colts belonged in Baltimore at Memorial Stadium.

The "sale-trade" saga was kept hush-hush for several weeks. Rosenbloom, the cool and calculating businessman, saw Irsay as an easy mark. By making the arrangement a trade of franchises and not a sale, Rosenbloom avoided huge capital gains taxes. On July 13, 1972, the 49-year-old Irsay officially took over as owner and president of the Colts.

Not much was known about Robert Irsay in Baltimore. His bio said he was born in Chicago, played football at the University of Illinois, served in the Marines for four years during World War II, and was discharged as a lieutenant in 1945. In reality there was no record of Irsay at the University of Illinois, nor did he play football there. He was in the Marines for six months and was separated as a sergeant, not a lieutenant.

It was apparent at the introductory press conference for Irsay and Thomas that Irsay had no business owning a professional sports team. Many wondered how such a crude individual had been able to amass millions of dollars in business. For someone who bragged about an intense sports background, Irsay talked like a novice. The Baltimore press corps was willing to give him a chance, however, and a honeymoon period began.

Thomas helped build two expansion franchises, the Vikings and the Dolphins, into Super Bowl teams. Although knowledgeable about football, Thomas, unlike Don Kellett and Harry Hulmes, was aloof, egotistical, impersonal, and unfriendly. Many of the players complained that he didn't even introduce himself.

McCafferty and his assistants were retained for the 1972 season. Everyone agreed that Don's 21-6-1 record and Super Bowl victory had established him after just two seasons as one of the most successful coaches in the game. When the Irsay-Thomas regime began, the Colts had the best record of any team in pro football since 1958. Their record of 136-54-5 was 12 wins better than second-place Cleveland's.

One of the men most responsible for that record, Gino Marchetti, was inducted into the Pro Football Hall of Fame on July 29, 1972. Picked for 11 straight Pro Bowls and named All-NFL seven times, Gino became an all-around brilliant defender. In testimonials at the induction ceremony it was brought out how Gino was often double- and even triple-teamed, but that only made the rest of the defense better.

After the Colts lost four of their first five games in 1972, Thomas fired McCafferty and replaced him with defensive line coach John Sandusky. One of those losses was a 44-34 shootout with the Jets on September 24, before 56,626 at Memorial Stadium. Joe Namath, the brash symbol of the AFL, and Johnny Unitas, the old master, staged a spectacular passing duel. Namath threw for 496 yards and six touchdowns; included among his 15 completions were touchdown passes of 65, 67, 79, and 80 yards. Unitas completed 26 of 45 for 376 yards and two touchdowns.

Johnny Unitas hands to Don McCauley against the Jets in 1972, Johnny's last great hurrah as Colt quarterback.

Sandusky then received orders from Thomas to change quarterbacks. Beginning with the October 22 game with the Jets at Shea Stadium, Marty Domres supplanted Unitas as the Colts' starter. Talk about tough acts to follow! Domres faced a huge challenge in replacing a living legend and was booed by the home fans. The Colts went on to lose five of their last nine games and finish with a 5-9 record, their first losing season since Unitas' first year in 1956. Johnny's last hurrah as a Colt occurred on December 3, 1972, against

Thousands of Colt fans had framed pictures of Johnny Unitas in their dens, game rooms, and bedrooms. Along with Brooks Robinson, he was Baltimore's favorite son.

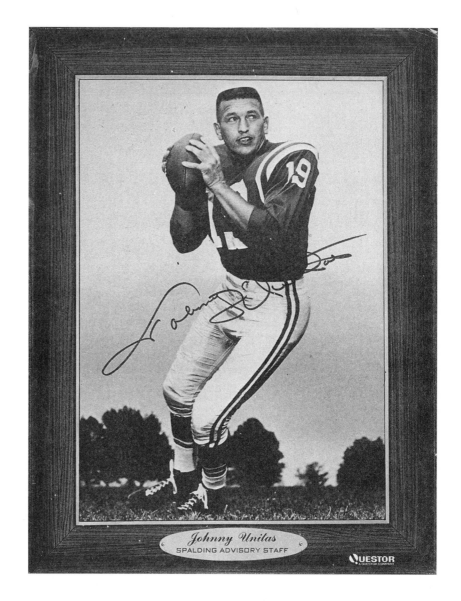

Johnny Unitas
SPALDING ADVISORY STAFF

QUESTOR
A QUESTOR COMPANY

Buffalo at Memorial Stadium in the final home game of the season. When Domres left the game with a muscle pull after tossing three touchdown passes, Unitas entered the game. With a plane flying overhead pulling a banner that said "Unitas We Stand!" Johnny hooked up with Eddie Hinton for 63 yards and a touchdown. It was the longest Colt pass play of the season. The fans went crazy in applauding their hero, and the Colts won the game 35-7. It was the 287th and last touchdown pass in Unitas' brilliant career as a Baltimore Colt.

Joe Thomas didn't waste any time in tearing the club apart after such a disappointing year. First he fired the entire coaching staff, including Sandusky; it was the same staff that had won a Super Bowl just two years before. That was just for starters. On January 22, 1973, Thomas did the unthinkable, dealing Unitas to San Diego for $150,000. In his 17 seasons in Baltimore, Unitas had completed more passes for more mileage (22 miles) and more touchdowns than any quarterback in the history of the National Football League. Plus, he had become a larger-than-life American hero. Like other great stars in sports, such as Otto Graham, Ted Williams, Mickey Mantle, Bill Russell, and Stan Musial, who played for only one organization their entire careers, it was taken for granted that as long as Unitas suited up, it would be in the uniform of the Baltimore Colts. In a cold, unfeeling manner, Joe Thomas abruptly changed that.

Johnny was saluted on Preakness Day, 1973, the day another immortal champion, Secretariat, won the Preakness Stakes in spectacular fashion. Only a few of those buttons were produced.

Johnny Unitas of the San Diego Chargers? It just didn't sound right. Johnny, although disappointed to be leaving his home, pretty much kept his thoughts to himself and was able to negotiate a $250,000 per year contract for two years in San Diego. He was making $125,000 a year in Baltimore, with a promise from Rosenbloom that he'd remain with the organization in a front office capacity after his playing days were over. But Rosenbloom was gone, and Thomas and Irsay never kept that promise. Since he didn't care for either Thomas or Irsay anyway, Johnny was able to arrange a buyout. As it turned out, Unitas spent one disappointing year in San Diego, and then retired from the game.

After Unitas was shipped away, other Colt heroes began leaving one by one. Thomas unceremoniously got rid of Tom Matte, John Mackey, Bill Curry, Danny Sullivan, Norm Bulaich, Fred Miller, Roy Hilton, Jerry Logan, Bubba Smith, and Jim O'Brien, among others. The impersonal way Thomas acted totally turned off loyal Colt followers and season ticket sales began to suffer. He refused to change his demeanor, however, and became the most hated individual in the history of Baltimore sports, rivaled only by Irsay. The way he dismantled a proud and revered franchise was almost criminal. In February 1973, Thomas hired Dolphin assistant Howard Schnellenberger to replace Sandusky as head coach.

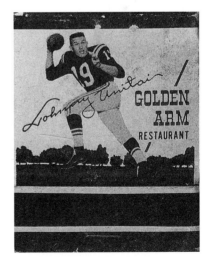

A matchbook cover from Unitas' Golden Arm Restaurant.

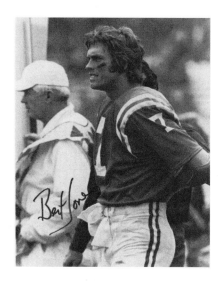

Bert Jones was picked number one in the 1973 draft and became the heir apparent to Johnny U.

The one move that Thomas made that wasn't questioned was his dealing away of tackle Billy Newsome and a fourth-round draft pick for the first pick of the New Orleans Saints in the 1973 NFL draft. Thomas picked LSU quarterback Bert Jones, a consensus All-American and the son of former Browns receiving great Dub Jones. With his other first-round pick, Thomas selected Joe Ehrmann, a talented defensive tackle from Syracuse who would replace Newsome. Several other draft picks from the 1973 draft, including Mike Barnes, Bill Olds, David Taylor, Ray Oldham, and Dan Neal ended up playing key roles for the Colts.

The 1973 Colts posted a 4-10 record under Schellenberger. Jones was brought along slowly, with Domres doing the bulk of the quarterbacking. Upset that former Penn State running star Lydell Mitchell wasn't playing, Thomas shipped the popular Don Nottingham to Miami during the season in order to give Mitchell his break. Lydell went on to lead the Colts in rushing with 963 yards.

Gracing the Colts press guide cover in 1973 was future Hall of Famer Ted Hendricks, one of the few star players that Thomas hadn't traded. Hendricks, however, was also gone by the following season, traded to Green Bay for linebacker Tom McLeod. The cover of the 1974 media guide was one of the classiest ever. Noted artist Jack Havey painted a Colt gladiator from behind, wearing his cape with "Colts" in white across the back. The colors were blue, white, and black and were extremely striking.

After opening losses to the Steelers and Packers, in which they were outscored 50-13, the 1974 Colts were on their way to a third straight loss in Philadelphia when all hell broke loose. Irsay came down the field just before halftime and ordered Schnellenberger to take out Domres and put in Jones. Schnellenberger, who had learned to coach football under Bear Bryant, told Irsay to get off the field and let him do the coaching. As linebacker Stan White told me about the incident, "Howard was going to play Bert in the second half, but after Irsay's demand, he couldn't, because it would seem like Irsay was coaching the team and not him. So he stayed with Domres." After the Eagles 30-10 victory, Irsay stormed into the locker room and announced that Schnellenberger had been fired and that Thomas was

the new coach. Thomas, perspiring heavily and in shock like everyone else, jumped up on a table and tried to calm the team. "Mike
Curtis screamed at Joe that there was no way the team would play for
him," remembers White. "There was bedlam and confusion." Curtis,
the "Mad Dog" of the Colt defense, was gone by the next season.

Thomas was ill prepared to coach and didn't want the job, but he
had no choice. He had picked the volatile keg of dynamite, Bob Irsay,
to work for. At least he could reasonably assume that no matter what
happened, he wouldn't be fired as coach unless he fired himself. With
wins only over the Jets and Falcons, the Colts limped home with a
2-12 record as 1974 went down as one of the great disasters in Colt
history. Jones got his feet wet under tough circumstances, throwing
for 1,610 yards and eight touchdowns. In one game, a 45-38 loss to
the Jets, Bert completed 17 straight passes for a then NFL record.
Mitchell's 72 receptions by a running back also set a league record.

After the season, Thomas recommended the hiring of dapper
Hank Stram or former Browns defender Paul Wiggin, but Irsay nixed
them both. Then Thomas suggested Ted Marchibroda, an NFL assistant on the Rams and Redskins for 14 years, and Irsay said yes. The
quiet, mild-mannered Marchibroda, one of the three quarterbacks
the Steelers kept instead of Johnny Unitas in 1955, was hired on January 15, 1975, the Colts' fifth coach in the past three years.

The Colts were about to embark on their last era of glory before
disappearing from the Baltimore landscape. Being a new head coach,
the unassuming Marchibroda, who "reminded you of an altar boy,"
according to former Redskin coach Bill McPeak, wasn't in a position
to demand control of player movement (Steadman 1978, 155).
Thomas was the boss in that department, and Marchibroda would
take the hand that was dealt him.

With Bert Jones at the helm, the 1975 Colts opened with a 35-7
upset win over the Chicago Bears in which the defense held Walter
Payton to zero yards rushing on eight carries. Four consecutive losses,
three of them to playoff teams of the year before, followed.

Then came the breakthrough. The Colts intercepted Joe Namath
seven times, the most in his career, and romped over the Jets 45-28
at Shea Stadium. After beating Cleveland at Memorial Stadium, the

Colts pulled off the greatest comeback in club history in Buffalo. They spotted the Bills a 21-0 and 28-7 lead before shocking the partisan crowd of 77,320 at Rich Stadium by rolling to a 42-35 win. The Colts scored five straight touchdowns, including a Domres to Bill Olds 15-yard pass on a fake field goal and an 89-yard bomb from Jones to Roger Carr less than a minute after a Buffalo punt. Jones passed for 306 yards and Lydell Mitchell ran for 112, his seventh straight 100-yard effort.

The Colts had evened their record at 4-4 and weren't about to look back. They trampled the Jets 52-19, dumped Miami 33-17, sacked Lenny Dawson seven times in beating the Chiefs 28-14, and notched a club record eight sacks in a 21-0 whitewash of the Giants to make it seven straight wins. In the win over the Giants, Lydell Mitchell ran for 119 yards to become the first Colt ever to rush for over 1,000 yards in a season. Suddenly that old feeling was back in Baltimore, as this new-look team captured the fans' fancy. Over 10,000 greeted the team at BWI airport when they returned from

Miami. The "Sack Pack" front four, Joe Ehrmann, Fred Cook, John Dutton, and Mike Barnes were reminding many of the Donovan, Marchetti, Joyce, and Lipscomb quartet of 15 years earlier.

Heading into the 13th week of the season, the Colts had a record of 8-4 while the Dolphins were 9-3. A win at home against Miami would give the Colts a huge boost toward the divisional championship and a date in the playoffs. A loss would eliminate them from playoff consideration. The game has become, along with the 1958 "sudden-death" game, one of the classic games in the history of pro football in Baltimore.

A crowd of 59,398 crammed themselves into Memorial Stadium to watch the Shula-led Dolphins meet the upstart Colts. On a foggy, damp day, the two teams battled for almost three quarters in a scoreless tie before Mercury Morris put Miami in the lead with a three-yard touchdown run with 2:07 left in the third quarter. The Colts marched 86 yards to tie the game on a seven-minute drive that was capped by Lydell Mitchell's six-yard run with 5:30 left. The game was tied after 60 minutes of play and the two teams headed for over-time. As in 1958, the Colts lost the coin flip, but the Colt defense, also as in 1958, did its job and Miami was forced to punt from midfield. Larry Seiple's punt bounced out of bounds at the Baltimore 4 yard line.

There then ensued one of the most dramatic drives in the history of the Colts; it was made even more dramatic by the fog-shrouded conditions that hampered visibility for both players and fans. The drive took 18 plays and featured a 17-yard pass from Jones to Raymond Chester, a 15-yard pass to Roger Carr, and a 13- yard run by Don McCauley. Finally, on fourth and three from the Dolphin 14, Toni Linhart booted a 31-yard field goal into the gloaming for a 10-7 Baltimore win. The Colts were now tied for the AFC East lead and the following week they knocked off New England 34-21 for their ninth straight win, a 10-4 record, and, on the strength of their two wins over the 10-4 Dolphins, their first AFC division title since 1970. The win over New England didn't come easily, as rookie Allen Carter took the opening kickoff back 99 yards for a Patriot touchdown. The Colt defense once again saved the day, as Nelson Munsey

opposite page

Lydell Mitchell was a workhorse at running back and set several Baltimore Colts records in the process.

John Dutton was part of a front four nicknamed "The Sack Pack."

intercepted a Steve Grogan pass and rambled 30 yards for a touchdown, and Stan White set an NFL record for linebackers with his eighth interception of the season.

The playoffs began the following week; the Colts were pitted against the powerful Steelers, the eventual Super Bowl winners, in Pittsburgh. Bert Jones left the game early with a severely bruised throwing arm and Marty Domres took over at quarterback. Behind 153 yards rushing from Franco Harris, Pittsburgh rolled to a 28-10 victory. The Colts led 10-7 in the third quarter, but the "Steel Curtain" defense put the clamps on the Colts from there on out. Jones returned in the fourth quarter and led a march to the Steeler 3 yard line. But on third and goal Bert was hit by Jack Ham and fumbled; Andy Russell picked up the loose ball and lumbered 93 yards for the final score that put the game out of reach.

McDonald's issued a four-print set of current Colt greats. Raymond Chester was one of them.

Despite the playoff loss, Baltimore was once again a Colt town. Their team was the talk of football, having gone from 2-12 the year before to 10-4. Marchibroda was voted "Coach of the Year" and Thomas "Executive of the Year." Jones had matured into one of the best young quarterbacks in the league. The "Ruston Rifle" set a club record with a 59 percent completion mark in passing for 2,483 yards and 18 touchdowns. He was intercepted only eight times, and just four times in the last ten games. He also led all NFL quarterbacks in rushing with 321 yards and three touchdowns. It was obvious that Marchibroda, known for his way with quarterbacks, was a great match for Jones. Domres, meanwhile, was traded to San Francisco.

Were the Colts now a contender or still a pretender? The 1976 season would dispel the doubts. This time the Colts wouldn't be able to sneak up on anybody. The price of winning meant a newfound respect. The exhibition season saw the Colts win two games but then drop four in a row, the last being a 24-9 verdict in Detroit in which the lackluster Colts played with little enthusiasm. Ehrmann collapsed from heat prostration during the game and was hyperventilating; he was taken to a hospital by ambulance for an overnight stay. The press was kept outside the locker room after the game while Irsay ranted and raved inside, criticizing the team's effort, and threatening to fire the coaches. On the bus to the airport, 15-year-old Jimmy Irsay got up in tears and apologized to the players for his father's actions. Marchibroda felt he couldn't continue with Irsay's outbursts and Thomas' interference. Two days later, before the season had begun, Marchibroda had a showdown with Irsay and Thomas on Irsay's yacht, the "Mighty I," docked in Milwaukee. When Irsay told Ted that Thomas was in charge, the coach decided, after a six-hour session on the boat, to quit. The players and the public were stunned over Marchibroda's decision.

The scene now shifts, a few days later, to St. Mary's Seminary in Catonsville, Maryland, where the Colts practiced. A group of players, led by Bert Jones, rebelled against Irsay and Thomas and threatened to boycott the season unless Marchibroda was brought back. Jones, who urged the fans to stay home on game day (which rankled Baltimore mayor William Donald Schaefer), composed a statement praising the coaching of Marchibroda. "Every player on this team will tell you that Ted Marchibroda is the man responsible for the success of this team and not the front office. You can put a pile of lumber on a lot but it does not make a house and Ted Marchibroda has made this pile of lumber a house. Yesterday, Irsay and Thomas forced Ted Marchibroda to resign. They were severely wrong in this. It is tremendously unfair to Ted, this town and the team. Ted's resignation was forced just because he asked for the ordinary powers given to any head coach in the NFL. He also asked that Irsay and Thomas respect ordinary rules of personal conduct in their dealings with him and the team. Ted is right. He should be allowed to have the decision authority given other NFL coaches. He has already proven his ability as a great coach and organizer and nobody should have to endure the personal abuse that I have seen Irsay and Thomas give him."

Bold words indeed from a quarterback with just one big year under his belt. After writing his thoughts in longhand on his personal Colt stationery, Bert ripped up the pages and tossed them into a waste can in one of the seminary offices. Recognizing that this was an important chapter in the history of the Colts, I felt Bert's words should be preserved, so I fished the scraps of paper out of the trash and meticulously taped them together like pieces of a puzzle. He had

Young Bert Jones, son of a former Cleveland Browns star, Dub Jones, was making people take notice he showed promise as the Colt quarterback of the future.

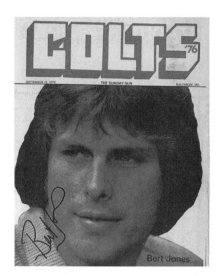

Bert Jones graced the cover of the *Sun* TV guide. He was hoping his performance would equal "Masterpiece Theater."

opposite page

Portions of Bert Jones' impassioned plea to keep Ted Marchibroda as Colt head coach.

written a couple of versions. I value this document as one of the significant contributions to Colt lore, similar in its own way to Tom Matte's wristband.

Chaos now gripped the franchise just days before the 1976 opener in New England. Thomas refused to back down and was adamant in not trying to persuade Marchibroda to stay. Three assistant coaches, Maxie Baughan, George Boutselis, and Whitey Dovell, also decided to quit. Baughan was offered the head job but refused, deliberately asking for an exorbitant figure that Thomas just laughed at. Finally, after commissioner Pete Rozelle got involved, Thomas bowed to the pressure and asked Marchibroda to return, granting him authority on all matters dealing with personnel. This was the beginning of the end for Thomas in Baltimore.

The players were determined to back up their faith in Marchibroda; they went out and ripped the Patriots in the opener, 27-13, with both Jones and Mitchell having banner days. The home opener the following week before over 50,000 fans was a 28-27 win over the Bengals, and after a three-point loss to Dallas the next week, Jones and company reeled off six straight wins en route to an 11-3 season and another AFC championship. The Colts wound up the regular season with a 58-20 pounding of Buffalo before over 53,000 fans.

Jones had his best year, passing for 3,104 yards and 24 touchdowns, and was named "Player of the Year" in the NFL. Mitchell ran for a team record 1,200 yards while catching 60 passes. He wasn't as flashy as his Penn State predecessor Lenny Moore, who had been enshrined at Canton the year before, but was dependable and a true workhorse. Wide receiver Roger Carr caught 43 passes for 1,112 yards, tops in the league. His average of 25.9 yards per reception was the best ever by a Colt. Kicker Toni Linhart led the league in points with 109. The Colts outscored the opposition 417 points to 246 and sent six players to the Pro Bowl.

Once again the powerful Steelers stood in Baltimore's way in the first round of the playoffs and once again the Colts were no match, losing 40-14 at Memorial Stadium as Pittsburgh outgained them 526 yards to only 170. Terry Bradshaw hit Frank Lewis for a 79-yard touchdown less than two minutes into the game and the rout was on.

Because the game was so one-sided, the crowd of 60,020 began leaving early which, as events would later prove, was a stroke of good luck. A few minutes after the game had ended a single-engine light plane began descending through the open end of Memorial Stadium, appearing as if it was trying to land on the field. When he realized he couldn't negotiate a landing, the pilot accelerated and tried to climb over the second deck. He was not able to pull up over the stands in so short a distance, however, and the plane crashed into the second deck behind home plate and the end zone. Fortunately, no one was sitting in the seats. If the game had been close or if the Colts had won, the fans would have still been there, filing out through the exits or reveling in a win. The pilot, Donald Kroner, was shaken up but not seriously injured. Kroner, who had a blue and white colored plane, had had his license revoked before for airborne indiscretions. He was charged with reckless flying, flying over the stadium, and destruction of property, and was sentenced to a jail term.

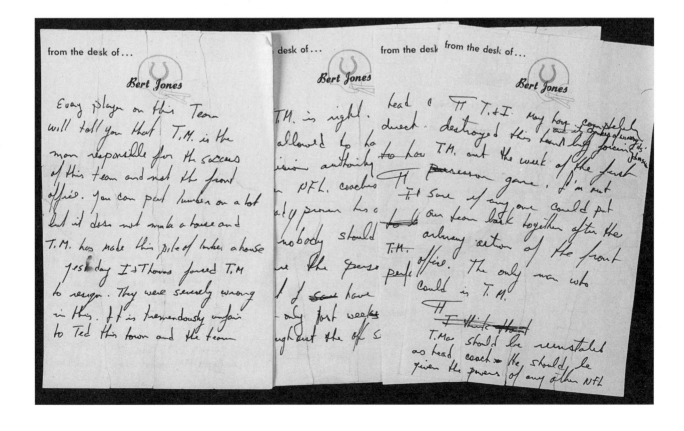

I remember being in the Steeler locker room getting postgame interviews and seeing the plane on television. It looked almost like a model plane it was so small. Thinking the incident had happened in some other stadium, I asked Steeler linebacker Jack Ham where the accident had happened, and he said, "Right here," so I quickly went up and observed the crash site, amazed that no one had been hurt. Colt Hall of Famer Artie Donovan had been sitting in a radio booth right below where the crash occurred and saw the plane coming right for him before it swooped upward. "I thought I was about to join my beloved mother in heaven," Artie said later. Instead of the football game, the plane crash made front page news all over the world.

A month and a day after the season ended, Joe Thomas lost his power struggle with Marchibroda and was fired as general manager of the Colts by the man he had helped introduce to the game, Bob Irsay. Thomas, returning from a luncheon honoring Bert Jones and offensive tackle George Kunz, was met at his Hunt Valley office by two lawyers who told him his services were no longer required. "It hit me like a death in the family," said Joe. Thomas never blamed Irsay for his departure but instead pointed the finger at "the little altar boy" (Marchibroda) for causing his ouster (Steadman 1978, 163). Earlier in the season, Irsay had offered Thomas a new contract. Thomas had balked at signing at that point because his wife Judi had been in an automobile accident and his concentration was focused on her and not a new contract. Irsay had offered him a sizable raise, but Thomas didn't think it was enough and asked to defer the talks until after the season. But by then Irsay had had a change of heart, and Thomas was gone.

Personnel chief and former player Dick Szymanski was picked to replace Thomas. His first move was to bring back Ernie Accorsi, former public relations director and later assistant to the president of the NFC, as his assistant. Ernie had grown up in Hershey, Pennsylvania, and having idolized the Colts from an early age, had a great perspective on their history and traditions. However, working for the "Mighty I," Robert Irsay, would prove to be the greatest challenge of his career.

With Szymanski's duties limited to negotiating contracts and

opposite page

Noted cartoonist Jack Davis drew this Natty Boh ad for bars and taverns.

Bert Jones in the huddle graced the 1977 press guide cover.

other front office duties, Marchibroda was now free to make his own personnel moves. He helped weave the Colts' third straight magical season. Nineteen seventy-seven was a lot like the previous two years in Baltimore, as the Colts won their first five games and nine of their first 10 en route to a 10-4 record and another AFC divisional crown. The emphasis was back on the field where it belonged.

Jones had another banner year, passing for 2,686 yards and 17 touchdowns. His backup, Bill Troup, attempted only two passes without a completion all season. In what would be his last season as a Colt, Lydell Mitchell ran for 1,159 yards and caught 71 passes for 620 more yards. In the process Lydell topped Lenny Moore's career rushing total of 5,174 yards. The Colts posted a 31-21 win over their old nemesis, the Steelers, to run their record to 6-1, and ended the season with a 27-point second half rally to defeat New England 30-24, and win a third straight division championship. The winning drive ended with 2:44 left in the game and covered 99 yards.

Despite the Colts' third straight year of success, the fans gave only grudging praise to their new team. There was a definite allegiance to the past in Baltimore and the latter-day Colts, although admired, paled next to the heroes of yesteryear. As popular as Bert Jones was, he couldn't compare with the legendary Unitas in fan adoration. Old traditions die hard in Baltimore.

Rather than the Steelers, the Colts met the defending Super Bowl champion Oakland Raiders on Christmas Eve at Memorial Stadium in the first round of the AFC playoffs. The game ended up as an NFL epic, a classic for the ages. Bert Jones and Ken Stabler locked horns before 60,763 fans in one of the longest games ever played. There was not one, but two overtimes, six quarters in all. An Errol Mann 22-yard field goal with only 26 seconds left in regulation tied the game at 31-31. This after the lead had changed hands eight times in the course of the game. Bruce Laird returned an interception 61 yards for a score for the Colts and Marshall Johnson ran a kickoff back 87 yards to give the Colts a lead in the seesaw game. Oakland ended the game at 2:17 of the second overtime period when Stabler hit tight end Dave Casper for 10 yards and the winning touchdown, Casper's third touchdown grab of the game.

If Mann had missed the field goal with seconds left in regulation the Colts would have prevailed. It was fourth down and a foot to go and coach John Madden didn't hesitate to send in the field goal unit. The Colts had their chances in overtime, with Jones overthrowing Raymond Chester, who was deep and in the clear. To this day Madden calls the game the greatest he's ever been a part of. Colt fans weren't aware of it at the time, but that overtime loss was the last bit of glory the Colts would enjoy in Baltimore.

A quarter of a century of mostly good memories were celebrated in 1977.

The year 1977 represented the 25th anniversary of the Colts' reentry into the NFL in 1953, and in a promotion that was sponsored by Wendy's an all-time team was picked by both fans and media and commemorated by posters that featured beautiful portraits of the greatest players in Colts history. The posters were passed out at a special luncheon, and not many reached the hands of the average fan. Named to the team on offense were center Dick Szymanski, guards Alex Sandusky and Glenn Ressler, tackles Jim Parker and George Kunz, tight end John Mackey, wide receivers Raymond Berry and Jimmy Orr, halfback Lenny Moore, fullback Alan Ameche, and quarterback Johnny Unitas. On defense, Art Donovan and Gene Lipscomb manned the tackles, Gino Marchetti and Ordell Braase were the ends, Mike Curtis, Ted Hendricks, and Bill Pellington were the linebackers, Bobby Boyd and Lenny Lyles the cornerbacks, and Rick Volk and Jerry Logan the safeties. Lou Michaels was picked as placekicker, David Lee as punter, and Don Shula outpolled Weeb Ewbank as coach. Of the 25-member team, nine are enshrined at the Pro Football Hall of Fame.

Many of the Colt players of the past, especially the Hall of Famers, enjoyed a rebirth during the 1970s, 1980s, and into the '90s in the form of the sports memorabilia market. Players would sign autographs at a memorabilia show on a weekend and walk out with more money than they had made for an entire year in their playing days. Johnny Unitas, especially, reaped huge fees in the autograph business.

In 1979, the Eastside Athletic Club, originators of the Ed Block Courage Awards, produced a beautiful 16 × 36 poster called "The

Former Notre Dame All-American George Kunz earned his way onto the Colts' all-time team.

Magnificent Seven," honoring the Colts' first seven Hall of Famers: Art Donovan, Gino Marchetti, Raymond Berry, Lenny Moore, Johnny Unitas, Weeb Ewbank, and Jim Parker. The artist was Fred Lesseg. There is also a smaller version.

In 1989, Goal Line Art, Inc. of Ridley Park, Pennsylvania, began issuing a collector's limited edition of Pro Football Hall of Famer cards. The artist, Gary Thomas, painted a portrait of every member of the Hall of Fame; limited to 5,000 sets issued nationwide, the 3 × 5 boxed set came in series of 30, beginning with Lance Alworth. Jim Parker was card number 22 in the first series. The second series in 1990 featured Raymond Berry, with Art Donovan in series three in 1991. Series four in 1992 included Weeb Ewbank and John Mackey, with Weeb wearing the cap and shirt of the New York Jets. Lenny Moore was in series five in 1993 and Gino Marchetti and Ted Hendricks were in series six in 1994, with Hendricks wearing the uniform of the Oakland Raiders. Johnny Unitas was also supposed to be in se-

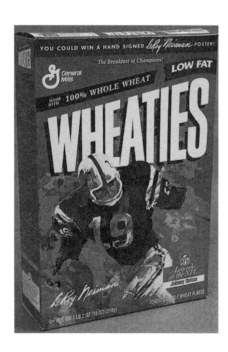

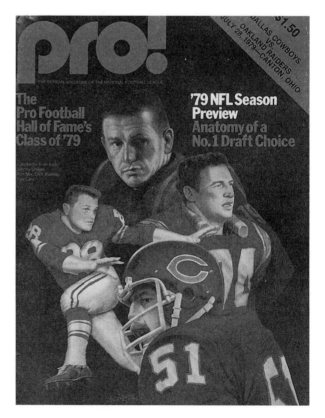

ries six but an asterisk was next to his name on card number 174 saying "Release not Authorized." Johnny relented in 1997 and the card
was finally issued. Beginning in 1995 Goal Line Art began putting out
cards for the current year's Hall of Fame inductees, since they had
by then covered the entire Hall of Fame roster. Don Shula was part
of the 1997 class, wearing, as might be expected, the colors of the
Miami Dolphins, rather than those of the Colts.

The Colts' downward spiral began in 1978. Without a buffer like
Joe Thomas, Bob Irsay became a constant thorn in Marchibroda's
side. Couple that with injuries to both Bert Jones and backup signal
caller Bill Troup in the preseason, and you've got the makings of a
shaky start. Jones was hurt in Detroit when defensive lineman Bubba
Baker rolled over on his shoulder. Bert was never the same after that.

Starting a third-string quarterback, Mike Kirkland, who had
never taken a snap in a regular season game, the Colts were so much
cannon fodder for Roger Staubach and the Super Bowl champion
Dallas Cowboys in the season opener, losing 38-0. There followed a
42-0 drubbing at the hands of the Dolphins for the worst start in Colt
history. By the end of the season, the Colts had registered just five
victories against 11 defeats. Jones tried to return against the Jets in
game seven but reinjured his shoulder after completing five of six
passes. He came back in week 10 to quarterback the Colts to a 21-
17 win over Washington on Monday Night Football. The Colts followed with a 17-14 win over Seattle to make it 5-6 on the year, but
Jones reinjured his shoulder late in the game and this time was lost
for the season. Five straight losses followed.

Perhaps the most dramatic win of the season was against New
England on Monday Night Football in the third week of the season.
On this rainy night in Foxboro, the Colts gave a national television
audience one of the most exciting fourth quarters of football ever
played. A total of 41 points were chalked up by both teams in that
dazzling final period. When the quarter began, the Colts trailed the
Patriots 13-7; when the final gun sounded, the Colts, thanks to little
Joe Washington's heroics, had posted a 34-27 win. Washington, on the
drenched artificial turf, tossed a 54-yard touchdown pass to Roger
Carr on the halfback option, caught a 23-yard touchdown pass from

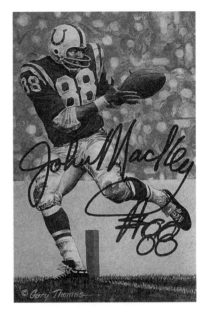

Tight end John Mackey was
one of the Colt Hall of Famers
in the limited edition Goal
Line Art cards.

opposite page

Leroy Neiman painted Johnny
Unitas for the front of a
Wheaties box.

Johnny Unitas was inducted
into the Pro Football Hall of
Fame in 1979, going in with
Dick Butkus, Yale Lary, and
Ron Mix.

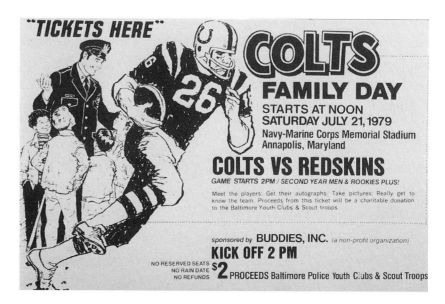

By 1979, Colts Family Day had become a longtime tradition in Baltimore.

Bill Troup, and capped the evening with a 90-yard kickoff return for the winning tally. The other memorable moment in 1978 was the 7-6 victory over Denver at Memorial Stadium in week eight. It took a great play by NFL Defensive Player of the Year Mike Barnes to assure the victory. The Broncos had the ball on the Baltimore 10 yard line with eight seconds remaining. Dependable Jim Turner came in to boot what would have been the winning field goal, but as the ball was snapped Barnes came pouring through to bat the kick down and preserve the win.

For the first time since 1964, the Colts printed a yearbook in 1978. Jones, who was the Colts' glamour player, graced the cover, and several local writers, including Cameron Snyder, who had been covering the Colts since 1953, contributed articles. Yearbooks would follow in 1980, 1981, and 1982, all published by former Colt marketing head Bob Leffler, who ran his own advertising agency.

Another 5-11 season followed in 1979, and after it ended Ted Marchibroda was fired as Colt head coach; he had compiled a respectable record of 41 and 33. Injuries took their toll, as six different starters missed most of the season. Bert Jones' career was at a crossroads because of the mounting injuries that were plaguing him. He missed much of 1979 and the veteran Greg Landry did most of the quarterbacking. The most positive development of the 1979 season was the construction of the $5 million Owings Mills training and office complex, which at the time was the envy of every franchise in pro football.

Former Cleveland Browns tackle Mike McCormack, who had been on the roster of the Dallas Texans when they moved to Baltimore in 1953, was dealt to Cleveland as part of a 10-for-5 trade, and had carved out a Hall of Fame career in nine seasons as a Brown, was named to replace Marchibroda. Called the "smartest lineman I ever coached" by his mentor Paul Brown in the Colts media guide, McCormack had served as an assistant under three great coaches, Vince Lombardi, George Allen, and Brown, before taking over the head job with the Eagles, where his teams stumbled to a 16-25-1 record.

Poor drafts had left the Colts thin in talent, but their first choice in the 1980 draft, Texas A & M's Curtis Dickey, made an immediate impression and, with Jones back in good form, the team made some strides in 1980. The Colts had won four of their first six and were 5-4 when Cleveland edged them 28-27 to even their record at 5-5. Still, they would have had a chance to win the division with a victory at Cincinnati on December 7. The Colts were leading 33-31 with 1:45 remaining, but the Bengals mounted a drive that was aided by a Larry Braziel pass interference call on the 6 yard line. Jim Breech connected on a 21-yard chip shot field goal and Cincinnati prevailed 34-33. The final record for the season was 7-9; Jones passed for 3,134 yards and 23 touchdowns, while Dickey ran for 800 yards and 11 touchdowns, and Roger Carr caught 61 passes for 924 yards. Amazingly, the Colts were only 2 and 6 at home, but 5 and 3 on the road.

The Colts opened the 1981 season with a 29-28 upset win over the Patriots in which top draft pick Randy McMillan ran for 146 yards and two touchdowns in his NFL debut. Then followed the worst stretch in the proud history of the Baltimore franchise, fourteen consecutive losses. In a 28-10 loss at Denver in week three, the Colts were outpassed 315 yards to 48 as Jones labored with a sore elbow. The following week, Bert threw for 357 yards, the second highest total of his career, in a 31-28 heartbreaking loss against Miami. A holding call on an apparent 31-yard touchdown pass from Jones to Ray Butler with less than a minute left cost the Colts the win.

The Colt defense couldn't stop anybody. Cleveland's Brian Sipe threw for 444 yards and four touchdowns in the Browns' 42-28 win, the third straight game in which the defense surrendered 40 points or more. McCormack benched the underachieving Dickey against the Jets. The following week in Philadelphia, in the tenth loss in a row, the Colt offense mustered only 36 yards rushing. That was the day that Irsay, seeing his team being routed 38-13, entered the scouts' booth in the second half, grabbed a headphone, and ordered McCormack to alternate Jones and Greg Landry on every other play. In my position as sports director of WMAR-TV, I remember standing on the sideline next to the Colts bench, watching the humiliated coach bowing to the owner's wishes. There was confusion and dismay among the players. Irsay even specified whether the play was to be a run or a pass. Bert said he did just the opposite of what Irsay barked into the headset. Just when you thought Irsay couldn't sink any lower, he managed to upstage himself.

Without a running game, Bert Jones was hung out to dry. He missed the Dallas game with a shoulder injury, came back in week 15 against the Redskins, who ripped the Colts 38-14, and then wound up his Colt career by tossing four touchdown passes in a 23-21 win over New England that snapped the losing streak at 14. For the year Bert passed for 3,094 yards and 21 touchdowns.

McCormack was unceremoniously fired after the game, and the following day former Arizona State coach Frank Kush was named the tenth head coach in Colt history. Kush, a hard-nosed, no-nonsense coach more suited to the college game, had amassed a 176-54-1 record in 22 years as coach of the Sun Devils before leaving after a recruiting scandal. His 1975 team had gone 12-0, beating Nebraska in the Fiesta Bowl, and he was named national coach of the year. One of 15 children, the Windber, Pennsylvania, native spent the 1981 season as coach of the Hamilton Tiger-Cats of the Canadian Football League, where he posted an 11-4-1 record and earned a first place finish in the Eastern Conference.

After graduating from Michigan State, where he played for Duffy Daugherty, Kush spent two years in the Army at Fort Benning, coaching and playing for the post football team. The military environment was to his liking, and he carried his drill sergeant approach over to coaching. His college preseason camps were both grueling and agonizing.

Kush wasn't nearly as successful in the NFL. The first big move he made was trading Bert Jones to the Rams for two 1982 draft picks. Bert had clashed with Irsay over his contract and had filed a grievance with the players' association. And so, on the eve of the draft, the nine-year vet was dealt to L. A., where he would not last the season. His career ended at the age of 31 after a serious neck injury that required surgery to fuse a bone from his hip into his neck. Next to Unitas, Jones was the most popular quarterback in Colt history, ranking above Y. A. Tittle and Earl Morrall. He was a great practical joker; I remember Bert bringing back ducks and geese from the Eastern Shore that he'd hunted on off-days and propping the birds up in other players' lockers. Bert was just an old-fashioned farm boy who made it big in the big city, but who fled right back to rural Ruston, Louisiana, to run the family lumber company when his playing days were over.

With the two picks from the Jones deal, the Colts selected Ohio State's All-American quarterback Art Schlichter and punter Rohn Stark. The Colts also had the second overall choice in the draft and picked Mississippi State linebacker Johnnie Cooks. Schlichter, however, was the prize. He had rewritten the Buckeye passing record book and ranked second all-time in Big 10 passing and total offense categories. In his four years in Columbus, Schlichter had led the Buckeyes to a 36-11-1 record, four bowl appearances, and two Big 10 titles. What the Colts and practically everyone else were unaware of was that Schlichter was addicted to gambling. He washed out of the NFL, spent years in jail and in rehab while trying numerous comebacks, before fading into oblivion.

Soon after the draft, Irsay inexplicably fired the man who hired Kush, general manager Dick Szymanski, and elevated Ernie Accorsi to the top job. "Sizzy" had joked for years that Irsay had fired him so many times he had lost count, but he would keep coming to the of-

Local ad man and former Colt front office exec Bob Leffler produced the last few Colt yearbooks.

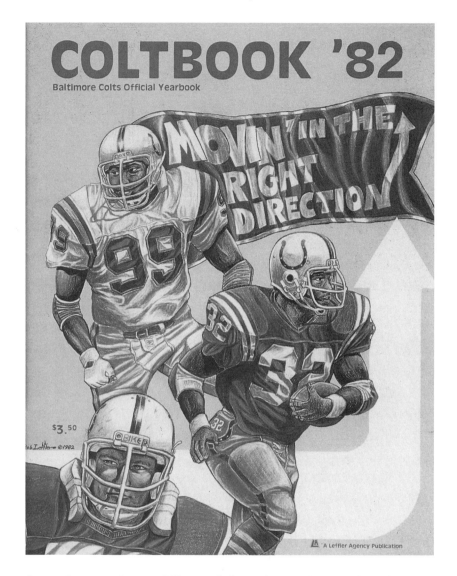

fice and Irsay, who would begin fading after his first drink at about 10 A.M., would make no mention of it. This time, however, the owner was serious.

As it turned out, the 1982 season was pretty much a washout. Kush had waived or traded away about two-thirds of the squad. After losses to New England and Miami to start the season, the Colts and the rest of the NFL shut down operations as the players went on strike. It was the first time ever a season had been interrupted by a work stoppage. Eight games in all were cancelled from each team's schedule, with one being made up at the end of the season. A total of

98 games were wiped out by the strike. When the Colts resumed on November 21 at Shea Stadium against the Jets, 57 days after the strike had begun, the scenario was pretty much the same: Baltimore was blanked 37-0. Buffalo shut them out the next week 20-0. For the year they didn't win a game, lost eight and tied one, the first time in Colt history that they hadn't won at least two games. The tie was against Green Bay on December 19, and only 25,920 bothered to come out. A makeup game was played at home against Miami on January 2. The Colts lost 34-7 and only 19,073 came out. The franchise was definitely at another crossroads.

The quarterback during this horrendous season was not Schlichter, but a fourth-round pick in the 1982 draft, Mike Pagel, who had played for Kush at Arizona State. Pagel had an outstanding preseason to win the job. The jury was still out on Kush. Was he in over his head or did the strike cost the young Colts a chance to mature? Thirty-one of the players on the 49-man roster were new, and most were young, inexperienced players.

The 1983 Colts had 12 first-year men on the roster. Unfortunately, one of them wasn't John Elway. Elway, the top quarterback in the draft after rewriting the record book at Stanford, was chosen by the Colts as the first pick in the NFL draft on April 26. It was just the third time in their history that they had had the first pick. Colt fans were ecstatic; Elway was seen as the player that would lead the Colts back to glory.

There were problems, however, as there always seemed to be with the Irsay-run Colts. Elway had been recruited by Kush in college, but elected not to play for him. He had also heard some very negative things about Irsay and was reluctant to play in Baltimore. He hinted that he might pursue a professional baseball career instead. Accorsi firmly believes (and has told this author) that Elway would have eventually softened and come to Baltimore when the pot was sweetened. It never came to pass, however, as Irsay panicked and, unbeknownst to Kush and Accorsi, traded Elway to Denver just six days after the draft for the Broncos' first pick, offensive tackle Chris Hinton, quarterback Mark Hermann, and the Broncos' first rounder the next year, who turned out to be Maryland guard Ron

Baltimore Colts

Mike Pagel was at quarterback and on the cover of the Colts' final press guide in Baltimore in 1983.

Solt. Who knows how the course of pro football history in Baltimore would have been altered if Elway had come to play for the Colts. Maybe they and not the Broncos would have been playing in five Super Bowls, winning two. And with such a great future in the offing, perhaps the move to Indianapolis would have been averted.

The loss of Elway wasn't the only downer in the spring of 1983. Trainer Eddie Block, associated with the Colts for 30 years, passed away on May 9. From 1954 until 1977, Eddie was head trainer, nursing players' physical as well as emotional needs; he became trainer emeritus after suffering a heart attack in 1977. One year later the Eastside Athletic Club inaugurated the Ed Block Courage Award, which began as just a Colt honor and then grew to honor players on every NFL team.

As fate would have it, the Colts' first home game of 1983 was against John Elway and the Broncos. A crowd of 52,613 came out to Memorial Stadium, many to boo the kid from California who had spurned Baltimore. Mike Pagel had passed for 292 yards the week before in the Colts' 29-23 overtime win at New England. Elway was booed unmercifully every time he took a snap; he was 9 of 21 for 106 yards. It took backup Steve DeBerg's efforts in relief of Elway to give Denver a 17-10 win. DeBerg hit 9 of 11 for 158 yards as he led the Broncos to two fourth-quarter touchdowns. When the two teams played later in the season in Denver, Elway threw for 385 yards on 23 of 44 and a 21-19 victory.

Despite having the youngest club in the league, the Colts posted a respectable 7-9 record in 1983, marking one of the great turn-arounds in NFL history. The running game blossomed under Kush and the no-name defense accounted for 36 take-aways (20 interceptions and 16 fumble recoveries) and 41 quarterback sacks. Linebacker Vernon Maxwell won NFL Rookie Defensive Player of the Year honors and the kicking combo of punter Rohn Stark and kicker Raul Allegre became one of the top tandems in the league. The rookie Allegre won two games with last-minute field goals and was voted Colt MVP by the fans.

December 18, 1983, ended up as a fateful day in Baltimore football history. It turned out to be the last game played by the Baltimore

Colts. Nobody knew it at the time, of course, and only 20,418 came out to see the Colts snap a four-game losing streak by knocking off the Houston Oilers 20-10. As sportswriter John Steadman, who never missed a game in Colt history, would write later, "The party was over, only the guests weren't told." Several fans at the game shouted invectives against Irsay. Many were upset that Irsay wouldn't give Curtis Dickey a new contract after the running back had rushed for 1,122 yards after just 232 the season before.

Irsay was as volatile as a Molotov cocktail, totally unpredictable and irrational. While the Baltimore media criticized his every move, Baltimore mayor William Donald Schaefer had shown amazing patience with Irsay, defending his actions and trying to remain calm in the face of the owner's threats to move the team. Schaefer felt that if he remained Irsay's friend and was honest with him, then the owner would keep the Colts in Baltimore.

On the heels of Irsay's bizarre conduct that brought embarrassment to both himself and his family, came an AP wire story quoting Irsay's mother as saying she hadn't seen her son in 35 years and that he was "the devil." His brother also called him uncomplimentary names: "He's a no-good son of a bitch," he told *Sun* columnist John Steadman. "He claims to be Roman Catholic. We were both bar mitzvahed at the same temple near Chicago." My own recollection of Irsay's private life is connected with a series I did on him for WMAR-TV in 1979. In talking about his family he said he had only one son, Jimmy, then a student at SMU in Texas. Then he thought a second and said, "Well, I do have another son, but he's retarded and in a home." That son, Tom, was 25 at the time, and I felt that Irsay's comments were particularly harsh.

Over the years, Irsay had flirted with moving the team. First it was Phoenix in 1976, then Indianapolis in 1977, and Los Angeles in 1979. Jacksonville filled the Gator Bowl for him for a pep rally with fireworks and bands in 1979. He had made it known that it wasn't a matter of if he was leaving, but where he was going.

We found out soon enough. Frustrated at not getting a new stadium, and jealous of Orioles owner Edward Bennett Williams, whose team played in the World Series in 1979 and 1983, winning in 1983 over the Phillies, Irsay lashed out at city and state officials who refused to take him seriously. In January 1984, it was revealed that Irsay had once again opened talks with Phoenix, which was hungry for an NFL team. Then followed the infamous BWI Airport press conference in which an obviously inebriated Irsay rambled on, with Schaefer present, about "having no intention of moving the goddamn team."

Accorsi, for one, had had enough and decided after the BWI episode that he could no longer work for such a ticking time bomb. Ernie felt that if the Colts were moving, it would be to Phoenix, because Kush was pushing for his old home state and had a buyer ready to come aboard in real estate developer Anthony Nicoli. Accorsi resigned on February 7, gaining a measure of distinction by being the only high-ranking Colt official not fired during the period of Irsay's ownership. Accorsi's departure left the front office devoid of leadership.

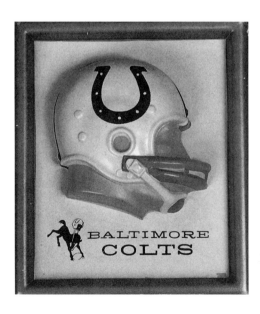

Indianapolis had recently completed the $82 million Hoosier-dome and was looking for a team, either expansion or otherwise. Irsay's right-hand man, Michael Chernoff, began talking with Indy officials about a move. Indianapolis promised a $15 million loan, sellouts of every game, and a new practice facility, among other things. Phoenix offered basically the same package.

The NFL, which had prided itself on having no franchise shifts since 1960 when the Cardinals had left Chicago for St. Louis, was faced with possible moves on two fronts. The Oakland Raiders wanted to move to Los Angeles, and the Colts wanted to move somewhere, or did they? Mayor Schaefer and Frank DeFrancis, Maryland's secretary of economic development, met with Irsay and offered him the identical $15 million loan and agreed to forgive the $2.2 million loan on the new training complex. On March 26, the Maryland legislature discussed buying the team for $40 million and then selling it to Maryland investors. The other proposal was the one that caused Irsay to move in the cover of night: it called for the state to condemn the Colts and begin eminent domain proceedings. Irsay and DeFrancis talked the next day and Irsay had a fresh set of demands, including a guaranteed home attendance of 43,000 fans a game and $6.6 million to buy the training complex. When word of this got back to the Maryland Senate, they voted 38–4 to grant Baltimore authority to seize ownership of the team. The measure still had to be passed by the House of Delegates. News reports later quoted Irsay as saying, "Schaefer stabbed me in the back with eminent domain." It can never be proven that the threat of eminent domain forced Irsay out of town, but that's the general opinion. He wanted to get out of town as fast as possible, before the bill could be enacted.

There was no phone call or any advance warning that the Colts were leaving. Irsay called Kush at his Arizona home on March 28 and told him to fly back to Baltimore. He was told that the team was moving, but Irsay wouldn't tell him where. Later that night, movers started packing 30 years of office equipment, training gear, game films, scouting materials, furniture, uniforms, helmets, club publications, and file drawers while a fleet of Mayflower moving vans headed for the Colt complex in Owings Mills. The scene was surrealistic, like

opposite page

The legacy of the Baltimore Colts was long and proud and helped pave the way for the resounding success of the National Football League.

something from a movie. A late March snow was falling; lights shone in the complex as the trucks pulled up. Word had rapidly started to spread that the Colts were fleeing Baltimore under the cover of a snowy night. One fan who quickly arrived was the team's number one fan, Hurst "Loudy" Loudenslager, who had played the Colt song at hundreds of airport arrivals and whose wife Flo had baked thousands of walnut cakes on players' birthdays. Tears streamed down his face.

Hardly anyone was informed about the heist. Colt employees, save for a few sworn to secrecy, had no idea what was about to unfold. Irsay hadn't even bothered to inform the league or commissioner Pete Rozelle. In a matter of a few hours the 15 Mayflower vans were on the road to Indianapolis. They had stripped everything except for a few potted plants from the Colt complex, taking everyone's personal belongings as well as team property.

There was disbelief as word spread of the Mayflower caravan. Both Mayor Schaefer and Governor Harry Hughes expressed outrage. "It's as if we were not being treated in good faith," said Hughes. "We felt we met every reasonable demand he made, but the demands kept changing." The day after the team left, the governor signed the eminent domain legislation and the city wired a $40 million offer to Irsay. It was too little too late, however. Nine months later U.S. District Judge Walter Black Jr. ruled that the team had already moved when the city acted. Not only had Irsay taken the tangible collection of what comprises a pro football franchise, he had taken a way of life. Of fathers and sons, and their sons, going to games. Of the blue and white, the horseshoe helmets, Johnny's hightops, Lenny's spats. He had taken a tradition, one of the proud legacies of the National Football League. About all he couldn't take, something that Indianapolis could never steal, were the memories.

SIX

The Long, Hard Journey Back

Since 1947, except for the two years, 1951 and 1952, in which the NFL abandoned the city, Baltimore had had a pro football team. There were some difficult times, especially in the early days, but the dedication of the ownership and the fans carried the Colts to paydirt. It took a buffoon from Skokie, Illinois, named Robert Irsay to spoil that tradition. The NFL was left with egg on its face, helpless to do anything about the Colts' move, for fear of legal challenges. The love affair of a city and its team, manifested in its Colt Corrals which numbered 31 strong, its band which kept on playing, and all the thousands of ticketholders, had been rudely broken off by a younger suitor, undeserving but with a brand-new domed stadium and a mayor willing to give the team owner all the riches he desired. Irsay, who died on January 14, 1997, didn't have the smooth ride he expected in Indianapolis. Mediocrity was the norm on the field, as the Colts posted five winning seasons, eight losing ones, and two seasons in which they broke even in the years that followed the Baltimore exodus. Ted Marchibroda returned to coach the team in Indianapolis.

In 1995, the wild-card Colts made it to the third round of the playoffs before losing to Pittsburgh. Fan apathy soon set in and empty seats began appearing at the Hoosierdome. There was even some talk in 1995 that the Colts were interested in coming back to Baltimore, but it never amounted to anything more than talk. The Indianapolis press guides were loaded with the exploits of the Baltimore Colts. Johnny Unitas, for one, wanted his name struck from the Indy record book, but the team wouldn't oblige. When all-time Colt tight end

John Mackey was inducted into the Pro Football Hall of Fame in 1992, he refused to have his ring presentation in Indianapolis. Instead he had it at Memorial Stadium in Baltimore during halftime of a sold-out NFL exhibition game between the Saints and Dolphins.

The fans of Baltimore were happy to be rid of Irsay, but the price was almost too much to bear. What happened after that midnight Mayflower escape wasn't a pretty sight either, as the city was used as a bargaining chip by New Orleans, St. Louis, Los Angeles, New England, and Oakland. Then, too, there was the travesty surrounding the expansion sweepstakes. Finally, shut out on all fronts by the NFL, the city swallowed its pride and went after an existing franchise in another proud city, just as Indianapolis had done to Baltimore. In 1995 John Moag, who had replaced the dignified Herb Belgrad as head of the Maryland Stadium Authority, offered Cleveland Browns owner Art Modell a $200 million rent-free stadium, and all sorts of other perks, from seat licenses and stadium naming rights to parking and concessions, that added up to the biggest Brinks job of the century. It was as if Moag had secured the rights to Fort Knox, handed Modell the key and said, "Everything in here is yours." How else do you explain something as implausible as the Cleveland Browns moving to Baltimore? It was as if the New York Yankees had decided to move to Chicago. Unheard of. But when you consider that greed was the paramount consideration, then you might as well forget about virtue, common decency, and all those other admired qualities that don't amount to a hill of beans in professional sports, where the almighty dollar is the holy grail. The fact that the move touched off the greatest uproar in the 75-plus years of the NFL was something very few of the principals bargained for. Certainly Art Modell, vilified and attacked to a far greater degree than Irsay ever was, didn't expect it. The fact that the announcement came during the season caused it to create a greater backlash than had been the case when the Colts left in late March.

In between the Colts leaving and the Browns' betrayal of Cleveland, Baltimore's football fortunes experienced a rocky ride. The University of Maryland and the Naval Academy played some games at Memorial Stadium, while on a professional level, the champion

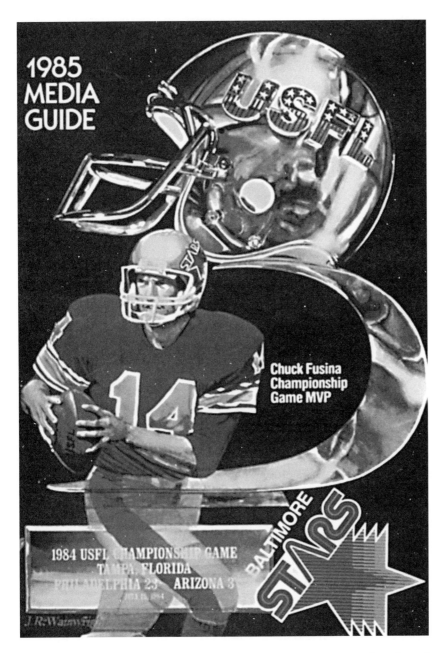

1985
MEDIA
GUIDE

USFL

Chuck Fusina
Championship
Game MVP

BALTIMORE STARS

1984 USFL CHAMPIONSHIP GAME
TAMPA, FLORIDA
PHILADELPHIA 23   ARIZONA 3

The Baltimore Stars of the USFL practiced in Philadelphia, played at College Park, and won a championship, never setting foot in Baltimore.

Philadelphia Stars of the United States Football League, who played in the spring but drew poorly in Philadelphia, moved to Baltimore in 1985. They moved, however, in name only. Because of the Orioles' use of Memorial Stadium, the Stars were forced to play their games at Byrd Stadium in College Park. Coached by Jim Mora, the Stars practiced in Philadelphia and bussed to College Park; the Harbor

Tunnel was about as close as they ever got to Memorial Stadium. Led by quarterback Chuck Fusina, running back Kelvin Bryant, and linebacker Sam Mills, the Stars won the USFL title, but their connection to Baltimore was extremely tenuous.

After a brief flirtation with the New Orleans Saints, the city focused its attention in 1988 on luring the St. Louis Cardinals to Baltimore. In short order there were Baltimore Cardinals T-shirts and sweatshirts hitting the clothing stores. Owner Bill Bidwill made numerous trips to Baltimore and met with the media on one occasion, before deciding on a family vote to move to Phoenix and its warm climate.

The focus then turned to acquiring an expansion franchise. The league decided to add two teams in 1994, and the city felt confident that with plans for a new stadium and its past proud tradition, it would win out over the likes of Jacksonville, Charlotte, Memphis, and St. Louis. Several ownership groups surfaced, led by Bob Tisch, brother of CBS boss Lawrence Tisch, who had great connections to the league; Leonard "Boogie" Weinglass, the pony-tailed self-made success story and former "Diner" guy who founded Merry-Go-Round Enterprises; novelist Tom Clancy, a Colt season ticketholder who had grown up near Memorial Stadium; and the Glasers, father Malcolm and sons Bryan and Joel, who eventually took over ownership of the Tampa Bay Buccaneers. As it turned out, having all of these groups vying for ownership was a hindrance rather than an asset.

In the summer of 1992, prior to the expansion decision, the city of Baltimore staged a preseason game between the Saints and Dolphins that was sold out six hours after the tickets went on sale. Sixty-nine former Colt players were introduced before the game to a thunderous ovation. The city was sending strong signals to the NFL to "Give Baltimore the Ball."

Fourteen months later, rather than taking Baltimore and St. Louis, the two cities that had been raped and pillaged, the NFL, behind the recommendation of commissioner Paul Tagliabue, opted for Charlotte and Jacksonville. Baltimore was too close to Philadelphia and Washington, said Tagliabue; the league wanted to open up virgin territory. Rather than select both cities at once, Tagliabue announced that Charlotte was in and that the other city would be named in a month to six weeks. The NFL wanted to give St. Louis more time to stabilize its ownership situation. So Baltimore still had a chance, but St. Louis was in the driver's seat.

So what happened? Jacksonville, whose backers tried to pull out of the expansion bowl when they heard that St. Louis was the front runner, got the nod, despite an 11th hour plea by retired commissioner Pete Rozelle to pick Baltimore, and despite the entrance of Al Lerner, a wealthy banker with ties to both Cleveland and Baltimore, into the ownership derby. The announcement came as a stunning and implausible defeat for Baltimore. Strangely, Art Modell, who was Lerner's friend and thought to be a Baltimore ally, voted against Baltimore getting a team. Was this because he was eyeing Baltimore for himself? In the final tally, only one owner, Philadelphia's Norman Braman, voted for Baltimore. Tagliabue, after the vote, said that maybe Baltimore should reevaluate plans to build a stadium and build a "plant or museum" instead. Talk about rubbing salt in the wounds. Pete Rozelle must have cringed when he read that statement. His successor obviously had no grasp of pro football history and Baltimore's contributions to the league.

Once more Baltimore was back to square one. Four months after the NFL expansion snub, the Canadian Football League came to Baltimore as part of an expansion experiment involving U.S. cities. Sacramento was the first American CFL outpost in 1993 and Baltimore, Las Vegas, and Shreveport joined the next season. Billing itself as "Longer, Wider and Faster," the CFL sported larger fields, 12 players on a side, and three downs instead of four.

Owner Jim Speros was from a football family; he had played at Clemson, and his father and two brothers had also played college football. Although short on money, Speros was determined to make Baltimore a CFL success. He hired veteran CFL coach Don Matthews, who brought in players such as quarterback Tracy Ham, running back Mike Pringle, and linebacker O. J. Brigance.

Speros wanted to name his team the Baltimore CFL Colts, which pleased the fans, but the idea was short-lived as the small-minded

They were called the Baltimore CFL Colts in 1994 until the heavy hand of the NFL forced the Canadian League team to drop the nickname, adding more insult to injury.

NFL successfully sued to prevent it even though the CFL and the NFL were two separate leagues and the name Colts had been used by the AAFC franchise three years before the Colts even joined the NFL in 1950. Thus the team basically was without a name the entire 1994 season. The Baltimore CFLs went 12-6 and averaged 37,347 fans at Memorial Stadium, tops in the league, as they tied the Winnipeg Blue Bombers for first place in the Eastern Conference. How many of those fans had free tickets is tough to tell. Speros was adept at promotion, working many different barter deals and trying to spruce up Memorial Stadium, which had been abandoned by the Orioles after the 1991 season.

Some notable achievements from the '94 season were Mike Pringle running into the CFL record books with 1,972 yards rushing and finishing second to Doug Flutie in MVP voting; Shar Pourdanesh being named the CFL's Most Outstanding Lineman; and linebacker Matt Goodwin, who blocked five kicks, being tabbed CFL Rookie of the Year. Baltimore beat Toronto in the first round of the playoffs in Baltimore and advanced to the Grey Cup final by beating Winnipeg on Donald "Iggy" Igwebuike's 54-yard field goal in the final minute. The storybook season came to an end when the British Columbia Lions beat Baltimore at Vancouver 26-23; 40-year-old kicker Lui Passaglia hit a 38-yard field goal on the final play of the game to win it.

In 1995, the CFLs had a new nickname, the "Stallions," as Speros stayed with the horse family. The Stallions dominated the Southern Division, winning 10 straight for a league best 15-3 record. Pringle, who gained 1,791 yards, was named MVP of the league, Mike Withycombe was the top offensive lineman, and Chris Wright, who amassed a league record 2,256 total return yardage, was the Rookie of the Year. Nine Stallions were named to the All-CFL team.

Preparing for the opening game of the 1995 playoffs, the Stallions learned that the Cleveland Browns were moving to Baltimore. Rather than fold their tents, the Stallions beat Winnipeg and San Antonio to reach the Grey Cup final against Flutie and the Calgary Stampeders, the only team Baltimore hadn't defeated in its two-year history. Tracy Ham outshone Flutie as the Stallions won the championship 37-20 in Regina, Saskatchewan, bringing the Grey Cup south of the Canadian border for the first time.

Unfortunately, the focus had been taken off the Stallions and their great 18-3 record by the Browns' decision to move to Baltimore. Six weeks later, Speros reluctantly announced that the Stallions were moving to Montreal; his losses were pegged at $1.6 million the first season and $800,000 the second. While several of the Stallions went on to play in the NFL, Speros left Montreal after the 1996 season and is now vice-president of a computer software company in the Wash-

The Baltimore CFLs came close to winning it all in 1994.

The Stallions went all the way in 1995, bringing home the Grey Cup and giving Baltimore championships in three separate pro leagues.

ington, D.C., suburbs. Matthews opted not to go to Montreal and signed to coach the Toronto Argonauts, where he won two more Grey Cups in three years. As with the USFL title in 1985, the Grey Cup symbolized another championship that the city would never get a chance to defend. The CFL dropped its U.S. experiment after the Stallions moved, closing down operations in Shreveport, San Antonio, Birmingham, Las Vegas, Sacramento, and Memphis. All that's left of the Stallions in Baltimore are the souvenirs, programs, ticket stubs, press guides, pins, and pennants.

Art Modell had planned to bring the nickname "Browns" to Baltimore, which is what Bob Irsay did when he moved the Colts, but the outcry was so great that Modell relented and decided to let Cleveland keep its colors, nickname, and tradition, and pick a new moniker for Baltimore. Modell was taking a terrific beating in the national press, and even members of Congress were trying to derail the Browns' departure out of Cleveland. *Sports Illustrated* did a cover article with a caricature of Modell throwing a body block at one of the Cleveland "Dawg Pound" faithful. Not even Walter O'Malley in

Brooklyn, when he moved the Dodgers to L.A., had taken the kind of abuse Modell was experiencing.

Baltimore fans had mixed feelings about the move. They knew what Clevelanders were going through, having experienced it themselves; at the same time, because the NFL had turned its back on Baltimore's expansion efforts, they were glad to get a team no matter what the circumstances. Governor Parris Glendening had said the stadium money was not going to be there forever, maybe a year at best; thus the hurried search for an existing NFL team.

It was on November 3, 1995, that word leaked out that the Browns, owned by Modell since 1961, were coming to Baltimore. I was in South Bend, Indiana, with the Navy football team, touring the new College Football Hall of Fame when word swept through the hallowed halls of college lore that the Browns were moving. The official news conference was three days later on Monday, November 6, in the parking lot of Camden Yards on the site of what would be the team's new stadium. The fact that the team had to play four more home games in Cleveland made it one of the longest wakes in the history of sports. The NFL tried to convince Modell to sell the Browns to Cleveland interests and await an expansion team in two or three years in Baltimore. He refused.

Modell got on with the task of establishing a new identity in Baltimore. Choosing colors, a logo and a nickname, and a new coaching staff all had to be done. Picked to coach the team was former Baltimore and Indianapolis Colt coach Ted Marchibroda, now 66 years old.

On Friday, March 29, 1996, Baltimore's new team was named the Ravens. The *Baltimore Sun* sponsored a name-the-team contest and a record 33,748 callers responded; the name "Ravens," based on Baltimorean Edgar Allan Poe's classic poem, won out over "Marauders" and "Americans." News reports described the raven as a "strong, soaring flier, mentioned in myths and legend as magical," but also noted that it is a "scavenger that preys upon the weak." On June 5, 1996, the Ravens unveiled their colors—black, purple, and metallic gold—at a noon fashion show at the Gallery at Harborplace. Players Vinny Testaverde and Rob Burnett modeled the uniforms. The hel-

opposite page

Johnny U. and all the old Colts helped to bring down the curtain on 33rd Street in 1997. The $10 program had many a tear stain after the emotional day had ended.

met logo was a shield sprouting a pair of wings with the letter "B" inside the shield. Right away, the souvenir and clothing manufacturers began cranking out Raven paraphernalia.

After the 1998 season, amateur artist Frederick E. Bouchat, a state security guard, sued the Ravens, saying that he had created the team's logo and not NFL Properties. He maintained that he sent the team his drawing, hoping to get a couple of season tickets out of the deal if it was accepted. He never heard anything back and was stunned when the Ravens unveiled their logo, which was almost exactly the way he had painted it. The jury sided with Bouchat and the Ravens had to torpedo all existing merchandise and create a new

logo, a sideview Raven, at huge expense; they are appealing the decision.

The Ravens went to Western Maryland College in Westminster for training camp, reviving an old Colt tradition, and played their first two seasons at venerable Memorial Stadium while the new downtown stadium was being built. Since the Ravens were beginning a brand-new history, leaving their past behind in Cleveland, public relations director Kevin Byrne decided to stock the records section of his first press guides with the records of the Baltimore Colts in the old All-America Football Conference and NFL.

The Ravens finished with a 4-12 record in their inaugural season, 0-8 on the road. In 1997, their last year at Memorial Stadium, they improved to 6-9-1, but were still last in the AFC Central. On December 14, 1997, the Ravens defeated Houston 21-19 in the final game at Memorial Stadium. A commemorative $10 program was sold featuring Vinny Testaverde and Johnny Unitas on the cover. Seventy former Colts, wearing replica jerseys, were introduced throughout the game. After the final gun sounded, the old-timers ran one final play at the Stadium. Unitas, unable to grip the ball because of the effects of an old football injury, handed off to Tom Matte, who in turn handed the ball to Lenny Moore who ran it in for the touchdown. It was Testaverde's last game as a Raven; he was signed by the Jets, and Coach Bill Parcells helped turn Vinny into one of the great success stories of the 1998 season.

The Ravens' new $200 million, 68,000-seat stadium debuted on September 6, 1998, with a 20-13 loss to Pittsburgh, a game in which the Ravens totally outplayed Pittsburgh but still ended up on the losing end. They limped home with a 6-10 record, the biggest win occurring on November 29 when Ravens quarterback Jim Harbaugh engineered a comeback 38-31 win over the Indianapolis Colts. It was bizarre seeing the familiar blue-and-white clad, horseshoe-helmeted Colts as the enemy in the town that had idolized and loved them with such passion; Johnny Unitas, the soul of the Baltimore Colts, stood on the sidelines and rooted against them like all the other Baltimore fans. And the former Cleveland Browns, now the Baltimore Ravens, were being cheered, while their owner, Art Modell, was still being re-

opposite page

Memorial Stadium had been a second home to Baltimore Colts too numerous to mention.

viled in Cleveland. It was confusing, to say the least. In a great gesture at game's end, Harbaugh ran over to Unitas and presented him with the football. During the game, Colts president Jimmy Irsay (son of the late owner), sitting in the press box, was berated and ridiculed by several fans who had spotted him. The verbal bombardment was so great he had to leave the press box and seek refuge. The fans have not forgotten, nor will they ever.

The day after the season ended on December 27 with a 19-10 win over Detroit, Ted Marchibroda was fired as head coach and Minnesota Vikings offensive coordinator Brian Billick was hired. Former Lions quarterback Scott Mitchell, benched in Detroit by Bobby Ross, was signed as the new hope to ignite the offense. By midseason, Mitchell had given way to Tony Banks as the Ravens finished with an 8-8 record.

Modell, cash-strapped and bogged down in enormous debt, was searching for a new minority partner as the century drew to a close. He found him in Stephen J. Bisciotti, a local businessman who had grown up rooting for the Baltimore Colts. It was hard to fathom how an owner who had drawn an average of 75,000 fans a game in Cleveland, benefited from a tremendously lucrative national television package, and gotten the greatest deal in sports history by moving to Baltimore still could be hurting for money. The NFL had to bail Modell out with a $65 million loan, which enabled him to restructure his massive debt.

As we look forward to the 21st century, the Ravens are starting to create their own tradition; the Naval Academy and West Point have agreed to return to Baltimore for the first time since 1944; Maryland is once again playing in Baltimore; Johns Hopkins, Morgan State, and Towson University are all fielding competitive teams; and the high schools are alive and well.

An entire generation has grown up without the Colts in Baltimore. That is a sad fact of life, made even sadder by the fact that they will never be back. For 35 years they were as much a part of the city as the "Bromo Seltzer" Tower and Fort McHenry. Their memory will live in Baltimore forever.

SOURCES

Bealle, Morris A. *Gangway for Navy: The Story of Football at the United States Naval Academy, 1879 to 1950.* Washington, D.C.: Columbia Publishing Co., 1951.

———. *Kings of American Football: The Story of Football at Maryland Agricultural College, Maryland State College, and the University of Maryland, 1890 to 1952.* Washington, D.C.: Columbia Publishing Co., 1952.

Brown, Bob, ed. *The House of Magic, 1922–1991: 70 Years of Thrills and Excitement on 33rd Street.* Baltimore: Baltimore Orioles, 1991.

Burgess, Hugh F., Jr., and Robert S. Smoot III. *McDonogh School: An Interpretive Chronology.* Columbus, Ohio: Charles E. Merrill, 1973.

Claassen, Harold. *The History of Professional Football.* Englewood Cliffs, N.J.: Prentice-Hall, 1963.

Clary, Jack T. *Navy Football: Gridiron Legends and Fighting Heroes.* Annapolis: Naval Institute Press, 1997.

Fitzgerald, Ed. *Johnny Unitas: The Amazing Success Story of Mr. Quarterback.* New York: Nelson, 1961.

Herskowitz, Mickey. *The Golden Age of Pro Football: NFL Football in the 1950s.* Dallas: Taylor Publishing Co., 1990.

Schaffer, G. Wilson. *Recreation and Athletics at Johns Hopkins: A One Hundred–Year History.* Baltimore: Johns Hopkins University Press, 1977.

Steadman, John F. *The Baltimore Colts Story.* Baltimore: Press Box Publishers, 1958.

———. *Football's Miracle Men: The Baltimore Colts' Story.* Cleveland: Pennington, 1959.

———. *The Baltimore Colts: A Pictorial History.* Virginia Beach: Jordan, 1978.

————. *From Colts to Ravens: A Behind-the-Scenes Look at Baltimore Pro-fessional Football.* Centreville, Md.: Tidewater Publishers, 1997.

Tittle, Yelberton A. Y. A. *Tittle: I Pass! My Story,* as told to Don Smith. New York: F. Watts, 1964.

INDEX

Numbers in *italics* denote illustrations.